LEON STILMAN

GOGOL

Edited by Galina Stilman

Hermitage Publishers

and

Columbia University

1990

Leon Stilman

GOGOL

Edited by Galina Stilman

Copyright © 1990 by Galina Stilman

Library of Congress Cataloging–in–Publication Data

Stilman, Leon.
  Gogol / Leon Stilman; edited by Galina Stilman.
    p. cm.
  Includes index.
  ISBN 1–55779–035–3
  1. Gogol', Nikolai Vasil'evich, 1809–1852––Criticism and
interpretation. I. Stilman, Galina. II. Title.
  PG3335.Z8S755   1990
  891.73'3–dc20
                                                            90–4901
                                                               CIP

A sketch by L. Stilman is on front cover

Published by Hermitage Publishers
P.O. Box 410
Tenafly, N. J. 07670, USA

with support and participation of Columbia University

ACKNOWLEDGEMENT

I wish to express my sincere appreciation to Helen Loewy for her invaluable assistance. I am very grateful to Professor Doris-Jeanne Gourevitch for her constructive criticism and her many helpful suggestions, and to Professor Ivan Marki of Hamilton College for his advice and encouragement.

My very special gratitude goes to Professor Marshal D. Shulman, of Harriman Institute, thanks to whom Leon Stilman's work on Gogol will see the light.

Galina Stilman

CONTENTS

CONTENTS

Chapter I

INTRODUCTION

Gogol's literary heritage is something in which the original images become visible once those superimposed by Gogol himself and by his critics have been removed. Gogol's literary career, which began in 1830, was very short; except for his early experiments in poetry (Hans Kuchelgarten) and a few early fragments. His last completed work, *Dead Souls,* appeared twelve years later, but it was virtually finished by 1840. During the remaining twelve years of his life − he died in 1852, in his forty-third year − he labored on the second volume of *Dead Souls* and produced various writings of moral and religious edification or glosses to his earlier works. These glosses and reinterpretations of Gogol − the moral reformer − created an even more distorted picture of his artistic creation than the picture composed by the critic and social reformer Belinsky.

Gogol's work does not lend itself easily to periodization. It is often classified according to the selling of his stories. The first period of his creative development is associated with the Ukraine: with his two collections of Ukrainian stories, *The Evenings on a Farmstead near Dikanka* (two volumes, published in September, 1831, and in March, 1832) and *Mirgorod* (January, 1835). This first Ukrainian period is said to be followed by the Petersburg stories ("The Portrait," "Nevski Prospect," "The Madman's Diary," "The Nose"), and finally by the third period, the scenery now being provincial Russia, with the *Inspector* and *Dead Souls.*

This division by areas, however, if it is a convenient simplification, is not supported by the chronology of Gogol's work.

One cannot disregard, in the first place, *Hans Kuchelgarten,* the long narrative poem, or "idyll in pictures," which preceded the *Evenings,* and which takes place in Germany (the hero Kuchelgarten also visiting Greece and other countries). Secondly, the "Ukrainian period" was not concluded with the publication of *Mirgorod* in 1835. In later years, in 1839 and 1840, Gogol reverted to Ukrainian themes, extensively reworking *Taras Bulba,* the Cossack epic hero (the late version, twice as long as the first, appears in all the

9

editions of *Mirgorod* since 1842), and writing a drama, which he destroyed, based on Ukrainian history. It may be said, therefore, that the Ukrainian "period" never ended: Ukrainian thematics recur in Gogol's work throughout his literary career.

Finally, the *Mirgorod* stories were completed not later December, 1834, when they were passed by the censor. A month earlier the censor passed *Arabesques*, a volume of miscellany, which included three of the Petersburg stories: "Nevskii Prospect," "The Portrait," and "The Diary of a Madman." A first draft of "The Nose," published only in 1836, was also written before the publication of *Mirgorod*. *Mirgorod*, consequently, was concurrent with the Petersburg stories (with the exception of the later "Overcoat"), and it was preceded by an unfinished comedy satirizing officialdom of the capital, and also by the early drafts of another comedy: *The Marriage*. Like the Ukrainian, the "Petersburg period" also extends to the late thirties and early forties with the greatest of the stories of this cycle: "The Overcoat."

Chronologically, therefore, after his early beginnings, there was in Gogol's life a period of intense creative activity during which he had written, or at least conceived, practically all his works. The years after 1836 were devoted to *Dead Souls* (begun in 1835) and to the rewriting of some of his earlier works; "The Overcoat" was the only important original work of these years, but its inception may be traced to a much earlier period.

To trace any general trend in the development of Gogl's art is hardly any easier than to distinguish separate periods in this development. *Dead Souls* was in many ways a final synthesis. But after the first volume of *Dead Souls* had been virtually completed, Gogol produced the second version of *Taras Bulba* in which he used even more elements borrowed from Ukrainian folk songs and legends, more rhythm, color and metaphor than in the first version. "The Portrait," completely unrelated to *Dead Souls* in its thematics and its stylistic method, was also extensively reworked in this late period. It seems therefore that even if Gogol strove toward a synthesis — and this was one of his contradictions — he also never abandoned or discarded any of his different methods and styles; they all preserved for him their validity and called for further experimentation.

In this book, an attempt is made to define the more important factors belonging to national tradition, to the past — that of his country; and to family reminiscences, to personal experiences, especially to the early years of his life. All this played a part in the formation of Gogol's personality — the man and the artist, and is directly or indirectly reflected in his work.

Gogol left his native Ukraine when he was twenty, and he left Russia when he was twenty-seven. Leaving Russia he deliberately separated himself from the source of new experiences which could be utilized as material in his creative work. *Dead Souls*, except for the first drafts of two chapters, was written not in Russia but abroad; it was based on reminiscence, not on observation; so were the earlier Ukrainian stories, written not in the Ukraine but in St. Petersburg. Very early in his life Gogol isolated himself almost completely, to live in a world of his own, a world of reminiscence and of subjective experience. Some insight into this world may be gained by going back to the sources of his personal and ancestral memories.

In the study of Gogol's personality and of his creative art several figures, historical or contemporary, must be introduced who either influenced him directly, or occupied an important place in his subjective world; among them was his hypothetical ancestor, Ostap Gogol, who lived in a period which attracted Gogol as a writer of historical romance; his father, a landed proprietor and a dilettante with various small talents; the former minister Troshchinski, a wealthy magnate and a distant relative of the Gogols who played a very important part in the life of the family; and finally Russia's greatest poet, Pushkin. The images of these men were present in Gogol's subjective world; they participated in his complex psychic processes; and the reflections of most of them appear, more or less clearly, in his creative work.

A number of examples will be given later to show how often Gogol turned to reminiscences of his early years in his fiction, especially in *Dead Souls*.

When, in 1903, Nestor Kotlyarevski published his extensive monographic study on *Nikolai Vasilyevich Gogol*, he found it necessary to introduce it by an apologetic statement: "All that is essential has been sufficiently clarified, yet he who would wish to return to Gogol once more is not condemned merely to restate what has already been said."

Today one would hardly consider as definitive those critical interpretations, biographies or text analyses which Kotlyarevski believed to supply final answers to problems of Gogol's art, of his life or of his personality. Nor, for that matter, was Kotlyarevski's own work definitive. The study of Gogol continued after Kotlyarevski; new factual knowledge has been gained, and much that seemed final has been re-examined and reinterpreted.

Gogolian criticism has a long and complex history which in many ways reflects the changing attitudes of Russian society towards literature. Several generations of critics followed the tradition established in Gogol's lifetime by Belinski (and was reinstated in the Soviet Union). This tradition interpreted Gogol's art as essentially realistic and primarily as a satirical exposure of social evils. Characteristic for this interpretation is the title of a work on Gogol published early in this century by a historian of Russian literature, S.A. Vengerov, "A Writer Citizen." The embarrassing fact, however, which this notion of the progressive and civic-minded Gogol, the "Writer Citizen," has to confront, is that the views Gogol stated himself toward the end of his career (and which, as he argued with some plausibility, had actrally never varied throughout his life) were the opposite of progressivism or of liberalism. Gogol was a Utopian conservative stronly marked with the belief that the political and social order is pre-ordained by God, and that instead of challenging this order, man should endeavor to perform his duty, as best he can, in that station which is his by divine predestination. This doctrine is reflected in the *Selected Passages from a Correspondence with Friends*, a collection of various moral and practical precepts including detailed advice on how best to keep the peasants in obedience and to preserve the sacred institutions of serfdom.

Soon after the *Correspondence* appeared in 1846, Belinski gave vent to his wrath and indignation in an eloquent letter to Gogol which was to become the political manifesto of the radical Russian intelligentsia. For Belinski, Gogol's book was an act of betrayal by a man in whom the critic saw his country's "hope, honor and glory, one of its great leaders on the path of consciousness, development and progress."

Gogol, it must be said, had never claimed such leadership, and therefore could hardly be made responsible for Belinski's disappointment. Old Taras Bulba, the hero of Gogol's Cossack epic, kills his son for betraying the country by falling in love with a Polish beuaty. He says to his son: "I gave thee life, and I shall take it from thee." Gogol – the Leader-on-the-Path-of-Progress – was largely the child of Belinski's fiery imagination; and his famous letter was the proclamation of the civic death of the "treasonable" author of the *Correspondence*.

Gogol's reinstatement in the progressive ranks was the work of Chernyshevski, son of a priest, economist and literary critic (1828-1889). In his famous "Essays on the Gogolian Period in Russian Literature," published in the mid-1850's, Chernyshevski attempted a posthumous reconciliation between Gogol and Belinski. His stand was that Gogol, misled and unenlightened (he "read the wrong books"), had nevertheless rendered an immense service to the cause of progress, for whatever his thinking and his preaching in his later years, the bulk of his work was a powerfully realistic exposure of social evils. Gogol was an ally, even if unwittingly and despite himself, but an ally just the same; and as such he was entitled to a place beside Belinski in the pantheon of Russian liberalism. Thus Chernyshevski's friend, the poet Nekrasov, in his poem, *Komu na Rusi zhit khorosho* (Who Lives Happily in Russia), asks himself whether the day will ever come when the muzhik will bring home from the fair the works and the likenesses of Belinski and Gogol. One may, nevertheless, wonder whether Gogol's works were the best choice for the muzhik in need of enlightenment, even accompanied by Belinski's critical commentaries.

It may be added that Gogol, in the *Correspondence* , pronounced himself against the muzhik's reading anything at all, with the possible exception of the Scriptures:

> In the first place, the peasant has no time for it; returning home after all his labors he sleeps like a log. . . . The village priest has a lot more to say that is really useful for the peasant than all those chapbooks.

"All those chapbooks," presumably, included Gogol's own works, by no means sacred.

Belinski and Chernyshevski's misrepresentations may be justified by the circumstances in which they fought their battle against serfdom and autocracy. In the days of Nicholas I, Russia had neither a parliament nor a free press, and literary criticism could sometimes be used as a cover for some amount of cautious social and political criticism, which became Belinski's tribune. That literary criticism was often nothing more than a vehicle for Belinski, was well understood by such men as the critic Alexander Herzen or Chernyshevski himself. Herzen wrote about Belinski, "one of the most remarkable figures of Nicholas's period," as he called him.

A concentrated attack on the view of Gogol proposed by Belinski and his followers began after the turn of the century. The reevaluation of Gogol was connected with the symbolist movement of the beginning of the twentieth century. In the interpretations suggested by Dmitri Merezhkovski, Valeri Bryusov, Andrei Bely, Innokenti Annenski, Vasilii Rozanov and a number of others, much is open to question. They had, however, the great merit of going beyond the traditional notion of the realistic social satirist and the humanitarian concerned with the "underdog," and of shifting the interest to Gogol's art and to the deeper and more obscure strata of his personality.

At the height of the symbolist movement, in 1909, Vasilii Rozanov wrote as follows of the Belinski school of thought:

> It is possible – it is even certain – that it was wrong. But this is not the point. . . . Granted that subjectively Gogol was neither a realist nor a naturalist: what "did the job" was not what he was subjectively; it was what he objectively seemed to be to his contemporaries, to his readers, to his spectators. LIfe and history . . . were shaped precisely by the fact that Gogol was taken for a naturalist and a realist, precisely by the fact that the *Inspector* and *Dead Souls* were regarded by everyone as copeis of reality and were certified true to the original.

Rozanov was undoubtedly correct in the sense that the image of Gogol created by the liberal Russian intelligentsia in the nineteenth century was a reality, and a highly operative factor, in the development of Russian society. But it was a social reality; how this image came into being, how Gogol became the unwilling leader and the absentee standard-beared of Russian liberalism – these are problems to be considered by historians of Russian society; they are extraneous to literature proper. The very fact, however, of this misunderstanding, this typically Gogolian story of mistaken identity, the appearance of the second image, of the "liberal double," undoubtedly had an influence on the real Gogol, who throughout his life suffered from the feeling that he could not be understood and was unable to communicate with others.

The mistaken interpretation of Gogol's art as essentially realistic could not be corrected, however, by stating that it has no connection with reality, that Gogol's characters are spooks and phantoms living in a world of distorted dimensions unrelated to, and incommensurable with, "objective reality."

Like all art, the art of Gogol is neither a "copy" nor a "reflection" of reality. And, it may be added, reproduction of reality (the unattainable ideal of "absolute realism," or "naturalism") is an impossibility for the obvious reason that "reproduction" is possible only in an identical medium: an image in black and white; but literature cannot "reproduce" because it operates with verbal symbols, a material essentially different from the material from which "real life" is made.

The art of literature, however, and specifically Gogol's art, is connected with reality (otherwise it would be unintelligible), it refers to reality in its own peculiar and very complex way. And the mistake of such critics as Belinski, and still more of Chernyshevski, was that they saw in literature primarily the references to reality, or, in other terms, that their main interest was in the reality referred to, rather than in the work itself (even if Belinski could discourse at length on problems of aesthetics). This transference from the work of art back to the reality recognized in it means the undoing of the work of art which can be discarded as useless once the recognition has taken place.

Belinski's interpretation of Gogol's art as realistic, erroneous as it was, deserves closer consideration for it is connected with the problem of realism in literature as it was understood in Gogol's days.

In 1835, before *Dead Souls*, or the *Inspector*, or "The Overcoat," Belinski made the following judgement:

> The distinctive character of Mr. Gogol's stories is: simplicity of invention, nativeness, perfect truthfulness to life, originality and a comical animation always conquered by a deep feeling of sadness and despondency. The reason of all these qualities lies in one source: Mr. Gogol is a poet, a poet of real life.

Further, addressing the reader, Belinski wrote:

> "How simple is all this, how natural and true, and at the same time how original and new!" Is it not surprising that the same idea did not occur to you, that you yourself could not invent the very same character, so ordinary, so familiar to you, so often seen. . . .

It is difficult to see how "simplicity" or "truthfulness to life" could possibly apply to the *Dikanka* stories dealing, all but one, with the supernatural, or to "Viy," the hair-raising story of witchcraft in *Mirgorod;* or how the Zaporog Cossacks in *Taras Bulba* , another one of the *Mirgorod* stories, could be called "familiar" characters; and the question "How is it that I did not invent all this myself?" is not necessarily suggested by the reading of these tales, nor of a story with a very complex structure like "Nevski Prospect."

True, at one point Belinski casually remarks that "in the (fantastic) genre Mr. Gogol is not quite successful. . . ." This would seem to condemn most of what Gogol had written by that time, but the remark applies only to "The Portrait" and in part to "Viy."

Elsewhere Belinski introduces the corrective concept of "poetical truth," giving as example Shakespeare's *The Tempest* which is "absurd," but "true poetically, for when you read it you believe everything, you find everything natural. . . ." But the whole point is that no one, unless his mind be unsettled, believes anything at all in *The Tempest*, and still less finds it "natural." We do not "believe" the poet, we are invited and we accept to follow him into the world of his creation without being deceived; the art of Shakespeare – or of Gogol – has little in common with the art of the conjurer or the illusionist.

Gogol was not alone to be interpreted by Belinski as a writer "true to life." He believed that Russian literature as a whole was moving away from what he termed "idealism" and "rhetoricism" toward a faithful representation of real life. The writers of the 1820's and 1830's, he thought, all strove to "bring the novel close to reality, to make it its mirror," but with Gogol this movement achieved its final success.

Belinski thought that reality had triumphed with Pushkin. Pushkin wrote in *Eugene Onegin*: "naturalness appears . . . as a truthful reproduction of reality." But Pushkin expressed his own views on art and reality in an unfinished article written in 1830: "While aesthetics, since the time of Kant and Lessing, have been developed so much in clarity and in scope, – we still repeat that the *beautiful* is imitation of beautiful nature, and that the principal merit of art is in its *usefulness*. Why then are painted statues less pleasing to us than those in bare marble or bronze? Why does the poet prefer to express his thoughts in verse? And what is the usefulness of Titian's Venus, or of the Apollo of Belvedere?"

To say that Belinski mistook romanticism for realism would be an oversimplification. Actually Belinski tried to define a very complex literary movement which contained within itself both romanticism and realism, not yet clearly differentiated or perceived as an antinomy; at that stage the different trends appeared as united in a common attack against the older convertions of classicism and of sentimentalism.

It has been pointed out more than once that the romantic movement, as practically all new schools and movements, attacked the existing conventions, those of classicism, in the name of truthfulness. Old conventions are always perceived as impeding a fuller and more genuine expression of truth, as narrowing the limits of art, as excluding valuable experience; and if the old conventions are overthrown, it is always in the name of reality as the only recognized norm.

Belinski, writing *O Gogole* (About Gogol), saw in the "new literature" a movement of emancipation from the conventions not so much of classicism, as of sentimentalism which he associated with

16

the name of the sentimentalist Karamzin:

Karamzin saw art through the eyes of the French of the eighteenth century. The French of that time understood art as the expression of the life not of the people, but of society, and even more, of high society, of the court, and considered *propriety* and *sentimentalism* foremost requisites of poetry. That is why their Greek and Roman heroes wore wigs and addressed the heroines as *madame*! This theory penetrated deeply into Russian literature.

Belinski, consequently, both observed and advocated the breaking away from the conventions established by the mannered, lachrymose and genteel Karamzin, and any non-conformism appeared to him as a victory of his ideal of "truthfulness." Karamzinian propriety and gentility restrained literature from performing its social function; the school produced literature for the candle-lit drawing room, for young ladies of good society. Belinski wanted, and welcomed, a literature for the people and about the people; and the new writers "despite the cries of the old-believers, brought people of all conditions into the novel, the authors doing their best to imitate the language of each one of them." The material which is not used in drawing rooms is an important point in Belinski's program. He mentions Karamzin's "Bednaya Liza" (Unhappy Liza) a story with a perfectly plausible and realistic plot (a peasant girl, seduced and abandoned by a young nobleman, commits suicide), and remarks that the old school

. . . may permit to depict peasants too, not otherwise, however, than clothed in theatrical costumes, manifesting feelings and notions alien to their way of life, position and education, and expressing themselves in a language which no one speaks, least of all the peasants. . . .

There is no doubt that this criticism was justified; but it leads to a paradox — Gogol is proclaimed to be "true to life" because his characters do not speak conventional language. The village blacksmith Vakula in one of his stories does approximate the language of a village blacksmith, but this blacksmith is carried from his Ukrainian village to St. Petersburg and back by an obliging devil; neither the devil, nor the blacksmith, however, would be admitted into a Karamzinian drawing room, and in this sense they are united in their opposition to the old conventions.

In Gogol's own writings a number of remarks may be found on

17

the relation between literature and reality. In an early essay, "A few words about Pushkin," he wrote:

> No one will disagree that a savage mountaineer in his warlike garb, free like freedom itself, his own judge and master, is much more colorful than some assessor . . . in his worn, snuff-stained frock-coat . . . But the one and the other are parts of our world: they both have a right to attention, although, for a very natural reason, that which we seldom see always strikes our imagination stronger, and to give preference to the common over the unusual is, for a poet, no more than a miscalculation — a miscalculation before his numerous public, not before himself; he loses nothing of his merit, he may even increase it, but only in the eyes of the few genuine connoisseurs.

And further:

> . . . the more common the object, the higher must be the post in order to extract from it the unusual, and, in such a fashion, it may be added, that his unusual be perfect truth.

These remarks referred to Pushkin's, not Gogol's own work; they were intended as an apology of Pushkin's works based on Russian material which came after the romantically exotic *The Prisoner of the Caucasus* or the *Fountain of Bakhchisarai*. But later Gogol repeated and developed his ideas on the "low" thematic material in *Dead Souls*, in the famous digression in Chapter VII, contrasting the writer who is admired and worshipped because he chose the exceptional in "slough of everyday images" and has never changed "the lofty harmony of his lyre," and the writer who has

> . . . dared to bring to the surface all that is constantly before our eyes, but what *indifferent eyes do not see*, all the frightful, the stupendous mire of the trivialities which ensnare our life, all the depth of the cold, the fragmented, the everyday characters which swarm our earthly road, a road at times bitter and tedious, and who with the firm power of his pitiless chisel has dared to expose them in sharp relief to the eyes of all!

Loneliness will be the lot of such a writer, all will turn away from him, for it is not understood that

> . . . equally marvelous are the lenses which survey the suns and which capture the movement of invisible insects; . . . that a great depth of the soul is needed to illuminate a picture taken

from life which is contemptible, and to elevate it to a pearl of creation.

It is important to bring out at this point that Gogol speaks of the choice between different strata, or segments, of reality: both the "savage mountaineer" and the official wearing a "snuff-stained frock-coat," both the "suns" and the "invisible insects" exist as components of objective reality. He justifies the choice of the officials (or the "insects"), but he emphasizes that the choice of "low" thematic material puts a particularly difficult problem before the poet; the unusual is striking because it is unusual, but from a "common object" the unusual (the aesthetically effective) must be "extracted," in the terms used in *Dead Souls*, everyday life must be so "illuminated" as to make it a " pearl of creation."

Gogol's views are not so much opposed to romanticism, as they are indicative of an internal differentiation of romanticism which has broadened its thematic material. But he lays the main stress on the treatment of the material, on making the commonplace unusual – that is, in contradiction to Belinski, not on the reality referred to and made recognizable, but on reality brought into art as material, creatively reworked, transposed, make unusual, and therefore perceptible to the "indifferent eye."

Gogol's theoretical views on art, which he stated in his earlier essays, clearly belong to the romanticist school. But his practical aesthetics, his creative art, moved along that stream of European literature which had rejected the restrictions of the classical and the politely sentimental conventions, which freely introduced new forms in literature and an ever broader scope of experience, objective and subjective. But gradually many of the forms and devices introduced in the post-classical period began in their turn to be felt as conventions. Gogol in his creative development followed different currents and experimented in different stylistic systems; often these experiments resulted in reinterpretation or in parody. Finally, in his mature works, such as *Dead Souls* or "The Overcoat," he integrated these various elements into an aesthetic system of his own which cannot be defined in terms of the romanticism-realism antinomy.

When at last it became apparent that the Belinski-Chernyshevski interpretation could not be made to account for all the complexities of Gogol's art and personality; when his work, seen in the perspective of the later nineteenth century, could no longer be labeled realistic without important reservations; when it had been established that contrary to Belinski and Chernyshevski's belief, Gogol borrowed not only from the "book of life," but also from books written by many Russian and foreign authors – then the older monolithic interpretation gradually began to give way to new interpretations based for the most part on the concept of dualism. One of the earlier attempts to analyze Gogol's "contradictions" was made by D. Ovsyaniko-Kulikovski (*Gogol*, St. Petersburg 1903); his much quoted work, smugly positivist and pseudo-scientific, operates with such ill-defined concepts as "intellect," "talent," and "genius;" geniuses are treated as a peculiar species, with much sympathy, for they are never happy and always have difficulties with their environment. At one point Ovsyaniko-Kulikovski writes:

Complicated by his genius, Gogol's nature, in itself contradictory and mysterious, shows a picture of a peculiarly complicated, bizarrely original psychic life. It may be said that his genius was in glaring contradiction with the most important and the most strongly expressed aspects of his nature and the peculiarities of his intellect.

Gogol's main contradiction, Ovsyaniko-Kulikovski believed, was the discrepancy between his "genius" and his "intellect." His psychic mechanism is described as follows:

The creative and the critical labors of this artist were immense. In other terms, immense was the expenditure of his mental forces. But unfortunately, the other work – that of the "learner," i.e. the accumulation of mental forces – was very weak. His tremendous intellect expended too much, and nourished itself too scantily. Hence – the lack of light, the absence of broad ideas. . . .

This strange interpretation of the great writer as a mental battery of sorts has often been quoted, and the passages from Ovsyaniko-Kulikovski did not fail to quote Goethe's "Zwei Seelen wohnen – ach! – in meiner Brust" and more than one attempt has been made to define the "two souls" struggling in Gogol's breast.

Merezhkovski (*Gogol*, Moscow 1903) applied to Gogol the favorite, almost obsessive antinomy between Christianity (or Spirit) and Paganism (or body). Despite his dogmatism, mysticism and exaggerations, Merezhkovski undoubtedly penertated deeper into the complexities of Gogol's art and personality than his predecessors; his picture of Gogol's basic "imbalance" is striking and convincing.

Another dualistic interpretation, less schematic than Merezhkovski's, was suggested by Vasili Gippius in his work, by far the best study of Gogol hitherto published. Gippius attempts to define the two elements of Gogol's polarity as the individualist's desire to withdraw from his social milieu, with its traditions, from the "soil," on the one hand, and the attraction which this tradition, this "soil" exerted upon him, on the other.

The attempts, more or less successful, to "define" Gogol seem to demonstrate that it is impossible to reduce the writer and his work to one basic antinomy, or to any other all-inclusive formula or definition. And instead of forcing upon him formulas and definitions, it is perhaps preferable to approach Gogol, the man and the artist, as a specific and unique phenomenon which was produced by many different forces and influences intersecting at a given point in space and in time, but which was not determined by, and cannot be attributed to, any one particular factor or to any one particular and definable conflict.

Gogol undoubtedly was characterized by what Merezhkovski called his "imbalance," but his contradictions or antinomies were many, and they were both external and internal. There is no doubt that Gogol's attitude toward the home, the "soil," the old way of life, was ambivalent. But it must be added that the old, patriarchal way of life with its security and its plenty, was disintegrating even in Gogol's young days; his "home," moreover, owing to family circumstances – especially to the early death of his father – did not so much offer him a peaceful shelter, as it made demands on him. The patriarchal idyl was for Gogol an idealized reminiscence, something he missed and yearned for, rather than a reality. And the homeless wanderer never freed himself from this yearning, which late in his life he rationalized in his *Correspondence* – this Utopia of stagnation – sanctifying landed property.

There was undoubtedly a sharp opposition between the rural, patriarchal and drowsy Ukraine with its bountiful earth and its mild climate, its rich folklore and its memories of a glorious past, and St. Petersburg, the northern capital of the Russian empire, the cold impersonal and competitive city of the bureaucrat and the tradesman. But this city was also the center of the new Europeanized civilization. It was an intellectual center with its university, its literary magazines and its literary salons; it was the city of Pushkin. The Ukraine of Gogol's young days, despite its remoteness and its provinciality, was not isolated from this center. Gogol's family and the school where he was educated were by no means immune to the new ideas and cultural trends; the "cultural dualism" was not only an opposition between the Ukraine and St. Petersburg: it was manifest in Gogol's environment in the Ukraine itself. An important aspect, or result, of this cultural penetration was the bilingualism prevalent among educated Ukrainians (the common people using Ukrainian only). Gogol's father, a literary dilettante of sorts, wrote a few rather coarse rustic comedies in Ukrainian, but generally he used Russian, and his correspondence is often colored with the lachrymose rhetoric of the Russian (or translated) pre-romanticists.

Gogol's own linguistic dualism, or rather the presence in his Russian of a dialectal substream (Ukrainian in his days was only beginning to rise to the status of a literary language) was of great importance in his work; this substratum manifested itself not only in occasional mistakes against the standards of literary Russian, but – and this is far more important – due to the very closeness of the two languages, it served to produce an extremely colorful, varied and expressive medium.

Gogol's subjective disharmony, his inner contradictions, may have been to some extent conditioned by the objective contradictions, social, cultural or national, to which he was exposed. But it is likely that they were largely independent of such conditioning. His main conflict was a conflict within himself; it appears in the form of a demand for ever-increasing, and finally impossible, achievement, made by an imperious force within him – a powerful urge, at once creative and self-destructive. Perhaps a counterpart of this conflict was his inability to love, his yearning for the remote, the immaterial, the sublime, his diffuse libido – a love without an object, or it seems, in the last analysis, a love for an exalted self-image.

Gogol's works, as long as they remained potentialities, were full of glorious promise; but they became inadequate – incommensurable with his demands and his self-ideal – when they were no longer *he*. *Dead Souls* was never completed; the first volume was merely an introduction; it only hinted at the tremendously significant whole. And what remained to be written of his *magnum opus*, this "Leviathan," as he once called it, seemed to grow to ever more grandiose proportions as his creative powers declined in his later years until his final undoing. The demand for the great deed was not satisfied by artistic accomplishment, nor by moral preaching, devout practices and pilgrimages; he could compromise with himself for nothing less than self-sacrifice, than total self-destruction.

Gogol's conflicts and oppositions are clearly apparent in his work. The diversity of his styles, however, the great variety of literary models, his work does not lack unity. It is by no means impersonal, not only in the sense that it bears the recognizable imprint of the author's artistic personality, but also because in the imagery, the situations and the characters in his work, one can decipher in more than one instance a language of personal symbolism, of concealed self-expression.

It is often useful, in the study of Gogol's work, to distinguish between what may be called his external and internal thematics. The external thematic material may be provided by Ukrainian scenery, popular beliefs or chronicles, or by the life of St. Petersburg officialdom and the street scenery of the northern capital, or it can be derived from literary sources, domestic or foreign, from some anecdote or incident. But internal themes overlap the different areas: that of the Ukraine, that of Petersburg, that of rural Russia; under different disguises, using a most varied material, this internal thematics follows its own course throughout Gogol's work, as a subjective and symbolic undercurrent.

It seems that at a relatively early period of his life, Gogol began to lose some of the acuity of his perception, some of his avid interest in the visible and audible world, in things and in people, in forms, colors, sounds and odors, in gestures and in words. Something became disturbed in his capacity to register impressions, to store them up, then to use them in the complex process of artistic creation.

Chapter II

GOGOL'S HOMELAND (THE PSYOL AND THE DNIEPER)

Nikolai Gogol-Yanovski was born on April 1, 1809, in Bolshiye Sorochintsy, a small town in the Ukrainian province of Poltava. Sorochintsy was not the home of the Gogols: they lived some forty miles away, in their property of Vasilyevka. But in Sorochintsy resided a physician, Dr. Trokhimovski, who enjoyed a great reputation in the region; he had a small clinic of sorts, and young Mariya Ivanovna Gogol – she was then eighteen – was placed there for her delivery.

Besides Vasilyevka, the Gogols owned a property near the town of Yareski where Mariya Kosyarovskaya married Vasili Gogol-Yanovski in the year 1805.

Both Yareski and Sorochintsy, Gogol's birthplace, lie on the river Psyol, a left affluent of the Dnieper. Vasilyevka is near the spot where the Goltva, a tributary of the Psyol flows into this river.

The title of one of Gogol's earliest stories is "Sorochinskaya yarmarka" (The Fair of Sorochintsy); it was written in 1830 and was included in the first collection of his Ukrainian stories published in two little volumes, in 1831 and 1832, under the title *Vechera na khutore bliz Dikanki*(Evenings on a Farmstead near Dikanka). Dikanka is a small town near the Vorksla, another left tributary of the Dnieper, flowing into it a few miles below the Psyol. On the Vorksla, to the south of Dikanka, lies Poltava where Gogol first went to school; this is the largest town in the region and the administrative center of the province (*guberniya* , now *oblast*); Poltava is some thirty miles from Vasilyevska.

In the "Fair of Sorochintsy" Gogol mentions the presence at the Fair of "merchants even from Gadyach and Mirgorod – two famous towns of the Poltava province. . . ." Gadyach, a town on the Psyol, some twenty-five miles upstream from Sorochintsy, is also mentioned in another of the *Dikanka* stories: "Ivan Fyodorovich Shponka i yevo tyotushka" (Ivan Fyodorovich Shponka and His Auntie). It is referred to as a far-distant place, just as in "The Fair" ("merchants came *even* from Gadyach"): the narrator heard the story of Shponka from an inhabitant of Gadyach and "last year" he chanced to travel through that town himself.

The other of the "two famous towns" — Mirgorod — lies on the Khorol, a right affluent fo the Psyol. Gogol used the name of this town as title for the second series of his Ukrainian stories published in 1835. The volume has these two epigraphs:

Mirgorod — a distinctly small town by the Khorol River. Has 1 rope manufactory, 1 brick factory, 4 water and 45 wind mills. — *Zyablovski's Geography.*

and

Although in Mirgorod buns are baked from dark dough, yet they are quite tasty. — *From a Traveler's Notebook.*

Severnaya pchela (The Northern Bee), reviewing *Mirgorod* , commented: "It is now the fashion to flaunt bizarre epigraphs which stand in no relation to the book."

The huge estate of Kibintsy was situated near Mirgorod, which was the residence of Dimitry Prokofyevich Troshchinski, a former Minister of Justice, a man of consequence and of great wealth. His Excellency Dimitry Prokofyevich was a distant relative of Mariya Ivanovna Gogol, and the Vasilyevka squires were often invited to Kibintsy for long visits.

Gogol's mother, Mariya Ivanovna Kosyarovskaya was born and raised in the Psyol area. Her parents and the Gogols were neighbors and she knew Vasili Afanasiyevich, her future husband, from her earliest childhood.

She recalls that one day — she was then in her fourteenth year — she asked her aunt, with whom she was staying in Yareski, for permission to go for a walk to the Psyol. This was granted, but a whole "detachment," as she puts it, of servant girls and women was sent along to accompany her. When they reached the river young Mariya heard

. . . a pleasant melody played on a wind instrument (a flute, or a clarinet?); it was easy to guess that this was Gogol because no one else had one; but how did he happen to be there that day? The music came from the other bank behind the trees and I couldn't see the musician, but the melody was charming. . . .

And when she was reminded that it was time to go home, "the music crossed to the other bank and followed me . . . hiding in the

25

gardens. . . ." (as Mariya Ivanovna Gogol describes it in her "Autobiographical Note").

Mariya married her flute– (or clarinet–?) playing Vasili about a year after this bucolic concert. She was then fourteen.

The Psyol, the banks of which were the scene of this idyll, is mentioned by the fifteen–year–old Gogol, then a student in a boarding school in the town of Nezhin, in a letter to his parents written shortly before returning home for a summer holiday: "I can already see all that is dear to my heart – I see you, I see my dear native country, I see the quiet Psyol shimmering through a thin veil . . ."

The "Fair of Sorochintsy" is one of Gogol's Ukrainian folk stories which combine rustic farce with grotesque demonology and with lyrical descriptions of nature, rich in rhythm and in metaphor. The story opens with a favorite image of Gogol – the archaic image common in folklore symbolism of the sky bending over the earth, his beloved, and pressing her to his bosom. Another animistic metaphor is used to describe the Psyol, and this metaphor develops into a labyrinth through which the reader barely manages to find his way:

The Psyol came into sight and even from afar our travellers could sense the cool breath contrasting with the oppressive, deadening heat. Through the foliage, dark and light green, of the birches and of the black and the white poplars carelessly scattered about the meadowland, there glittered fiery, yet icy, sparks, and the river – the Beauty – magnificently bared her silvery breast on which fell luxuriantly the green curls of the trees. Willful – like she (the Beauty) is during those rapturous hours when the faithful mirror so enviably catches her proud and dazzlingly brilliant brow, her lily–white shoulders and her neck of marble shaded by a darker wave descending from her light–brown head, when she casts away some ornaments only to replace them by others, and there is no end to her caprices – nearly every year it (the river) changed its vicinity choosing for itself a new course, surrounding itself with new, variegated landscapes.

The description of another river, the famous description of the Dnieper in Chapter X of "Strashnaya mest" (The Terrible Vengeance), another of the *Dikanka* stories, is in many ways related to the description of the Psyol in the "Fair of Sorochintsy":

Glorious is the Dnieper on a calm day when freely and

smoothly it rushes through woods and hills its plentiful waters. Not a stir is there, not a rumble. You look and you cannot tell when it moves or stands still, this majestic breadth; and it seems that it is all cast in glass, that a blue road of mirror — measureless in breadth, endless in length — lingers and winds along in a green world. And a delight it is then for the blazing sun to glance into this mirror from the height and to plunge its beams into the coolness of the glassy waters; and for the woods that border — to reflect in the waters brightly. Green-curled ones! They crowd together with wild flowers to the waters, and bending over, peer into them, and never tire of the sight, and never have their fill of admiring their bright images — they smile at them and greet them waving their branches.

Despite the obvious similarities between the two descriptions, the images of the Psyol and of the Dnieper differ considerably. The first of these two images — that of the Psyol — seems to have been, for Gogol, a feminine image; the second, that of the Dnieper, masculine.

Both *Psyol* and *Dnieper* are in Russian, grammatically, masculine nouns. But in the description of the Psyol, after introducing the name of the river, Gogol substitutes for it the generic *reka* (river), or *reka-krasavitsa* (river — the beautiful); both these nouns are feminine and call for the use of the feminine pronoun *ona* (literally: she) and of feminine endings of modifiers and preterit verbs. In the description of the Dnieper, however, the noun *reka* (river) is never used as a substitute for the masculine name of the river; the pronoun used is *on* (literally: *he*), and the modifiers and preterits are in the masculine.

Thus in the description of the two rivers, Gogol restores symbolic value to grammatical categories and uses them to express the feminine quality of the image Psyol and the masculine of the image Dnieper.

The passage in the "Fair of Sorochintsy" quoted above continues thus:

The cart with the pssengers whom we have already met mounted the bridge, and the river in all its beauty and grandeur as one single piece of glass spread itself before them. The sky, the green and blue forests, people, carts loaded with earthenware, mills — everything was overturned and stood or walked upside down, without falling into the blue, beautiful abyss.

The "blue abyss" of the Psyol is bridged and despite the

"grandeur" of the river one may safely stand over its very middle and see in it the amusing, reversed reflections of people and familiar objects.

Not so the Dnieper: trees and flowers gaze into it from its banks —

> But into the Dnieper's midstream they dare not glance: none of the sun and the blue sky glances at it. Rarely will a bird reach the midstream of the Dnieper.

The image of the Dnieper on a sunny day is the first part of a triptych: the second depicts the Dnieper on a warm sunny night, the third during a storm:

> But when mountains of dark blue clouds go scudding across the sky, when the black forests shake to the roots, and the oaks crack, and the lightning zigzagging between the clouds lights in one flash the whole world — oh, then terrible is the Dnieper.

After the sequence of pictures (the triptych: summer day, summer night, storm) placed outside of the time through which moves the story, there is an imperceptible, typically Gogolian, transition: the narration resumes and the stormy night becomes the background of a scene — a lonely boat dances up and down on the billows, then it reaches the bank and the Sorcerer, one of the central characters in the story, emerges from the boat and descends deep underground into a little cave to perform there the rites of his evil art.

The motif of reflection in the water is present, both in the passage from "The Fair of Sorochintsy" (Psyol), and in the passage from Chapter X of "The Terrible Vengeance" (Dnieper). It is also present in *Hans Küchelgarten*, a poem which preceded "The Fair of Sorochintsy" by some two years:

> Enchantingly all things are overturned
> and upside down in silv'ry waters shine.

The motif appears once more in Chapter II of "The Terrible Vengeance," in a description of the Dnieper at night; under the haze of a pale moonlight a dugout glides in midstream:

> It is a delight to glance from the middle of the Dnieper at the high hills, at the broad meadows, at the green forests! Those hills are no hills: they have no bottom, above and below alike is a sharp-pointed summit, under them and above them is the

lofty sky. Those woods that spread over the hills are no woods: it is the hair growin over the shaggy head of Old Man Forest. He washes his beard in the water and deep under it, and high over his hair is the sky. Those meadows are no meadows: it is a green belt girdling by its middle the round sky, and in its lower half and in its upper half wanders the moon.

In the "Fair," the images reflected in the river form a topsy-turvy world in which the woods and the water mills are overturned and the peasants with their carts walk or stand upside down.

In the description of the Dnieper at night (in Chapter II of "The Terrible Vengeance"), the power to correct visual perception is destroyed — the hills are not hills, the woods are not woods, the meadows are not meadows — and as the metaphors grow in intensity the real world and the upside-down world merge into one phantasmal image. Gogol's nocturnal Dnieper is doubtlessly reminiscent of the Rhine of the romantic poets — of Uhland or of Robert Southey known to him in Zhukovski's translations. But even if Gogol borrowed some of his imagery from the romantic stock, it had undoubtedly for him the significance of personal symbolism.

The Psyol, a feminine image, is radiantly beautiful and it is friendly world; his home lies to the east of the Dnieper, on its left bank. The Dnieper limits this world. The "masculine" Dnieper is "glorious," it has "no equal in the whole world." But it is "measureless in breadth" — "none but the sun and the blue sky glance into it in its midstream." It is radiant on a sunny day, but on a stormy night it may change into a wrathful deity.

The Psyol flows through a friendly, familiar country — the parental home — then joins the Dnieper. The Dnieper is "endless in length." upstream, on its hilly right bank, is the ancient and glorious city of Kiev. Downstream are the rapids, the wide open steppes, the Black Sea. It is a symbol of the ancestral world: the mighty river flows through space, and through the centuries: a flow of historical memories. It was the Boristhenes of Herodotus, with the Scythians inhabiting the steppes along its banks; it was the route of the Norsemen to Byzantium; on one of its islands, just below the rapids, was established in the sixteenth century the stronghold of the Zaporoghian Cossacks, and down it they sailed, in their boats, into the Black Sea, to raid cities on its Asiatic coast, and Constantinople itself.

The Dnieper appears in Gogol's stories dealing with the past of the Ukraine: in "The Terrible Vengeance," in *Taras Bulba*. The cognizance of a larger world beyond the narrow limits of "home," of the familiar Psyol area, is presented in "The Terrible Vengeance" as a supernatural awe-inspiring revelation:

> Outside of Kiev appeared an unheard of miracle. The nobility and the Hetmans assembled to marvel at the appearance: suddenly one could see far away, all around, to the very ends of the world. Far off one saw the blue glimmer of Dnieper's estuary, and beyond it spread the Black Sea. Traveled men recognized the Crimea rising out of the sea like a mountain, and the maushy Sivash. To the left one saw the Galician land. "And what is that?" the people crowding there inquired of old men, pointing at grey and white crests that shimmered cloudlike far in the sky. "Those are the Carpathian mountains!" the old people replied: "there are some among them from which snow does not retreat in all eternity; and the clouds take harbor there for the night."

Chapter III

THE PAST, THE COSSACKS, HETMAN OSTRANITSA,

OSTAP GOGOL, TARAS BULBA

Gogol turned to the past of his country as writer of his historical romance even before he attempted to deal with his past as a romanticist historian. In his fiction, he introduced the region where he grew up, and his hypothetical ancestor, Ostap Gogol, as well as only one historical figure, the leader of the uprising of 1638, Stefan Ostranitsa.

In one of his early letters from Petersburg (dated February 2, 1830), Gogol asked his mother to

> . . . collect all ancient coins and curiosities that are found in the vicinity . . . incunabula, any other old objects, antiques, and especially arrows which were found in abundance in the Psyol. I remember they used to get them by the handful. You would do me a very great favor if you sent me some.

He gave the following reason for his request:

> I want to win the grace of a certain grandee, a passionate lover of native antiquity, upon whom it depends to better my lot.

It is believed that the "grandee" was actually Paul Svinyin, an amateur archaeologist and the publisher of *Otechestvennye zapiski* (Fatherland Annals) – the magazine in which appeared in February 1830, Gogol's "Bisavryuk," or "The Eve of St. John the Baptist," a story later included in the *Evenings*. The reason for making a "grandee" out of Svinyin was evidently that Mariya Ivanovna would better understand, and readily approve, of her son's offering a gift to an influential official, while the usefulness of a gift to a magazine publisher would hardly be appreciated in Vasilyevka.

31

But whether in this instance Gogol wanted to buy the favors of a bureaucrat in high position, or of a publisher, he himself had a great interest in the past of his native country, in those long centuries of history of which his homeland had been the scene, and which he knew, had impregnated its very soil with relics of the past.

The arrows found in the Psyol, near Gogol's family home, may have been the relics of battles fought with the Mongol invaders, or earlier, with the Polovtsy nomads. The border between the Russian lands and the steppe empire of the nomads fluctuated, advancing into the steppes or retreating, between the revers of Sula and Psyol. The main defense barrier was the Sula; and "the horses neighing beyond the Sula" in the *Lay of the Host of Igor*, signaled the approach of the Polovtsian horde. During the Kievan period, Gogol's homeland was a wedge advancing into the steppes on the southern periphery of Kievan Rus. This principality was the first on the path of Khan Batu when, in 1240, he swept over the south of Russia, leading his hordes toward central Europe.

In an essay on the origins of the Ukraine published in 1834, Gogol wrote:

From Asia, from its very center, from its steppes which had disgorged so many peoples upon Europe, rose the most terrible one, the most numerous one: . . . The dreaded Mongols, with their innumerable herds of horses, such as had never been hitherto seen in Europe, and their carts, flooded Russia, lighting their path with flames and conflagrations . . . This invasion imposed two centuries of slavery upon Russia and barred it from Europe . . . Southern Russia suffered most from the Tatars. Cities and prairies burned out, forests scorched, ancient Kiev destroyed, a desert, a wilderness – this was the spectacle that the unfortunate country offered! The horrified inhabitants fled to Poland or Lithuania; many boyars and princes moved to northern Russia.

This picture is generally correct: the area was completely devastated, and most of the population that escaped slaughter fled either to the northeast where woods and marshes afforded some protection from the Mongol horsemen, or westward to the Galician lands later incorporated in the Polish–Lithuanian state.

It is possible that some very sparse population remained or returned before long, as Gogol assumes in the following passage which is worth quoting, whatever its historical accuracy, for the views it expresses on the Ukrainian and the Great-Russian peoples:

After the first shock, little by little settlers began to arrive from Poland, from Lithuania, from Russia, Slavs . . . of the purely Slavic tribes which in Great-Russia had begun to mingle with Finnish peoples, but here had preserved their integrity, with all their childish superstitions, their songs, legends, the Slavic mythology which they so naively blended with Christianity.

During the centuries which followed the Mongol invasion the Russian lands came together into two states, around two centers: Moscow in the northeast, and Lithuania in the southwest:

Southern Russia, under the powerful protection of the Lithuanian princes, became completely separated from the northern part. All communication between them was broken off, two states were formed, both called by the same name of Rus, one under the yoke of the Tatars, the other under one sceptre with the Lithuanians.

The border of the rapidly expanding Lithuanian state with a population predominantly Russian (Ukrainian, Byelorussian and Russian proper), and Greek-Orthodox, had advanced, in the fifteenth century, to within some ninety miles to the west and the south of Moscow. Early in the sixteenth century, Muscovy began a counter offensive and made important gains. Kiev, however, which is on the right bank of the Dnieper, and the lands bordering its left (eastern) bank below Kiev were to remain under Polish-Lithuanian dominion for another 150 years.

This area, practically a no-man's-land, was resettled, beginning in the middle of the sixteenth century, by a population coming from the west. The vanguard of this movement into the steppes was formed by bands of armed freemen, the Cossacks, who provided protection to the settlers against the incursions of the Crimean Tatars.

In 1557, the Cossacks established "beyond the rapids" (*za porogami*) of the lower Dnieper, on the island of Khortitsa, an advanced outpost, the later famous *Zaporozhskaya sech* (Ukrainian *sich*), that legendary brotherhood of fearless warriors and feckless freebooters, excellent horsemen and seamen, who fought and looted Turks, Tatars and Poles and gradually extended their power over the vast prairie land of southern Ukraine.

Gogol, whose chronology was never too accurate, placed the origin of the Cossacks "if not in the late thirteenth, then in the early fourteenth century" (the late fifteenth century would be closer to historical fact); he gives the following account of the origins, the character and the way of life of the Cossacks –

. . . a motley gathering of the most desperate men of the neighboring nations. The savage mountaineer, the Russian who had been robbed, the peasant fleeing from the despotism of the Polish lord, even the Tatar renouncing Islam, were perhaps the first founders of this strange society beyond the Dnieper . . . This multitude had no fortified places, not a single citadel. Dugouts, caves and caches in the cliffs of the Dnieper isles, in the thickets of prairie grass, they used as shelter for themselves and their booty. The nest of these predators was invisible; they attacked suddenly, and seizing their booty, retreated . . . All were free to join this society, but under one condition: that of adopting the Greek faith. . . . They were not the severe catholic knights, however: they made no vows nor did they fast; they did not seek to tame themselves through abstinence and mortification of the flesh; they were indomitable like their Dnieper cataracts, and during their wild feasts and drinking bouts they would forget the whole world. . . . It was a sight worth seeing, this inhabitant of the cataracts, in his half–Tatar, half–Polish garb . . . galloping on his horse with the impetuosity of an Asiatic, disappearing in the thick grass, springing with the swiftness of a tiger from his invisible hiding place, or emerging suddenly from a river or a swamp, covered with mud and mire – a terrifying appearance for the Tatar who would take to flight. . . .

Much in this portrayal is imaginative, and of Gogol's literary inspiration (one may think, among other sources, of Fenimore Cooper and his American Indians). The furiously galloping horsemen were united, however, in a strong community, and this community, Gogol believed, was the nucleus of the Ukrainian nation:

This assemblage took on little by little one common character and nationality, and the closer to the end of the fifteenth (sexteenth?) century, the more it was increased by new arrivals. Finally entire villages began to settle . . . around the mighty stronghold. . . . The sword and the plough had become companions and were owned by every peasant. And in the meanwhile some rakish bachelors began to carry away, together with the sovereigns, zecchinos and horses, also the daughters of the Tatars, and to marry them. Due to this blending, their features, formerly varied, assumed one common physiognomy, prevalently Asiatic. And thus was shaped a people belonging to Europe by its faith and its habitat, but at the same time, by its

34

way of life, its customs, its clothing completely Asiatic – a people in which met so strangely two opposite parts of the world, two different elements: European prudence and Asiatic unconcern, simple-heartedness and slyness; powerful activity, and the greatest indolence and self-indulgence; striving for improvement and development – and at the same time an inclination to exhibit contempt for any kind of improvement. (Much of this is repeated and amplified in *Taras Bulba*.)

To these views on the formation of the Ukrainian nation and the Ukrainian national type and character, Gogol added an interpretation of the historical destiny of his people; he believed that "the way of life, even the character of a people" depended largely on geographic factors: "much in history is determined by geography." He described the geographical position and characteristics of the land as a vast plain with no natural frontiers:

Whether in the north with Russia, or in the east with the Tatars, or with the Crimeans in the south, or in the west with Poland – everywhere its border was the steppe, everywhere was the plain, on all sides open land. Were there, even if only on one side, a natural border of mountains, or the sea – and the people inhabiting the land would have a separate state. But this open and defenseless land was a land of devastation and attack, a place where clashed three warring nations, its soil manured with bones and fed with blood. A single Tatar raid destroyed all the labors of the tiller; the meadows and the fields were trampled by horses and scorched, the slight dwellings destroyed, the inhabitants scattered or driven away into captivity together with their cattle. This was a land of fear, and therefore none but a warlike people could be molded here, a people strong by its unity – a desperate people whose whole life was nurtured and nursed in warfare.

Considering the time when they were formulated, Gogol's geopolitical views are interesting, even if they overemphasize the geographical factor. It may be useful to present in a brief outline the phases of the struggle between the "three warring nations" mentioned in Gogol's essay, since the earlier phase of this struggle forms the background of his historical fiction.

The resettlement of the Ukraine in the latter part of the sixteenth century was mainly due to the new conditions within the Russo-Lithuanian state which at that time formed with the Polish Kingdom a more or less united Polish-Lithuanian-Ukrainian state. In this political formation, Polish institutions and customs, and the

Roman Catholic faith gradually became predominant. New and oppressive forms of landlordism together with the increasing pressure of the Roman Catholic Church against Greek Orthodoxy caused large masses of peasantry to move southeastward, into the no-man's area of the steppes, nominally under Polish sovereignty. The Orthodox faith became for this peasantry a powerful symbol of social and national resistance (the union of the two churches proclaimed, after years of preparation, in 1596, in Brest, met with serious popular opposition).

The settlers, as they advanced towards and then across the Dnieper, were followed by the Polish landlords; Poland's political and social regime was gradually extended to the newly settled area now reaching the borders of Muscovy. The land in this area was very fertile, and the picture of "prosperous Ukraine" grew at that time, in Poland, to almost legendary proportions. A Polish author, writing about 1590, gave a description of the Ukraine which Gogol's descriptions of his homeland often seem to echo:

> The Ukraine is the richest land known. Its steppes are to be compared with the Elysian fields. They are boundless, broken only from time to time by gentle hills, valleys and groves. Their aspect is fertile and lively. There is such a wealth of cattle, game, and birds that you might think it were the home of Diana and Ceres. Such quantities of honey are taken from the countless hives that you would forget the Sicilian Hela and the Attic Hymettus. Grapes grow there in plenty and the vine can be easily cultivated. Walnuts are in such plentiful abundance that the Ukraine might once have been an Italian land. It would be impossible to enumerate all the fish ponds, lakes and rivers. But why should I vainly scatter magnificent descriptions when I might say in a word that Ukraine is the promised land that our Lord spoke of to the Jews, the land that flows with milk and honey. Once to have been in the Ukraine is never to leave it; it draws everyone as a magnet draws steel on account of its many advantages. The sky above the Ukraine is smiling, its climate is healthy, its soil fertile.

This "promised land," "flowing with milk and honey," was to become, for many decades, the scene of savage strife and destruction.

Cossack revolts against Polish domination began toward the end of the sixteenth century. The beginning of the next century was a period of collaboration, and the Cossacks took an active part in the Polish campaign against Moscow. But when the war ended and the lands to the east of the Dnieper were in their turn divided between a small number of Polish magnates, the Cossacks and the armed peasantry rose once more. From 1630 to 1632 they fought under Taras Fedorovich, or Taras Tryssylo (whose name, it is believed, suggested to Gogol the name of the hero of his Cossack epic: Taras Bulba). After a few years of respite, a new uprising was led by Pavlyuk, and after his capture and execution, by Ostranitsa (1637–1638).

Ten years later began the great epic of Bohdan Khmelnitski – the climax of the national movement of the Ukrainian people.

One of Gogol's earliest efforts in narrative prose was published in 1831 as "A Chapter from an Historical Novel"; together with another piece of historical fiction, this "Chapter" was later included in *Arabeski* (The Arabesques), a volume of miscellany published in 1835, with the following footnote:

> From a novel entitled *The Hetman*. Its first part was written and burned, for the author himself was dissatisfied with it; two chapters published in periodicals appear in this collection.

Some fragments were spared in this burning, if it ever took place: they were found in Gogol's papers and published posthumously. These different fragments were apparently interrelated as parts of an unfinished historical novel, *The Hetman*, on which Gogol worked in the early 1830's, concurrently with the *Dikanka* stories. This unfinished novel served in many ways as a preparatory and experimental stage for Gogol's major effort in historical fiction, *Taras Bulba*, written in 1834, and extensively reworked in 1839 and 1840.

Ostranitsa, the hero of *The Hetman*, also appears in *Taras Bulba*. Taras Bulba, himself a fictitious character, is assigned the role of one of the colonels under the orders of Ostranitsa, and the uprising he led forms the historical background of the last chapters of *Taras Bulba*.

Gogol's choice of Ostranitsa as his only historical hero may be due to the fact that the campaign of 1637–1638 was fought in an area familiar to Gogol. The major battle which the Cossacks won against the Polish forces took place near the town of Goltva, in the immediate vicinity of Gogol's Vasilyevka. The itinerary of a Polish emissary sent on a secret mission is indicated in one of the fragments; it was a route which Gogol traveled many times – between Vasilyevka and the town of Nezhin where he went to school.

Ostranitsa's first victory on the Goltva was also his last one: it was followed by several reverses, and Ostranitsa, abandoning the struggle – and his army – fled eastward, to the safety of the region which was under the sovereignty of Moscow. In 1639 the Polish government requested from Moscow the extradition of Ostranitsa, but met with a refusal. The none-too-glorious story of Ostranitsa became in the Ukrainian tradition a story of heroism and martyrdom: Ostranitsa, this story went, won a decisive victory over the Polish forces; he accepted their surrender, and the solemn promise that no retaliation would be taken; the Poles, however, broke faith before long: they treacherously captured Ostranitsa and his lieutenants in a monastery during a service they were attending, and brought them to Warsaw where they were savagely executed.

The plot of the unfinished *Hetman* seems to be based neither on the tradition of the Cossack chronicles, nor on historical fact, but on the author's imagination: this plot, apparently, assumed that after the failure of the uprising in 1638, Ostranitsa was not captured, and still less executed, but escaped to the Zaporozhye whence he returned several years later (the action takes place in 1645), to take part in a new uprising.

In *Taras Bulba* the scene is occupeid by fictitious characters, and Ostranitsa is kept in the background. The campaign is treated briefly ("There is no need to describe all the battles in which the Cossacks showed their valor, nor to retrace the course of the whole campaign: all this is recorded in the pages of the chronicles . . ."), but the episode of the siege of the small town of Polonnoye is told in some detail. Having cornered the Polish Crown-Hetman Nicholas Potocki, the Cossacks laid siege to the town and refused to lend an ear to the offers of peace and the tempting promise of the Polish general. But Hetman Potocki and his men were saved by the local Orthodox clergy, who marched toward the Cossacks in a solemn procession and persuaded them to spare the besieged Poles. The Cossacks gave in, but had the Polish leaders take a solemn oath first that the Orthodox Church would by respected and the Cossack freedoms and privileges restored. One voice rose, however, in violent protest against the Cossacks' leniency and gullibility, that of old Taras Bulba. Followed by his men, he left to continue the struggle; and in a farewell speech Taras sounded this solemn and sinister warning:

Ye believe ye have bought tranquility and peace; ye believe ye are high up now? That ye will be, not the way ye reckon, though: they will tear the skin off thy head, Hetman, they will stuff it with buckwheat chaff, and for many a day will it be seen in the market places! And ye too — my good men: your heads will not be saved either! In damp dungeons will ye rot, immured in stone walls, unless like sheep, ye are boiled alive in

38

kettles!

These sinister predictions were soon to come true:

A short time later, following the treacherous act at Kanev (Ostranitsa's capture in the monastery near the town of Kanev), the Hetman's head was hitched up on a pole together with those of the highest dignitaries.

The "historical" episodes relating in *Taras Bulba* to Ostranitsa's decisive victory over the Poles, to their flight to Polonnoye, to the intercession of the clergy, and to the capture and execution of Ostranitsa, are entirely apocryphal. It has been shown that Gogol borrowed these episodes from an historical compilation known as *Istoriya Rusov* (History of the Russians), a work whose authenticity is in serious doubt. One of the borrowings is Taras Bulba's gruesome prophecy concerning the fate of Ostranitsa: that his executioners will tear the skin off his head, stuff it with chaff and expose it in the market place. This manuscript gives a lengthy, gruesomely elaborate account of the tortures inflicted on Ostranitsa and his companions by their Polish executioners:

This execution was the first in the world of its kind, and theretofore humanity had never heard of anything so cruel and barbarous, and posterity will hardly believe the event, for not even the savage and most ferocious Japanese would have been capable of such an invention; and carrying it out would have horrified the very beasts and monsters.

Gogol borrowed a few details from the account, but used them for the description of the execution of Taras Bulba's son, Ostap (the author lowers the curtain over the sinister scene with the words: "We shall not pain the reader with the picture of the infernal tortures . . ."). As for the death of Ostranitsa, the composition of *Taras Bulba* did not permit a detailed direct description; it is dealt with by a brief reference, and the dramatic accent is given by presenting Ostranitsa's end as a fulfillment of old Taras's prophesy.

Borrowings from *Istoriya Rusov* may be found not only in *Taras Bulba* (it was the main source of the first, *Mirgorod*, version), but also in the *Hetman* and in "The Terrible Vengeance." The work enjoyed considerable prestige in those days.

Another historical character who played a prominent part in the events of the second half of the seventeenth century should have attracted Gogol's interest, a man whose name he bore, and whom the

Vasilyevka squires believed to be their ancestor — the Cossack colonel, and later Hetman, Ostap Gogol.

The chronicles and documents of this particularly agitated period in the turbulent history of the Ukraine often mention his name; he is referred to as Colonel of Mogilyov or of Podolye, or of the Dniester region.

One may find in the Cossack chronicles the account of a battle fought in the winter of 1655, when three Cossack colonels were besieged by the Poles and the Tatars in the town of Uman; one of these colonels was Ostap Gogol. The chronicle says the Cossacks fought valiantly, using the shafts of their sleighs when no ammunition was left, and frozen bodies of killed enemy formed a rampart around them; the supplies were gone, there was left "only frost and snow — free for all, but mixed with blood . . ." This ferocious battle ended in a complete victory of the Cossacks.

In 1658 and 1660, Moscow's *voyevodas* (generals-in-chief) stationed in the Ukraine mentioned in their reports Colonel "Ostafei" (Ostap) Gogol; he and his men did faithful service to the Tsar killing many Poles and Tatars during the siege of Mogilyov. Three years later, however, in May 1663, the Hetman of the right-bank Ukraine, which was under Polish control (the left bank had its own Hetman), reported to the King of Poland that Colonel Gogol, whose conduct had been so completely unsatisfactory in the past, now intended to go over to the King's service; and a few months later, that Ostap Gogol had sworn allegiance to the KIng.

During the rest of his life — his death was reported in 1679 — Colonel Gogol was thoroughly involved in the complex history of the struggle of the Ukrainians to achieve independence both from Poland and from Muscovy. A particularly interesting incident in this eventful life occurred in 1674, when Gogol was an ally of Hetman Doroshenko, who sought to advance the Ukrainian cause through an alliance with Turkey.

In the summer of 1674, Doroshenko sent a messenger to the Crimean Khan. The courier traveling across the steppes with a small escort carried a letter for the Khan and also a present which certainly would have pleased him — several Zaporoghian Cossacks taken prisoner by Doroshenko (Doroshenko was not on friendly terms with the *Sech*). The company however failed to reach the Tatar Khan: somewhere in the steppe it was intercepted by Zaporoghians and brought to the *Sech*. Doroshenko's courier was Ivan Mazepa, the future Hetman, who seemed to specialize in secret and dangerous missions. His talents did not fail him in this predicament: his captors were so impressed by his cunning, his eloquence and the amount of information he possessed, that instead of being submitted to the customary procedures, which were applied in the *Sech* when dealing with captured enemies, Mazepa was set free, and not only that: he left the *Sech* entrusted by the Zaporoghinas with a secret mission. The circumstances of Mazepa's capture were duly reported to the Tsar and with the report was forwarded the intercepted letter to the Khan. In this letter Doroshenko made various recommendations, among others to establish contacts with "well disposed people"; one of these was Gogol, in the Dniester region.

King Jan Sobieski was crowned in December, 1675, and Colonel Ostap Gogol attended the ceremonies in Lvov. Some time in the fall of the next year, the Colonel was made by the Polish government "Hetman of His Majesty's Zaporoghian Forces," a purely nominal title, for the Poles had no control over the Zaporoghians.

In September 1676, Gogol's former associate, Doroshenko, finally gave up his struggle: he surrendered to the Russian General, Prince Romodanovski and was taken to Moscow, where he was treated with extraordinary leniency: after some two years in prison, he was made *voyevode* in a northern province and later was granted a small estate where he ended his days in 1698.

Gogol's influence rapidly declined despite his promotion. In 1677, Moscow received reports that the Hetman was being deserted by nearly all his followers, who passed to the side of Moscow.

On April 8, 1678, Gogol sent a personal message to Moscow, advising that the Sultan whom he now called the "enemy of the Holy Cross," was planning a new invasion; he proposed joint action against the Turk. (This course is understandable; Muscovy and Poland were no longer at war, and the Turks, their common enemy, had a Hetman of their own.) Gogol's offer was duly forwarded to Moscow, but was apparently left without reply.

Among historical documents published in 1853 were several letters written by Vasili Kochubei to a friend, Colonel Novitski: one of these letters, dated January 27, 1679, has the following postscripts:

And here is some news, in case it has not reached you yet: that Gogol's days have come to an end.

Thirty years later Vasili Kochubei, one of the highest dignitaries in the Cossack hierarchy, was falsely denounced to the Russian Government, and tortured to death by Hetman Ivan Mazepa, the aged lover of Kochubei's daughter, Matryona Kochubei; shortly thereafter, on the eve of the battle of Poltava, Mazepa betrayed the Russians and went over to the Swedes. This was the first time in his long career that he chose the losing side.

The concluding lines of Pushkin's poem about the battle of Poltava and the tragedy which preceded it mention Dikanka, the family estate of Kochubei, and the ancient oaks, planted there by the friends of the innocent martyrs which carry their memory to their descendants.

A year after Pushkin's poem, the name of Dikanka appeared once more in the title of a volume of Ukrainian stories "published by beekeeper Redhead Panko." Certain parallels may be found between "The Terrible Vengeance," one of Gogol's *Dikanka* stories, and Pushkin's *Poltava*. In Gogol's story the rivals are the husband of Katerina and her incestuous father, the "sorcerer." In Pushkin's poem, the conflict is between Kochubei, the father of young Mariya (historically Matryona) and her seducer, old Hetman Mazepa. The relations between Mazepa and Mariya Kochubei, if not incestuous as in Gogol's story, were illicit, and the great difference of age between the lovers may have a connotation of incest. On the other hand, the husband of Katerina in "The Terrible Vengeance" and the father (Vasili Kochubei) of unmarried Mariya in *Poltava* are the lawful guardians, or "possessors," of the young women; they both perish at the hands of their enemies who are both traitors, and are both endowed with great power — supernatural, in the case of Gogol's sorcerer, political in the case of Mazepa. And finally: both are defeated in the end by a power even greater than theirs. The story and the poem are strikingly close in the scenes of the insanity of Katerina and Mariya: their deranged minds produce horrifying and revealing syntheses: of the murderer (the sorcerer, or the old Hetman) and of the victim (the husband, or the father).

It is difficult to say whether there was in this case any borrowing or influence, or merely a fortuitous encounter between Pushkin's historical and Gogol's fictitious heroes. As if presaging this encounter, the names of Mazepa and of Ostap Gogol, two historical characters, more than once appear side by side on the pages of the chronicles and documents of the seventeenth century, as in the episode of Mazepa's mission to the Crimean Khan, when he rode across the steppe carrying the message with the name of Ostap Gogol. And this final encounter: the letter announcing the death of Ostap Gogol bears the signature of Mazepa's victim and Pushkin's hero, Vasili Kochubei.

There can be no doubt that Gogol knew the main facts, if not all the details, of the stormy career of Colonel and later Hetman Ostap Gogol. In his copy of *Istoriya Rusov* he could read, and certain did read, the following passage dealing with Doroshenko and with his associate:

> Witnessing the progress of Samoilovich and the favorable
> disposition of the people toward him, Doroshenko was rant
> with rage and set to exterminate in barbaric fashion those
> towns, together with their inhabitants, which had joined
> Samoilovich. He dispatched his troops which were under the
> orders of their Colonels, Grigori Doroshenko, Ostap Gogol,
> Andrei Sotski and Andrei Doroshenko, to the city of Korsun,
> ordering them to take up a defensive position there. When the
> trans-Dnieper Cossacks saw Doroshenko's savage conduct
> toward their brethren, the local inhabitants, and his ignominious
> friendship with the Turks, those implacable foes and oppressors
> of Christianity, some of them removed to Little Russia, or to
> the Slobotskiye regiments, while those living closer to the
> borders of Poland, sought protection from the new Polish King,
> who, accepting them most readily, appointed as their Hetman
> Yevstafi – Ostap – Gogol chosen from their own dignitaries.
> And these Cossacks, numbering 14,700, with their new Hetman
> Gogol, took part in all actions under King Sobieski, famous for
> his eminent successes over the Turks, and lent him notable
> support in the victory won over the Turkish Vizier and his
> army before the capital city of Vienna . . . Jan Sobieski . . .
> returning from his glorious victory over the Turks at Vienna,
> appointed as Hetman of the trans-Dnieper regiments, Yakim
> Kunitski, elected by the Cossacks among their dignitaries, in
> place of their Hetman Yevstafi Gogol who was killed in the
> battle of Vienna.

This story of the death of Ostap Gogol is a myth: Ostap Gogol
died four years before the battle of Vienna, and there is no mention
in any reliable source of the Cossacks in connection with the battle
of Vienna.

Nikolai Gogol knew Bantysh-Kamenski's *History* well, and
apparently had no liking for its author. (He once wrote a letter
dated March 13, 1634, to his friend Pogodin: "What business do you
have taking up the defense of Bantysh! Don't you know he is [an
unprintable word is omitted] and has embezzled lots of materials
and manuscripts from many honest people?") In Bantysh-Kamenski
he no doubt found this paragraph:

> At that time (in 1676) Jan III invested with the Hetman's mace
> Yefstafi Gogol, who had served with Doroshenko as Colonel of
> Podolye and who had gone over to Poland in 1674. He was
> ordered to reside in Polesye occupying the town of Dymer and

several Lithuanian villages; his salary was to be paid by the Treasury.

Gogol was also familiar with Riegelmann's compilation which mentions Ostap Gogol a number of times and reports, among other facts, his mission to Turkey to ask for assistance in the name of Doroshenko.

To label Ostap Gogol a traitor would be an oversimplification: he did not owe unconditional loyalty to the Moscow Tsar; and whether, in its struggle, the Ukraine should choose as its ally Muscovy, or Turkey, or Poland, or Sweden, was then an open question. Later the perspective changed and the choice made by Khmelnitski became final. And the Cossack chronicles developed a violently anti-Polish tradition which culminated in *Istoriya Rusov*; the *Istoriya* was essentially a modernized literary rearrangement and amplification of older compilations, which in their turn were in the main adaptations and amplifications of the oldest account of the Cossacks' struggle with Poland: the *Eyewitness's Chronicle*. *Istoriya Rusov* belongs to the domain of political propaganda, rather than to historiography, and if it was written, as it had been suggested, in the middle period of the reign of Alexander I, then its purpose was to rouse opinion against Alexander's pro-Polish inclinations, and against his plans of territorial restitutions to Poland (cf. the memoir presented to Alexander I by Karamzin).

The popularity of pseudo-Koniski in the early 1830's, on the other hand, may be related not only to the romanticists' interest in the colorful history of the Cossacks, but also to the Polish revolution and to the anti-Polish feelings in Russian society which gained even such men as Pushkin (cf. his "To Russia's Slanderers" 1831). Such was then the tradition behind Gogol's historical fiction – a tradition to which he closely adhered – and the political atmosphere when he wrote the *Hetman* chapters in his *Taras Bulba*. And it is understandable that the colorful, if problematic, ancestor was embarrassing: in the perspective of Gogol's days he was clearly a traitor.

The descent from Ostap Gogol had received official recognition, in the late eighteenth century, thanks to the efforts of the paternal grandfather of Gogol, Afanasi Demyanovich Yanovski, who became Afanasi Demyanovich Gogol-Yanovski. Grandfather Afanasi's purpose was to establish his noble birth; he actually had no proof of his noble origins, but he did produce a document showing that Colonel Gogol was a nobleman, and the authorities which were not too strict in matters of evidence, believed his statement that Colonel

44

Gogol was his ancestor. What is remarkable in the cdocuments produced by grandfather Afanasi, is that it tells the story of the noble Colonel's treason; it reads as follows:

In recognition of the friendly disposition toward us and the Polish Kingdom of noble Hohol (this spelling renders the Ukrainian pronunciation of the name), our Mogilyov Colonel, which he now manifested by returning to our camp, by swearing allegiance to us and by surrendering the fortress of Mogilyov to the Polish Kingdom, and to encourage him to render further service, we do grant our village known as Olchoviec . . . to him and to his present spouse; and after their death their son, noble Prok (Prokop) Batacko (?) Hohol will also enjoy the right during his lifetime. . . . Made in our camp, by Kalnik on the 6th of December, 1674.

It would certainly be an overstatement to derive Gogol's historical fiction from the troublesome ancestral image. But the theme of treason recurs with a strange insistence in his historical narratives, and on the other hand it was perhaps to cancel out this image that Gogol created his super-patriotic and super-heroic Cossacks, such as old Taras, the indomitable fighter, the implacable enemy of the Poles, who dies with these words (added, however, only in the revised text) which he shouts to his Polish executioners:

Just wait, the time will come, the time is near, when you'll learn what it is, the Russian Orthodox faith! Even now they can sense it, the nations that are far distant, and those that are near: there will rise in the Russian land its Tsar, and in the whole world there won't be a force that will not submit to him!

Old Taras, it will be remembered, warned Hetman Ostranitsa against sparing the defeated Poles; Taras fought on, even after victory was won, never making peace with the enemy, pursuing his vengeance until his own destruction, until he found death at that very spot where Colonel Ostap Gogol committed the treasonable act which won him the favors of King Jan Sobieski. The epic of Taras Bulba ends when, after his raids deep into Polish territory, five Polish regiments move to surround him; in an attempt to lead his men out of the snare, he retreats toward the Dniester, the Turkish border. On the precipitous bank of the river, the Cossacks find the ruins of an abandoned fortress; here Taras decides to make a stand. After a fierce battle, the Cossacks break through; but Taras turns back; he dropped his pipe, and he cannot suffer that it become a

Polish trophy. This costs him his life! Onrushing Polish soldiers overpower him; he is chained to a tree and burned alive, while his men, obeying his last orders, jump from the cliff into the Dniester and escape.

The choice of the fortress over the Dniester for the scene of the death of his hero suggests a disguised reminiscence of the fortress of Mogilyov on the Dniester which Ostap Gogol surrendered to the Poles.

There is also a traitor in *Taras Bulba* – the younger of his own two sons, Andri, who succumbs to the charms of a young Polish beauty (the love scenes in *Taras Bulba* are among the worst pages Gogol ever wrote); he goes over to the Poles whom the Cossacks, led by he father, are fighting. In a melodramatic scene, father and son meet on the battlefield, and Taras kills his son with his own hands: there is no mercy for a traitor.

This theme was also present in the earlier *Hetman* fragments. In one of these fragments Ostranitsa is shown caught in a conflict which, it must be admitted, is not conspicuously original: a conflict between personal happiness and patriotic duty: he is eager to avenge the outrages suffered by his countrymen at the hands of their Polish oppressors, but he loves a young Cossack girl, and his love diverts him from his plan for a new uprising against the Poles. When he first meets his sweetheart after his return from the Zaporozhye, he persuades her to escape with him:

> We will go to Poland, to the King. He surely will give me some land. Or else we could go to Galicia, or even to the Sultan; he too would give me land. Then we will not be separated, and will live well, better even than on our farms here.

Later Ostranitsa soliloquizes:

> It hurt to see the Catholic mock the Orthodox folk, but it was a gay sight at the same time. Just wait, you Pole, and you will see how they will trample you, the free, knightly people! But what happened? Bragging – that's all there was! A fair lass turns up – and I forget everything, everything goes to the devil. Oh, those eyes, those dark eyes! The Lord Almighty wanted to destroy people for their lawlessness, and so he sent you. Our folk prepared to avenge the outrages to the Christian

46

faith and the humiliation of the people. I gave no thought to it, I was well-nigh forced to take up my sword. . . . I came here once more with a band of companions; but it is not justice, or vengeance, or the thirst to atone and to gain glory by prowess and blood that brought me here – but you, o, dark brows, you alone! . . . My head buns, what am I to do! . . . I'll go to the King, I'll persuade Ivan Ostranitsa to get a charter for me and the royal pardon.

The basic conflict is banal, but it is strange that Gogol chose to depict the hero of the Cossack tradition on the verge of committing treason, and Ostranitsa's plans of "going to the King" and obtaining a "charter" and a "land grant" are curiously reminiscent of the Mogilyov colonel.

Ostap Gogol not only went over to the Poles, he also maintained contacts with the Turks. In the *Hetman* fragments, in Ostranitsa's recollections of his young years (another soliloquy), there are these lines:

I was captured by the Tatars. It's no good, for a Christian, to live in their midst, to drink mare's milk and to eat horseflesh.

The motif of the sojourn among the infidels is prominent in "The Terrible Vengeance." The "sorcerer" si guilty of the worst of all treasons: he has forsaken the Chrisitan faith. Early in the story he returns to the Ukraine after many years spent in "foreign lands" and takes up quarters with his daughter and her husband, the valiant Cossack Danilo. Soon he betrays himself by refusing the food and drink he is offered. Danilo notices that his father-in-law will not drink spirits, as all good Christians do, and remarks: "Even the dirty Catholics are fond of vodka; the Turks alone don't drink." He is even more suspicious when the old man refuses to share in the *halushki* (kind of dumplings) prepared by Katerina. "This is Christian food!" protests Danilo. "All god's saints and holy men ate *halushki*." When pork is also refused, Danilo comments that "only Turks and Jews don't eat pork." The old man respects those "wrong" taboos, but his incestuous passion for his daughter violates that taboo which is most universally accepted.

To all the horrors and crimes committed by the "sorcerer" Gogol also adds the crime of treason: he kills his son-in-law during a battle between the Cossacks and the Poles, acting as an ally, if only as a chance ally, of the latter.

Gogol's interest in this theme of treason may obviously have been completely independent of the story of the Mogilyov colonel. It does, however, seem that, here and there, in his historical romances, it comes to light, like a deeply buried substratum, that, in spite of grandfather Afanasi's conviction, the question whether the colorful Ostap Gogol was actually Gogol's ancestor, remained unanswered.

Chapter IV

GOGOL'S ANCESTRY AND HIS NAME

The battle of Poltava in 1709, in which Peter I defeated Charles XII of Sweden, was the last dramatic event in the left-bank area, and Hetman Ivan Mazepa was the last great figure in Ukrainian history. In the course of the eighteenth century, the Ukraine was incorporated by gradual steps into the Russian Empire. Catherine II did away with the traditional Cossack administration, and "guberniyas" on the Russian model were organized instead. The office of the Hetman was abolished in 1764. After Mazepa, three Russian-appointer Hetmans held office. One of them, Daniel Apostol, Hetman from 1727 until his death in 1734, built the church in Bolshiye-Sorochintsy — a beautiful specimen of Ukrainian baroque — in which Gogol was baptized.

In one of Gogol's *Dikanka* stories, "Christmas Eve," young Vakula, a blacksmith in the town of Dikanka, wins the beautiful Oksana's promise to marry him; but he must first give her a present: a pair of shoes worn by the Tsarina. Vakula, needless to say, performs this task. He goes to St. Petersburg and returns — with a pair of shoes given to him by Empress Catherine. Within twenty-four hours, riding a devil, a petty demon, whom he easily outwits and forces to service him as his mount. The plot of the story (only the main theme has been mentioned here) uses various motifs borrowed from folklore which are combined with an "historical" episode. Arriving in the capital, blacksmith Vakula meets some Zaporoghian Cossacks: they are the delegates sent to submit various grievances to the Empress. Vakula follows the delegation to the Court and seized an opportunity to ask the Empress for the shoes. She very kindly orders a servant to give a pair of her favorite shoes to Vakula. The delegates are received by Catherine in the presence of a favorite of hers, Potyomkin, Field Marshall, Vicerly of New Russia, and one of them addresses the Empress; the Zaporogs do not know why they had incurred Her Majesty's disgrace:

. . . first we heard that you ordered fortresses to be built against us everywhere; then we heard you want to turn us into carabineers; now we hear of new calamities. Of what offense is it guilty, the Zaparog Host? Is it of leading your army over the Perekop, and helping your generals to chop up the Crimeans? . . .

The Zaporogs appear in this story — as though taking a final bow — at the very moment when, by orders from St. Petersbutg, they were destined to leave the historical scene. The delegate's speech alludes to the war with Turkey during which the Cossacks gave the Russian forces valuable support, and to the measures taken by the Petersburg Government against the unruly *Sech*. The Turkish war ended in 1774, and a year later, by orders of Catherine, the *Sech* was destroyed.

Serfdom was introduced in the Ukraine (New Russia) gradually, by a series of measures completed in 1783. After the second partition of Poland in 1793, the Petersburg government extended its policies to the newly-annexed right-bank (Polish) Ukraine.

By the end of the eighteenth century, the Ukraine was a peaceful region on the periphery of the Russian Empire. The so-called *Hetmanshchina*, along the Dnieper's left bank, with the ancient Kiev and Poltava lands, was living in a drowsy provincialism, resting, as it were, after the storms that had swept over it. Farther east, toward the Don, extended the newer "Slobodskaya" Ukraine (where, in the seventeenth century, Hetman Ostranitsa had found refuge after his defeat); and to the South, down to the Crimea and to the shores of the Black Sea, now firmly held by the Russian Empire, spread the endless expanses of rich virgin soil, a tremendous potential of wealth, a vast territory now made safe for settlement and cultivation.

It was in this area that Gogol's Pavel Ivanovich Chichikov was planning to settle his mythical peasants, the phantoms he had purchased: the "dead souls," or so at least he told one of the local bureaucrats interested in his plans:

"But allow me, Pavel Ivanovich," said the president, "How is it that you are buying peasants without the land? Or maybe it is for transplantation?"

"It is for transplantation."

"Well, if it's transplantation, then it is a different matter. And where to?"

"It is to . . . to the province of Kherson."

"Oh, the land there is excellent," said the president, and he referred with great praise to the tallness of the grass there. "And the land is in sufficient quantity?"

"It is; as much as is needed for the peasants purchased."

"Is it a river or a pond you have?"
"A river. However, there is a pond as well."

The steppe appears here in a modernized aspect. The romantic steppe where roamed the Cossacks and the Tatar horsemen, the tall grass hiding the mount and the rider, through which Taras Bulba with his two sons rode to the *Sech* to join the free Zaporoghian host was no more. It still had something legendary about it, but the myth was of a new kind, it was concocted by the "speculator" of the early nineteenth century.

In the year 1697, during the Hetmancy of Ivan Mazepa, a priest identified in his certificate of induction as *Jan Yakovlevich* (that is, by his given name and patronymic, no family name being mentioned), was made vicar of the church of the Holy Trinity in the town of Lubny, some thirty miles to the west of Mirgorod. In 1723 this ecclesiastic was transferred to the parish of Kononovka, a small town in the same vicinity. He was succeeded in this parish by his son Damyan (or Demyan) who assumed the family name of *Yanovski* (or Janovski, from *Jan*, the Polish first name of his father). Damyan Yanovski had two sons; one of them in due course took over the parish which he later passed on to his progeny; the other son, Afanasi, was the grandfather of Nikolai Gogol-Yanovski.

Attempts have been made to identify Afanasi Ivanovich *Tovstogub* of the "Old-time Squires," with Gogol's grandfather to this similarity of names, the following biographical data, to be found in the "Old-time Squires," recall the life of grandfather Afanasi:

Sometime, in his young days, Afanasi Ivanovich served with the companies and later was a second major (he earned this title in 1782), but that was very long ago, it belonged to the past, and Afanasi Ivanovich himself would hardly ever recall it any more. Afanasi Ivanovich married at the age of thirty, when he had plenty of gallantry and wore an embroidered camisole; he even abducted, quite deftly, Pulkheriya Ivanovna, whom her relatives were unwilling to give him in marriage. . . .

Like his namesake, grandfather Afanasi was second major, and according to a family tradition, his future wife, Gogol's grandmother, eloped with him and married him without her parents' consent; the young couple, according to this story, was later forgiven, and even received the Vasilyevka estate and other property.

Despite these similarities in thebiographies of the two Afanasis, the "old-time squire" is not a portrait of Gogol's grandfather. The general pattern of the life of Afanasi Demyanovich Yanovski (later Gogol-Yanovski) was advancement: advncement through education, through marriage, through promotion in government service. Born in 1738, a son and grandson of village priests, he was educated at the Kiev Theological Academy (he claimed knowledge of Latin, Greek, German and Polish, in addition to Russian and, of course, Ukrainian). His marriage, if it did not bring him wealth, at least made him a fairly well-to-do landowner. His wife, Tatyana Semyonovna Lizogub (Gogol's grandmother), who belonged to a wealthy family of the old Cossack nobility, brought her husband as dowry some landed property, including the estate later known as Vasilyevka (unless this property was later donated by her parents), with some three hundred serfs.

In 1785, Catherine II issued an edict which made the right to own "inhabited estates" (i.e. serfs) a privilege of the nobility. Being a noble thus became a necessity for Afanasi Demyanovich, who thanks to his marriage, owned such "inhabited estates," and three years after the edict he filed a petition for the recognition of his noble origin (he stated in the petition that he owned 268 serfs registered in the name of his wife, and by inheritance five serfs, two male and three female).

Afanasi Demyanovich's petition present his genealogy as follows:

My ancestors, Gogol by name, were of the Polish nation; great-great grandfather Andrei Gogol was Colonel of Mogilyov, great grandfather Prokop and grandfather Jan Gogol were Polish nobles; of these the grandfather, after the demise of his father, Prokop, leaving his estates in Poland, came over to the Russian side, and, making his abode in the town of Kononovka, in the district of Lubny, was considered a noble; by father Demyan, attaining the schools of the Kiev Academy (where he did assume, after his father Jan, the surname Janovski), was ordained priest and was inducted into the parish of the same town of Kononovka.

In support of his claims Afanasi Demyanovich produced the Polish document quoted above, dated December 6, 1674, in the camp of Kalnik, by which the King of Poland made a grant of land to "noble Hohol," his Mogilyov colonel, as a reward for the surrender of the fortress of Mogilyov to the Poles. The document, of course, proved nothing as far as Afanasi Demyanovich's claim went, but its authenticity can hardly be doubted. The fact that Ostap Gogol, Colonel of Mogilyov, surrendered this city to the Poles in the summer of 1674 is evidenced by Samoilovich's report to Moscow and other contemporary documents. It is also a fact of historical record that in the winter of 1674 Jan Sobieski, elected but not yet crownned king of Poland, set up his camp in the vicinity of the neighboring cities of Bratslaw and Kalnik (the act was signed "in the camp at Kalnik"). It may be added that the language of the document is unquestionably seventeenth century Polish. The village of Olchoviec, finally, which was donated to Ostap Gogol, is in Podolye, not far from Mogilyov. The fabrication of the document would have required an amount of knowledge which no one in the entourage of Afanasi could possibly have.

The best proof, however, of the authenticity of the document is its content: a fabricated document would certainly not relate that the alleged ancestor had committed a treasonable act and had received an estate as salary for his treason.

But if the document produced is authentic, as undoubtedly it is, it does not follow that Ostap Gogol, Colonel of Mogilyov, was an ancestor of the Yanovskis, the descendants of the Kononovka priest, Father Jan. To establish the link there is nothing but the statement of Afanasi Demyanovich, and in his statement he made at least three mistakes. According to Afanasi Demyanovich's petition his grandfather Jan was the son of Prokop Gogol, and the grandson of the Mogilyov colonel. Grandfather Jan's patronymic, however, was *Yakovlevich* (son of Yakov — Jacob); this is established by the two certificates of induction, dated 1697 and 1723. And Jan therefore was not a son of Prokop Gogol. Second, the petition states that Jan was "considered a noble" and that only his son Demyan (the petitioner's father) became a priest. This, of course, was a voluntary omission; Afanasi Demyanovich could hardly have concealed that he was the son of a priest, but he preferred to pass in silence over the fact that his grandfather too was a village priest. Finally, the petition calls the alleged ancestor — the Mogilyov colonel — Andrei. The Polish document does not mention the first name of the grantee and Afanasi Demyanovich mistakenly supplied the name Andrei.

If the document had actually been preserved in the family and handed down from father to son, finally to reach Afanasi Demyanovich, it would only be natural if some family tradition, some memory, had also been preserved and passed on with the document, and it is strange that even the name of his ancestor was unknown to Afanasi Demyanovich. He was apparently also ignorant of the fact that Ostap Gogol, in 1676, was promoted to the high dignity of Hetman; a fact which obviously would have enhanced his claim of nobility.

To say the least, it is questionable that Afanasi Yanovski was actually a descendant of Ostap Gogol, the Mogilyov colonel, even though the document he produced was genuine, as apparently it was.

It may be added that grandfather Afanasi's brother, a priest by the name of Kirill, and his descendants, continued to be known as Yanovski, without the addition of Gogol. A son of Kirill, Merkuri, was a priest in the neighborhood of Vasilyevka in Gogol's days; young Gogol, when he was about to leave his family, expressed concern over the fate of his mother in a letter to his second cousin Kosyarovski of September 8, 1828:

> . . . perhaps greedy heirs will leave her without a shelter. You know that grasping pope, father Merkuri, who avidly watches our property and who has already sneaked a goodly morsel taking advantage of family rights.

Gogol's paternal grandfather consequently, was a descendant and a member of a family of poor village priests, who did not follow the clerical vocation traditional in the family, but instead embraced an administrative career, and obtained the recognition of his very doubtful title of nobility.

Clerical ancestry carried little social prestige in Gogol's days, as is attested by the following episode told in *Dead Souls* about Chichikov, the buyer of the dead souls:

> Once, during a heated conversation, and perhaps after a drink or two, Chichikov called the other official a "priest's son," and the other one, although he actually was a priest's son, for some reason took bitter offense, and immediately answered him back, forcefully and with unusual sharpness, in these very words: "That's a lie, I am a state councilor, and not a priest's son; you're one yourself!" And he even added pointedly, further to increase the vexation: "Yes, and that's how it is!" Although he had thus parried him effectively, by turning upon him the very appellation he himself had used, and although the expression "and that's how it is" was, no doubt, a strong one, yet he was not content with this, and so he sent, in addition, a secret report about him.

Gogol published his *Hans Kuchelgarten* in 1829, under the penname "V. Alov." The reception it had in the press was such that the young poet hastened to withdraw the copies of

54

Kuchelgarten from the bookstores and to destroy them. "V. Alov" vanished forever, together with his Germanic hero.

During the following year the young author signed "P. Glechik," "G. Yanov," and "oooo." "G. Yanov" was the pseudonym he used to sign an article entitled "A Few Thoughts on the Teaching of Geography to Children" (January 1831); the opening lines of this article read as follows:

> Great and amazing is the sphere of geography: a land where the South is seething, and in every creature pulsates a redoubled life, and a land where horror is inscribed in the distorted features of nature, and the earth is changed into an icebound corpse; giant mountains surging into the sky; a vista full of charm, sketched by a negligent brush, and glowing deserts and steppes; a bit of land isolated amidst the boundless sea; peoples and art, and the boundary of all life! – Where could one find a subject appealing more powerfully to youthful imagination? What other science could be more beautiful for children, or could as swiftly elevate the poesy of their infant souls!

The signature "N. Gogol" appeared for the first time on the pages of the *Literary Gazette*, in its issue of January 16, 1831, under a piece entitled "Zhenshchina" (Woman).

Then came the two little volumes of the *Dikanka* stories (September 1831 and March 1832); they appeared anonymously, with the mention "edited by Redhead Panko, Beekeeper."

After *Dikanka* Ggol no longer used any pennames, signing his works with his own name. Gogol-Yanovski, however, was cumbersome, and *Yanovski* was dropped. During his first year in Petersburg, Gogol did some tutoring to supplement his meager salary of government clerk. One of his pupils has the following recollection: "The double name of our teacher, Gogol-Yanovski, ambarrassed us at first; somehow we found it simpler to call him Mr. Yanovski rather than Mr. Gogol; but at once he protested against this vigorously. 'Why do you call me Yanovski?' he said. My name is Gogol, and Yanovski – that's just an addition; the Poles invented it.'"

Afanasi Demyanovich Yanovski, the son and grandson of Kononovka priests, had added to his name that of his hypothetical forefather – a ghost for whom he secured official recognition – then, two generations later, with Nikolai Vasilyevich, *Yanovski* faded out and *Gogol* , the surname of the legendary ancestor, now stood alone, unadulterated. The circle was closed.

With his unusual sensitivity for the verbal symbol, Gogol always took great care and showed great inventiveness in the choice of names for his characters.

His own name combined *Yanovski* and *Gogol*, an indifferent, rather common name with a Polish flavor, and a name suggesting Cossack origin, unusual and expressive, though with a slight comical connotation. *Gogol* is the name of a bird (*golden-eye*, or *whistle wing*); in Russian it occurs in the expression *khodit gogolem*, literally "to go about like a golden-eye," that is to swagger, to be jauntily superior in manner.

In the concluding paragraph of *Taras Bulba*, Gogol uses the name of the bird – his own name – restoring to it its original meaning, and bringing out its poetical quality:

> No small river is the Dniester, and along it are many inlets, many spots thickly grown with sedge many shoals and soundless pools; all aglitter is the mirror-like river, ringing with the sharp whoops of swans, and the proud golden-eye [*gogol*] swiftly wings over it, and the sandpipers, the red-breasted snipe and different other birds are many in the rushes and along its banks.

In a notebook Gogol used in 1842 to jot down miscellaneous information, one finds the following item: "*Golden eye (gogol)*, large – the size of a large duck, white with red feathers around the head something like cuffs; the legs are far back, toward the tail. Hard to shoot because as soon as they catch sight they immerse the whole body, and only the neck remains above the water. Cannot run on land. Swims proudly and swiftly, lifting its long nose. Sometimes places its goslings on its back and swims with them. Dives far and stays long under water."

A reminiscence of the theme of the family name may be found in another of Gogol's early works, his "Povest o tom kak possorilsya Ivan Ivanovich s Ivanom Nikiforovichem" (The Story of How Ivan Ivanovich Came to Quarrel with Ivan Nikiforovich).

The two gentlemen of Mirgorod quarreled over a barter proposed by Ivan Ivanovich to his friend and neighbor Ivan Nikiforovich; the offer was that of a sow and two sacks of oats in exchange for a shotgun. Ivan Nikiforovich, the owner of the firearm, refused the deal, whereupon a heated argument developed over the comparative value of the commodities considered. During this argument Ivan Ivanovich, the owner of the sow and the oats, was insulted by Ivan Nikiforovich.

Ivan Ivanovich – Pererepenko by his last name – lodged a complaint against Ivan Nikiforovich. In this complaint, which

56

initiated an endless litigation, he stated that he had been called

> . . . a name insulting and slighting to my honor, *viz.*, that of *gander*, the fact notwithstanding that it is known to the entire Mirgorod county that at no time did I bear the name of this vile animal, nor do I intend so to be named henceforward. As for evidence of my noble birth, such evidence is that in the parish register kept at the Three Saints Chruch is recorded the day of my birth and likewise the baptism which I received. A gander, however, as is known to anyone with some little amount of learning, may not be entered in a parish register, for a gander is not a human person, but a bird . . .

In a typically Gogolian fashion, the plaintiff shifts from the idea of insult to the idea of mistaken identity; from the idea that Ivan Nikiforovich had wronged him by calling him a gander, to the idea that he was wrong in calling him a gander. And Ivan Ivanovich undertakes, quite unnecessarily of course, to rectify the "error" and to prove, calling the whole county to witness, that he is not, and never was, known by the name of the "vile animal."

He further turns to the quite irrelevant question of his gentle birth, offering as evidence thereof the fact that his birth and baptism are recorded in the local parish register, which evidence is obviously no evidence at all. He argues finally that it is not even possible to bear the name of *gander,* for gander is the name of a bird, and for that reason cannot be entered in a parish register reserved for human beings.

Gogol – the golden eye – is also a name of a bird (it is a member of the *anseridae* or goose, family). Of course, Ivan Ivanovich refects the bird name that was given him, while Afanasi Demyanovich Yanovski went through long procedures to prove that another bird name, *Gogol*, was the name of his ancestors; Nikolai Gogol also accepted this name, discarding the "human" name Yanovski.

It seems plausible, nevertheless, that Ivan Ivanovich's complaint was a reminiscence – or a reflection, even if an inverted reflection – of the story of Gogol's family name.

It may be added that in his complaint Ivan Ivanovich mentions the fact that his parent ("of blessed memory") was in the ecclesiastic profession; so was the parent of Afanasi Demyanovich – the Kononovka priest Demyan Ivanovich Yanovski.

Afanasi Demyanovich met with some difficulty in establishing his rights to the name Gogol and his noble birth: his petition was granted some four years after it was presented. Ivan Ivanovich's complaint may well be understood as a caricature of Afanasi Demyanovich's petition, and possibly also of the objections he encountered: *gander* cannot be entered in the parish register – *Gogol* cannot be entered in the register of nobility. The evidence produced by Afanasi Yanovski to prove his noble birth is questionable, and apparently was questioned. The evidence offered by Ivan Ivanovich (the parish register) was, of course, anything but convincing.

One may consequently conjecture that Gogol had some knowledge of the procedure through which his grandfather obtained recognition of his noble ancestry – also that he was not entirely unaware of the fact that this ancestry was of a rather doubtful nature.

Gogol was conscious of the meaning of his name; he had spent the fall of 1836 on Lake Geneva (working in Vevey on *Dead Souls*), and in November he wrote from Paris to Zhukovski telling him about his solitary wanderings along the northern bank of the Lake, and of his visit to the castle of Chillon:

> I even carved my name, in Russian letters, in the dungeon of Chillon; I was not bold enough to sign it under the glorious names of the author and of the translator of the "Prisoner of Chillon" [Byron's Russian translator was Zhukovski], and there was no room either: a certain Burnashov signed his name right under theirs. At the base of the last column, the one that is in the shade, one day a traveling Russian will decipher my bird's name, unless some Englishman will be sitting on it.

In 1967, Leon Stilman, visited the dungeon of Chillon and could not find Gogol's "bird's name" carved in Russian letters "at the base of the last column, the one that is in the shade."

Chapter 5

PARENTS

Vasili Afanasyevich, Gogol's father, Afanasi Demyanovich's only child, was born in 1777. He studied at the Seminary at Poltava where he was in the care of a tutor whose main concern was to avoid overburdening young Vasili (or Vasyuta) with excessive work. This tutor reports, in March 1795, to his pupil's parents:

> Vasyuta, thanks to God, to the extent of his forces and abilities, and correspondingly to these, is making progress in his studies, and gives good hope to do so in the future; I urge him to study, but always with due consideration for his physical forces which appear not too great.

Even if he did not overstrain himself in Poltava, Vasili Afanasyevich, according to his wife's Autobiographical Notes

> . . . knew grammar very well, arithmetic in all its parts, geography, Latin, versification, knew well mythology; having a solid natural intelligence, he had knowledge of architecture, and drew, in his spare time, the facade of our house, explaining what the plan would be, where what room would be and how it would be most convenient to live.

Once the education of his son was completed, Afanasi Demyanovich concerned himself with his future. At one time he considered a military career for his son, and steps were taken to enlist him in the Guards. Such an enlistment, often at a very early age, followed by automatic promotion, so that actual service began with an officer's rank, was a traditional privilege of the nobility. Paul I, however, who had come to the throne in the meantime, put an end to these conditions: regardless of birth, service in the Guards was now to begin in the ranks and was to be actual. The project was therefore abandoned, and through various connections a job, or rather a sinecure, was obtained for young Vasili in the Ukrainian postal administration. He resigned from government service in 1805. The same year he married Mariya Ivanovna Kosyarovskaya. The

59

couple made their home at Vasilyevka.

Vasili Afanasyevich has been shown as a landowner preoccupied with the management of his property and the raising of his family; as the factotum of his "benefactor" Troshchinski; as the manager of the Kibintsy theater and an amateur playwright; as a man sociable and good-natured, doing his best to take care of many things, rather harassed and toward the end showing signs of fatigue and discouragement.

Some aspects of Vasili Afanasyevich's personality are brought to light in the story of his courtship and marriage. Young Vasili often visited his parents' small property in Yareski. Mariya, Anne Troshchinskaya's niece, spent most of her childhood in her aunt's neighboring estate. When he came to Yareski, Vasili never failed to pay his respects to Madame Troshchinskaya, and this lady noticed that during his visits he showed an unusual interest in her little niece Mariya – or Mashenka – playing dolls with her for hours at length.

Years went by and the time came of theidyllic promenades on the banks of the Psyol and of the bucolic concerts. And when Mashenka reached the age of thirteen, Vasili – he was then twenty-seven – timidly spoke to her father of marriage. At the time, as she innocently remarks in her reminiscences, ". . . I loved him so, that I was unable to decide whom I loved more, my aunt or him . . ." Some time later Vasili declared his feelings to her and asked her if she shared them. Mashenka's reply grieved him immensely: she answered simply that she was "fond of him like she was of all people," choosing to conceal her love which by then seems to have exceeded even her affection for her aunt.

Several of Vasili's letters to his youthful bride have been preserved; two of these epistolary effusions (neither of them dated) read as follows:

To my great sorrow I may not speak to you, I have to be cold with you. I must conceal under apparent gaiety my intense love and my sadness engendered by terrible fantasies! Ah, could it be that you do not love me! that you have changed your intentions: but I do not know anything, and despair relentlessly gnaws my heart. I must leave today – without having spoken to you! Oh, how unbearable for me is this separation, the more so that I am not sure of your love. Reassure me, were it only with one single word, have pity for one who suffers! Farewell. . . . Your ever devoted Vasili.

Dearest Mashenka! Different obstacles deprived me of the

felicity of being with you this day! The weakness of my health gives birth to terrifying imaginations, and fierce despair gnaws my heart. Farewell, my best friend in the whole world! I beg you to be well and not to worry about me. Be assured that no one in the world could be loved as strongly as you are loved and respected by your eternally faithful friend, unhappy Vasili. . . . Pray, do not show this unfortunate expression of passion to your parents. I do not know myself how I can write this.

"Unhappy Vasili" was evidently a character of his time, and much in his prose and in his attitudes was merely the sentimental cliché of the kind made popular in Russian by Karamzin. His literary sources went back even farther: Mariya Ivanovna reports that in the early years of their marriage her husband read with her "a very old book" – *Cadmus and Harmonia*; this was a novel of classical antiquity by Mikhail Kheraskov (published in 1786), one of the Russian imitations of Fénelon's *Télémaque*, a work of appalling length filled with improbable adventures and didactic allegories.

The pre-romantic pattern is evident in Vasili's love for landscape gardening (he jotted down in his notebook that "Bacon, Milton and Addison created the taste for English gardens. . . ." and other relevant information); in the building of arbors and grottoes in the Vasilyevka garden; in giving various names to sites in the neighboring country, such as "The Valley of Rest;" in prohibiting laundry to be done in the Vasilyevka pond lest the noise should frighten away the nightingales of which he was particularly fond.

The *Zeitgeist* may certainly account for young Vasili's tearful effusions, for the "despair gnawing his heart," as well as for the arbors and the nightingales. But if Vasili sought to emulate Karamzin's heroes or Werther, he could borrow from them only the style, the mode of expression. Literary models do not account for his tender devotion for a little girl, a feeling which developed into a passionate love when Mashenka reached what even then was scarcely considered the nubile age. Vasili insisted, it may be added, that his fourteen-year-old bride join him one month after their marriage – which she did – although it had been agreed that she would spend a year with her parents. In this unusual romance Vasili was not imitating literary models: it reflected his own personality, and it may be conjectured that if he fell in love with a child it was because of a certain lack of virile self-confidence, because of a fear of more mature femininity.

It is also significant that, in his love letters to a girl of thirteen (he was twice her age), he speaks not only of his moral agonies, but also of his ill health, of his weakness, as if wishing to deny his

61

strength of a man, and to cancel his superiority. A fear of womanhood, then, may be the explanation of his affection for a child, an affection which grew into passionate love after a long period of an innocent, and reassuring, relationship.

Vasili and Mashenka seem to have found perfect happiness in their marriage, despite the many worries they had to face.

Vasili Afanasyevich, the young Vasilyevka squire, devoted himself with earnest zeal to the management of the property. This property was by no means negligible. The totoal acreage owned by the Gogols amounted to about 1,100 desyatinas (approximately 2,900 acres). Vasili Afanasyevich took care to round off the properties, and between 1804 and 1823 he entered into fourteen different transactions: purchases of small plots or exchanges. The number of serfs owned by the Gogols in the middle 1830's (no figures are available for an earlier date) exceeded 400 (the only known purchase was made in 1813, of a family of four, of "Great-Russian stock," for the price of 4,000 rubles).

The crops grown were mainly wheat, rye and barley, but also millet, oats, flax and tobacco. The grain was milled locally; some wheat flour was marketed, bringing in an average of about 2,000 rubles a year. The rye was used for distilling. A small distillery had long existed on the estate; it was destroyed by fire in 1817 and was rebuilt the next year. A plan was adopted for enlarging and modernizing the distillery, which was put into effect by Mariya Ivanovna after her husband's death, and 2,300 rubles were invested in new equipment. The sale of liquor brought approximately 2,650 rubles in the year 1820, for which figures are available. Especially profitable was the retail sale of liquor in the tavern owned at Vasilyevka by the Gogols (another tavern was later opened in the village of Yareski where the family owned a small property).

The Vasilyevka squires also engaged in raising cattle, sheep and pigs; imported animals were purchased to improve the domestic breed.

In addition to the distillery and the wind-mills, there were also on the property a fullery, a tannery and a brick factory. Some of the output was marketed.

Vasili Afanasyevich took the initiative of organizing in the village of Vasilyevka a fair which was held four times yearly. The Vasilyevka fairs were very successful and facilitated the marketing of the produce of the estate.

The second chapter of Gogol's "Fair of Sorochintsy" has the following epigraph (in Ukrainian):

Lord Almighty! is there anything you can't find at that fair! wheels, glass, tar tobacco, straps, onions, all the peddlesr with their goods . . . so that even if you had, say, thirty rubles in your pouch, or thereabouts, even then you couldn't buy up the whole fair.

This passage is subscribed: "From a Little-Russian Comedy." The author of this "Little-Russian Comedy" was Vasili Afanasyevich, Gogol's father, the founder of the Vasilyevka fair.

To summarize: the economy of the Vasilyevka squires was a manorial economy, primarily agricultural, but with some manufacturing based on raw materials produced or found on the estate (e.g. rye for distilling, clay for brick manufacturing, etc.); the economy depended on serf labor; finally, part of the produce was marketed.

During the Soviet period especially, the social and economic status of the Gogol family has been the object of extensive research and of much controversy. The opinion seems to have prevailed that Gogol's parents belonged to the middle stratum of the Ukrainian land-owning class rather than to its lower-middle category, their existence developed atypically: their life did not follow the customary pattern of either of these strata.

A very important, largely determinative, factor in the life of Gogol's parents was their relationship with Dmitri Prokofyevich Troshchinski, their wealthy and powerful relative and neighbor.

Mariya Ivanovna was related to the Troshchinskis through her paternal aunt, Anna Matveyevna Kosyarovskaya; this aunt, who brought her up, was married to a brother of Dmitri Prokofyevich.

Aunt Anna had a son – a cousin of Mariya Ivanovna Gogol – who played a prominent part in the relations between his wealthy and influential uncle, Dmitri Prokofyevich, and the Gogols. Mariya Ivanovna writes in her reminiscences that her cousin Andrei (he was her elder by seventeen years) always treated her as his sister. This may well apply to Mariya Ivanovna's childhood. In later years, however, the relationship seems to have been affected, in some measure at least, by the great difference in social position between the cousins.

Andrei Troshchinski who had received an excellent education ("he spoke Russian," says Mariya Ivanovna, "in the Petersburg tongue, as we called it in Little Russia, and also French and German . . .") and had served with the Guards, retired in 1811 with the rank of major-general to devote himself to the management of the estates of his uncle's entourage and later inherited most of his fortune.

In Mariya's childhood reminiscences there is a recollection of

Dmitri Prokofyevich himself. He once came to visit her aunt Anna when she was in her care. He was accompanied by two old gentlemen wearing decorations; the visitors were very kind to her. Her aunt told them that little Mariya (she was then seven) could perform a dance to the accompaniment of her own singing. It is not known whether the dance was performed on that occasion, but in later years demands were often made on the talents of Mariya and of her husband to provide entertainment for Troshchinski when he retired to his estate at the end of a most successful career. Mariya recalls that Troshchinski was inspecting the postal services in the Ukraine when he visited her aunt. At that time (Mariya was seven in 1798) he actually held a high position in the postal administration.

Born in 1754, into a family of Cossack gentry of the Mirgorod district, Dmitri Troshchinski, a pupil of the Kiev Theological Academy, took service in the Ukrainian Military government. Passing from the local administration to military and diplomatic service, he advanced rapidly. In 1787 he was introduced to Empress Catherine II. Later Catherine conferred upon him one of the highest court titles, that of Secretary of State, and shortly before her death in 1796, he received from her, in recognition of his services, a grant of huge properties in the Ukraine.

Troshchinski's career continued during the reign of Paul I and of Alexander I, who made him Postmaster General, then Minister of the Domains. In 1806 Troshchinski resigned and retired to Kibintsy, one of his Ukrainian estates. In 1814 he visited the capital and was received by Emperor Alexander, who pressed him to accept the post of Minister of Justice.

After two years in this high position, Troshchinski (he was at that time seriously ill) was honored by a personal rescript of the Emperor which read:

Dmitri Prokofyevich! It is my wish that after recovery from your present illness, and a prompt resumption of your former position, you continue the business of your office with your former diligence. Entirely confident in you, I entrust you with the duty of redoubling surveillance in order that business before the Supreme Senate, as well as that before all the courts under its authority, may follow its course with utmost regularity; that laws and decrees be everywhere applied unfailingly; that the poor and oppressed may find in the courts defense and protection; that justice be not perverted, be it by partiality for individuals, or by ignominious bribery, repugnant to God and hateful to me, and that those guilty of this abominable vice be not permitted to continue in service and be prosecuted with all the severity of law . . .

Young Gogol, shortly before graduation and on the threshold of life, once expressed the belief that he would best render service to his countrymen and to mankind in general if he entered the judicial branch of the government (and it is not impossible that he had in mind the inspiring example of Troshchinski, who in the noble service of Themis had gained the highest honors, as well as vast estates with thousands of serfs); Gogol did not take service in the judiciary; but he did attack "ignominious bribery" as a dramatist. Nicholas I, Alexander's successor on the Russian throne, attended the première of the *Revizor* (Inspector) and applauded the play with some ostentation. The "abominable vice," now exposed by Gogol, had survived the courageous efforts of Minister Troshchinski. It also survived Gogol's famous satire.

Toward 1816, Troshchinski reached the apex of an unusually successful career. Soon thereafter he entered upon his decline: his daughter, Nadezhda, died in 1817. Troshchinski had never married and his illegitimate daughter, Nadezhda, was his only child; she lived separated from her husband. His own health was slowly deteriorating. On the other hand his position in the government was affected by the changing trends of the policies of Alexander I, and especially by the rise of the notorious Arakcheyev (Count Aleksey Andreyevich Arakcheyev [1760-1834], favorite of Alexander I, became Minister of War in 1808 and his name became the symbol of intolerance and despotism as a result of his reactionary internal policy). In January, 1816, his daughter Nadezhda wrote to her cousin, Andrei Troshchinski:

> Arakcheyev is here now . . . He rules over everything, he decides everything, makes reports (to the Emperor); a minister over the ministers, without being answerable to anything . . . All the ministers go to him to pay reverence, except ours . . .

In 1817, Troshchinski, a faithful and dignified servant of three Russian monarchs, asked to be relieved of his duties. This was granted — together with a yearly pension of 10,000 rubles supplementing the income from some 190,000 acres of land, with 6,000 serfs, which he owned). After a few years the former minister retired once more to his native Ukraine where he died in 1829, at the age of 75.

The sumptuous manor-house of Kibintsy where Troshchinski spent his last years contained beautiful art collections, and an excellent library; hosts of domestics, attendants, spongers and hangers-on of every description made up the household, and often the house was thronged with guests, some distinguished, others whom the master hardly knew. There was a domestic orchestra, and amateurs as well as serf-actors performed plays on the domestic stage. To add to the entertainment provided by the theater and the orchestra, there were also fools and jesters at the Kibintsy court, and even personages whose duty it was to act as hecklers of these fools and jesters; a certain unfrocked priest, mildly insane, served as the object of various practical jokes. Amidst this rather strained merrymaking, Dmitri Prokofyevich himself, according to the testimony of a contemporary was

. . . . somewhat stiff and not especially affable. He did not customarily converse much with his guests and liked to play solitaire in their presence. Before dinner . . . the guests would tensely await their host. Dmitri Prokofyevich finally appeared, always wearing full dress with medals and decorations, pensive and morose, his old, intelligent face expressing ennui or lassitude.

The Gogols were drawn into the orbit of Kibintsy soon after Troshchinski established his residence there. Manifold connections developed between the Kibintsy magnate and the modest Vasilyevka squires, and Vasili Afanasyevich was called upon to perform a variety of duties. He assisted Troshchinski as secretary when he was elected marshal by the nobility of the province, and at one time held the position of marshal of the district.

Vasili Afanasyevich acted, on the other hand, as a factotum in the management of Troshchinski's vast estates. All contracts, bills and reports passed through his hands. He not only compiled the accounts for the completed year, but also had to submit projects and considerations for improvements of the economy.

No less important among Vasili Afanasyevich's duties were those connected with providing entertainment for Troshchinski; it seems that the dominant concern in his entourage was the veteran stateman's boredom, and Vasili Afanasyevich showed himself very helpful in dispelling it.

Vasili Afanasyevich was a lively and sociable person, a man of many small talents, a dilettante, dabbling in literature, in architecture, in landscape gardening, a collector of various bits of information, of various odds and ends, anecdotes, rhymes and aphorisms which he jotted down at random in his notebooks between memos concerning business matters to which he had to attend.

The talents and the readiness to oblige of this jack-of-all-trades were soon appreciated and put to use. As early as 1813, he was placed in charge of Troshchinski's domestic theater. In a letter dated April 12 of that year, Andrei Troshchinski, the retired Major-General, expressed to him his gratitude for assuming these responsibilities; the General was prone to use rather solemn language in his correspondence, and he worded his letter as follows:

> I also wish to compliment you greatly for the pleasure you gave, in a family spirit, to our benefactor (his uncle was ordinarily designated by this term) by agreeing to take upon yourself the duties connected with the theatrical performances which, in a harmonious family life, and especially for aged persons having sojourned in high society, provide an amusing pastime.

In addition to managing the Kibintsy theater, Vasili Afanasyevich also appeared on the stage. So did Mariya Ivanovna, and on one occasion Andrei Andreyevich informed her: "Dmitri Prokofyevich wrote to me that you had distinguished yourself in playing the parts assigned to you."

It is possible that young Nikolai was also given the opportunity to demonstrate his talents on the Kibintsy stage. In October 1824, then a student at the Nezhin Gymnasium, he asked his father to let him know whether he would go home for the Christmans holidays (he actually did, that year), and, in the affirmative, to send him his part. "Be assured," he added, "that I will do it well."

And finally: some of the plays produced at Kibintsy were written by Vasili Afanasyevich. According to Mariya Ivanovna, "her husband wrote many poems and comedies in verse, in Russian and in Little-Russian." All that survived of the poems is a quatrain quoted from memory by Mariya Ivanovna; the following translation does not sacrifice much of its poetic quality:

> In Nature only is my pleasure,
> I never grudge another's treasure;
> My favorite motto: I'm content
> With that which Fate to me hath sent.

Vasili Afanasyevich is known to be the author of two comedies in Ukrainian entitled *Sobaka-vivtsya* (The Dog-Sheep) and *Prostak, abo khitroshchi zhinky perekhitreni moskalem* (The Simpleton or the Ruse of a Woman Outwitted by a Muscovite). Only the text of the latter has been preserved. From all that remains of his heritage, it would appear that he did not lack a sense of humor and a certain amount of skill, but that his was not a talent outstanding in stature or originality. The *Simpleton* is largely an adaptation of a work of the father of the new Ukrainian literature, Ivan Kotlyarevski, the comedy *Moscal-charyvnik* (The Muscovite Wizard). Like its model, Vasili Gogol's *Simpleton* was a rustic farce. The main protagonists, a slow-witted peasant and his shrewd wife, were given the names of two domestics in Troshchenski's employ, Roman and his spouse Paraška, who enacted the two characters in the play. Roman was a flunkey of sorts whose extraordinary stupidity caused much merriment at Kibintsy. The dumb flunkey playing the part of a dumb peasant fooled by his wife, was thus unwittingly portraying himself, and this was found to add much drollery to the performance.

It was not unusual at Kibintsy for the domestics to provide a bit of entertainment for their masters: in a letter (not dated) to the wife of Andrei Troshchinski, her good friend, Mariya Gogol describes the festivities on the occasion of the wedding of cook Vasili. Troshchinski himself opened the ball with the bride, and Mariya with the groom. Later a manservant by the name of Sashka performed a comic ballet number to the accompaniment of music he had composed. The merriment reached its peak when the servants were told to dance the mazurka, and did a caricature of this dance.

The attitude toward the peasant as an essentially farcical or low comedy character, is typical for the eighteenth century, and peasant speech, imitated on the stage — a droll distortion of the educated language — was a convenient medium for comedy. The Ukrainian language, a patois for the educated listener of that time, added a further comic note.

There is evidence that a Russian comic opera which enjoyed lasting popularity, Ablesimov's *Miller, Wizard, Cheat and Matchmaker* (first performed in 1779), was produced on the Kibintsy stage in 1824.

It must also be noted that a close friend of Troshchinski was Vasili Kapnist (1757-1823), a talented satirical poet and dramatist, and one of the most brilliant figures of his age. After his retirement from government service in 1783, he lived on his estate in the Mirgorod district and was a frequent visitor at Kibintsy where Gogol's parents often met him. Kapnist wrote a comedy for the Kibintsy theater, and appeared on the stage together with one of his daughters. Another daughter, Sofya, Skalon by marriage, was a close friend of Gogol's throughout his life; so were some of the other members of this highly cultured and very wealthy family. In January 1824, Gogol wrote to his parents that he had learned "to my greatest regret" of the death of Vasili Vasilyevich Kapnist.

Mariya Gogol also met, in her young days, the greatest literary celebrity of his age, the poet Derzhavin, who came to visit his friends Troshchinski and Kapnist in their Ukrainian estates. Derzhavin made this visit in 1813; he was then seventy. Gogol's mother had a vivid recollection of the trio — the poet, the satirist, and the statesman — three brilliant representatives of the age of Catherine the Great. Men of that age had healthy tastes, solid appetites, and a vigorous love for pleasure and for beauty. At Kibintsy there were jesters to provide entertainment, and some rather coarse farces were performed on the stage. But at the same time, according to Mariya Gogol's testimony, the domestic orchestra played not only Mozart, but also the works of a modern composer, Beethoven, who was then becoming fashionable.

Mariya Ivanovna Gogol recalls, in her autobiographical notes the brilliant society she met at Kibintsy and the lavish entertainment she enjoyed there; there is a faint note of melancholy, however, in her reminiscences when she speaks of the change in her own and her husband's life after Troshchinski's arrival:

I never went out for any receptions or balls, finding complete happiness in my family; we were unable to part from one another even for a single day, and when he had to drive out into the fields in his little droshki, he always took me with him. If it happened that I had to stay at home, I feared for him, imagining that I would not see him again. . . . Once it had been impossible for him to return when I was expecting him, and he was tormented, thinking all the while of what would happen to me, and I fell ill with a fever. We hardly ever parted before the arrival from St. Petersburg of D.P. (Dmitri Prokofyevich). He would not let us return home, being very fond of my husband. There (in Kibintsy) I saw everything I may have sought in the world: balls, the theater, fine society from both capitals, but I was always happy when I could return to Vasilyevka.

At Kibintsy the pleasures in which she could share had their counterpart in the many absorbing duties demanded from her husband.

It is not easy to weigh the burden of these duties against the advantages derived by the Gogols from Troshchinski's benevolent disposition. It does not seem that Vasili was ever paid any salary for his services. Troshchinski's appreciation and the privilege of his hospitality were, apparently, considered sufficient compensations.

Occasionally Troshchinski used his influence to assist the Gogols.

Thus, in 1822, he obtained a scholarship for their son Nikosha; the fee in the boarding school where he was studying, 1,200 rubles a year, weighed heavily on the family budget, and thanks to Troshchinski's intercession the Gogols were freed from a serious worry. Mariya Ivanovna wrote to him on this occasion in a style clearly attributable to Vasili Afanasyevich, although he was said in the letter to be ill and unable to write himself; the missive ended thus:

. . . accept, unprecedented benefactor, my gratitude feebly expressed in the present which is moistened with tears flowing from the feelings of my heart filled with limitless devotion and perfect respect which I here attest on behalf of our entire family, having the honor to remain, etc. . . .

As for direct financial assistance, it does not seem that Troshchinski did more than grant some loans to the Vasilyevka squires whose circumstances were anything but easy. In June 1829, four months after Troshchinski's death (and four years after the death of her husband), Mariya Ivanovna described to one of her cousins her situation with regard to the Troshchinski estate:

My angel and benefactor, Dmitri Prokofyevich, used to pay for me to the Treasury and seldom accepted (repayment), and apparently, just for the sake of having a record, noted how much I owed him, and it comes out that it is 4,060 rubles, and now this note has been found, and I am to pay this money, but since I have no means whatsoever to pay it, I offered Andrei Andreyevich to accept my Yareski property, consisting of 70 desyatins of land; this was agreeable to him, but he will not give more than thirty rubles a desyatina, so what this amounts to, is that my property will be lost and the debt will not be paid, but it's all in God's will, man proposes and God disposes . . .

The debt, it must be said, was not settled at that time (and it remained unpaid for a number of years); it should be noted, nevertheless, that at the time of the "benefactor's" death the total debt of the Gogol family, accumulated over a number of years, barely exceeded 4,000 rubles, and that the "benefactor's" heir took a very businesslike attitude with regard to the settlement.

Toward the end of his life Vasili Afanasyevich's zeal for serving the Kibintsy magnate seems to have subsided. He had to be reminded of his duties, as he was in one instance by a letter from

Andrei Troshchinski's wife dated August 8, 1824:

I must tell you, my dear friends, that our gray-haired little old man is seriously angry at you and won't listen to any reasons for your not coming here, saying that since you shun him he is ready no longer to count you among his friends. So I beg you, dearest friends, be here tomorrow, and don't antagonize him unnecessarily: you know that he does not like it.

There have been found in the Gogol family archives several drafts (not dated) of Vasili Afanasyevich's letters to Andrei Troshchinski and to his wife, and any one of them may have been the draft of a reply to the letter just quoted; one fragment reads:

I am vexed that . . . I did not return to Kibintsy . . . This worries me all the more because I am not capable of atoning for this offense due to my failing health and to those grievous circumstances which, to my regret, you do not wish to take into account, knowing perfectly well both about my attacks and about our domestic situation . . .

Further on, Vasili Afanasyevich protests that were it only possible, he would at once hurry to Kibintsy knowing that this is his "duty toward [my] honored benefactor Dmitri Prokofyevich."

The word "duty" which Vasili Afanasyevich uses in his letters is significant; for even if direct coercion could not be used against him, even he could not be forced to come to Kibintsy at Troshchinski's first call, he nevertheless obviously felt that the Kibintsy magnate had certain rights over him; and it seems that these rights, and his own obligations to serve when his services were needed, and to come when he was called, were taken for granted by all concerned. Troshchinski, apparently, did not take the trouble to write to the Gogols himself, but his nephew Andrei Andreyevich's letters to Vasili Afanasyevich often sound like orders to attend to some business concerning his uncle's estatess.

The fact that no salary was paid to Vasili Afanasyevich; that his "benefactor" felt free to compensate him as he pleased (as by granting some subsidies or by obtaining through his connections some favor for his protégé); that the Gogols were expected to abandon their own estate and to reside at the Kibintsy manor-house if Troshchinski happened to feel lonely (thus changing, even if temporarily, their status of independent squires for that of retainers of the magnate) – all this combines to form a pattern reminiscent of a relationship between a vassal and his suzerain.

Gogol in his young years had a perfect understanding of Troshchinski's importance and of his role of "benefactor" of his family. It may be interesting to quote some of the references to the magnate in his letters.

In September 1826, Troshchinski was expected to visit at Vasilyevka in person; Gogol wrote to his mother:

> Let me know when his excellency Dmitri Prokofyevich will be in our house, what he will find to his liking, what will please him; I am eager to know the opinion of the great man, even about trifles; be so kind, dear mother, and don't miss anything.

Mariya Ivanovna satisfied his curiosity and he wrote to her two weeks later:

> I read avidly your charming account, dear mother, about the visit of the honored guest . . .

Further in the letter, answering his mother's suggestion that he offer "his excellency" a specimen of his literary efforts (seventeen-year-old Gogol apparently had gained some measure of literary reputation in Vasilyevka and in Kibintsy), he wrote that he thought of doing this, but then

> . . . reasoned that presenting some ephemeral trifle would do me little good and would be of little help in giving a favorable impression, so I resolved to prepare myself for more important tasks and to do something worthy of benefactor of Little-Russia.

The young man perfectly realized the importance of producing a "favorable impression" on men in high position.

After Troshchinski's death, the title of "benefactor" was transferred to his nephew Andrei; he was in Petersburg when Gogol arrived there, and gave him some financial support. On October 27, 1829, Gogol wrote to his mother:

> I sense the invisible hand of the Almighty protecting me: He sent me a guardian-angel in the person of our benefactor, his excellency Andrei Andreyevich who has done for me only what a father could have done for his son; his benefactions and his advice will be forever engraved in my heart.

Another letter followed two weeks later:

I did not answer you earlier because . . . I handed over a letter to Andrei Andreyevich, in his own hands, according to his desire, and unsealed; consequently you should not be surprised if I flattered him a little in it; however, he actually has done a good deal for me: thanks to his graciousness I have warm clothes for the winter, and he also paid the rent for my apartment which I owed.

In a little less than two years Gogol received from his "benefactor," a man of tremendous wealth, and his mother's first cousin, in all about one thousand rubles; and Mariya Ivanovna found it necessary to explain to her cousin her son's excessive expenses by his passionate love for books and his exaggerated generosity toward the poor.

The relationship between his family and its "benefactor" undoubtedly had an influence on Gogol; he had witnessed in his early days a situation of extreme inequality and had seen his parents depend on the favors and caprices of a man of great wealth and great power – and he understood the importance of gaining favors and of satisfying caprices. In bureaucratic Petersburg, where Gogol moved from the Ukraine, hierarchism was exceptionally strong, and the theme of hierarchy – of the "little man" and the "general" – is a dominating theme in his Petersburg stories. But among the Ukrainian landowning gentry hierarchism was little known, and Gogol's early awareness of inequality was the result of the special relationship between his parents and the Kibintsy magnate.

Gogol's ostensible reaction toward this situation was his eagerness to please and to gain the favor of the "benefactors." But on a deeper level he reacted by a daydream of one day becoming himself a Troshchinski: power and glory could be gained through effort and perseverance. He worshipped the "great man," but he also secretly identified himself with him. This phase of the development of Gogol's personality will be discussed in a later chapter.

When Vasili Afanasyevich pleaded ill health to explain his failure to appear at Kibintsy, this was by no means an empty excuse. He had been ailing, his wife recalls, during the last four years of his life. When it was finally realized that his condition was serious, he made one more trip to Kibintsy, to seek advice from Troshchinski's house physician. He died in March 1825, in Kibintsy, some six months after the warning that through his absence he had incurred the "benefactor's" displeasure.

Vasili Afanasyevich left five children when he died; Nikolai, or Nikosha, as his parents called him, the oldest of his children, was then sixteen. He was a student in the town of Nezhin, some 120 miles from Vasilyevka, in a boarding-school where he had been placed four years earlier.

The story of Nikosha Gogol's school years, up to his father's death must now be retold.

Chapter VI

SCHOOL

In August 1818, nine-year-old Nikosha and his brother Ivan, one year younger, were sent to school in nearby Poltava. During their first summer vacation which the two boys were spending at home, in Vasilyevka, little Ivan fell ill and died. A few months later, Nikosha returned to Poltava, this time alone, taking lodging with a tutor who was to prepare him for the second grade of the local gymnasium.

In the meantime Vasili Afanasyevich learned that a new school with very high standards and an advanced curriculum would soon open in the town of Nezhin. Vasili Afanasyevich was anxious to give his son the best possible education, and he immediately concerned himself with obtaining information and with securing Nikosha's admission.

The Nezhin school, known as the Prince Bezborodko Gymnasium for Higher Learning, owed its existence to Count Ilya Bezborodko who conceived and, in 1805, submitted to the government in St. Petersburg the project which he backed with the donation of a piece of land in Nezhin and of a substantial sum of money, together with the promise of a sizable annuity. He dedicated the Gymnasium to the memory of his older brother, Prince Alexander Bezborodko, Catherine the Great's Minister and Chancellor under Paul I, who died in 1799 leaving him most of his tremendous fortune. The powerful protection of Prince Bezborodko, a Ukrainian by birth, was a major factor in the career of his countryman Troshchinski.

It took fifteen years to complete the building of the Gymnasium, and Count Ilya did not live to see its inauguration in 1820.

The year 1805, when Count Bezborodko initiated his project, was an important date in the history of education in the Ukraine: that year the University of Kharkov, the first university in the Ukraine, was inaugurated. Kiev, the ancient capital, had to wait another thirty years for its university. Kharkov, the main city of the prospering "Slobodskaya" Ukraine, and the administrative and economic center of Russia's southern provinces, also became an important cultural center with its new university.

Whatever the intentions of the Russian government, the spreading to the Ukrainian provinces of the new education, western and secular in its spirit, but administered and controlled by the Petersburg government (a Ministry of Education was created in 1803), did not merely result in a Russification of the Ukraine: it also contributed to a revival, even if on a limited scale, of Ukrainian national consciousness. Kharkov became an important publishing center. Several magazines published articles on Ukrainian history, ethnography and folklore written for the most part in Russian, but also some fiction in Ukrainian.

In the notebooks of Gogol's father for the year 1817, there is a memo about sending money for a subscription to one of these magazines, the *Ukrainski vestnik* (The Ukrainian Herald).

The new culture, coming to the Ukraine from the North, was the product of direct contacts between Russian and western Europe which developed in the course of the eighteenth century, especially during its latter half; it was superceding the once flourishing, but now moribund Ukrainian culture, strongly marked by Polish influence, but shaped in the very process of resistance to the political and religious domination of Poland and of the Roman Catholic Church.

This culture was the culture of the Catholic resurgence, with its scholasticism, its rhetoric and its baroque style, heavily ornate, but elegant, artificial and intricate, yet harmonious, adorned with gilt ornament in architecture or with elaborate allegory and metaphor in literature.

Muscovy, which in the second half of the seventeenth century was cautiously feeling its way towards Europe, received a powerful influx of this culture, western and "Latin" by its origins, but digested by the Ukrainians and placed by them at the service of Orthodoxy. The learning and the magnificent rhetoric of Kievan preachers and theologians greatly impressed the Muscovites (later the Old-believers fought the southern influence, contaminated with unholy "Latinism").

In the seventeenth century the Kiev Theological Academy (founded in 1632 by Metropolitan Peter Mohyla) became the center of Ukrainian scholasticism. The Academy trained a number of men who played a prominent part in the political and cultural history of Russia. One of the last among them, a pupil and later a professor of the Academy, was the learned and crafty Archbishop Feofan Prokopovich — statesman, author and theologian, Peter the Great's chief advisor in matters of Church policy. But as the "age of enlightenment" advanced, the inadequacy of the old system and the need for secular education were becoming more and more obvious.

Gogol, in *Taras Bulba*, subjects to a sharp and lucid criticism the very principles of scholasticism which dominated in the seventeenth century:

> The learning of that time was divorced from life in an appalling fashion: all those scholastic, grammatical, rhetorical and logical refinements were completely out of touch with the times, and could never be applied or found in life. . . . The most learned in those days were only more ignorant than the others because they were completely removed from experience.

This severe judgement is followed by a picture of the mores of the *bursa* (the seminary boarding-school) and of its inmates, young lads whose coarse, but healthy instincts were in constant rebellion against the tedium and the constraint of the seminary.

The passage from *Taras Bulba* is paralleled in "Viy" by a description remarkably vivid and direct, apparently based on memories still alive in Gogol's days, if not on personal observation, of the unruly community of over-age and over-grown divinity students held within some limits of discipline by vigorous and frequent floggings; of those moustached "philosophers" and husky "theologians," as the senior students were called, clad in their long and shabby frocks, who clashed in savage battles, pilfered the market place, and used liberally of liquor, snuff and tobacco; who wandered during the vacations about the city and the surrounding country, collecting small gifts from the inhabitants for whom they chanted Latin verses or presented puppet shows, or plays (interludes, or scenes from "school dramas" based on Biblical subjects):

> Sometimes a comedy was played, and in such a case some theologian barely exceeded in height by the Kievan bell tower would always distinguish himself, enacting Herodias or Pentephria, the wife of the Egyptian courtier. For this they would be rewarded with a piece of homespun, a sack of millet, the half of a cooked goose or some similar gift.

Gogol's grandfather Afanasi was a pupil of the Kiev Academy; so was Dmitri Prokofyevich Troshchinski; Vasili Gogol had studied at the Poltava Seminary. But in Gogol's days, the new secular education, western and classical in spirit, had become available in the Ukraine.

Young Nikosha Gogol was admitted to the newly established Nezhin Gymnasium in May 1821. Placement examinations were held the next month. Nikosha's performance was very poor, with the exception of religion and sacred history: he was the last but one among some forty candidates (the youngest aged eight, the oldest, among them Nikosha, twelve). The students were placed in three divisions (or "museums" as the divisions and their dormitories were called). In January 1822, each division was subdivided into three grades, and Nikosha was assigned to the third, that is, the senior grade of the first division.

The nine-year curriculum included an impressive variety of subjects: religion; Russian, Latin, Greek (optional), French and German languages and literatures; ethics and logic; history (ancient, medieval, modern, and the history of Russia); geography; pure and applied mathematics (including calculus); physics and elements of chemistry; natural history; technology and military science; economics and financial science; natural law, Roman law and the different branches of Russian law.

Nikosha returned to Nezhin to enter upon the arduous path of learning in the fall of 1821, after a summer spent in Vasilyevka.

Following him there arrived in Nezhin a cartload of victuals, and with it a domestic of the Gogols whose services – he was a cook – Vasili Afanasyevich contributed to the new Gymnasium with the understanding that this domestic, Simon by name, would also give Nikosha whatever assistance or protection he might need.

The victuals were intended for one of the supervisors, who also gave instruction in German, his native language, one Seldner, a man apparently of rather limited intelligence and a permanent butt for the students' practical jokes. Seldner, it was agreed, would care for Nikosha's health and general werfare, and supervise his studies, and in consideration thereof various produce of the Vasilyevka estate would be sent to him from time to time.

Soon after Nikosha's arrival Seldner reported that the boy was in good health and perfectly content; this was corroborated by a short letter from Nikosha himself.

The very next day, however, eluding Seldner's surveillance, Nikosha sent his parents the following message:

I was much grieved hearing that you would come only in October. Oh! how I wish you came as soon as you possibly could, and learned about the fate of your son. Before the vacation I wrote that I was fine here, but now it is all the contrary. Oh! if only Dearest Parents you came this month, you would se what is happening to me. I have been so sad after the vacation that day after day tears well forth from my eyes in a stream and why – that I do not know myself but especially when I remember you — then they just flow in a torrent. And I have now such a pain in my chest that I cannot even write much. . . . Goodbye, Dearest Parents, tears will not let me write any further. . . .

He adds, however, a plea for "my good Simon who is so solicitous with me that not a night has passed without his admonishing me not to weep for you Dearest Parents. . . . He is paid no salary and has to cook for us all. . . ."

This letter caused considerable alarm. Vasili Afanasyevich, it seems, was taken ill after reading it. Urgent inquiries were made. Seldner replied September 1st. He was distressed by the boy's unreasonableness; the boy was perfectly happy, and in excellent health — the school physician, Karl Karlovich Fiebing, had just examined him. But he was lazy, and two weeks before he had to be left without tea after dinner. That is what incited him to write the letter and to send it, Seldner's interdiction notwithstanding, causing so much unnecessary worry to his parents.

After this incident Nikosha refrained from further complaints, and his letters became rather colorless and impersonal. This may have been due to the lesson he was taught: his parents did not come when he cried out for help, they let themselves be reassured by Seldner. There was also Seldner's tightened censorship. But on the other hand there is no doubt that Nikosha soon accommodated himself to life at school and the separation from his parents. As for Seldner, Nikosha soon learned that he need not be feared and could be ridiculed with impunity. He ceased to play any part in Nikosha's existence when the new principal, Doctor Orlay, a personal acquaintance of the Gogols, took charge in the fall of 1821.

Doctor Ivan Orlay, a Ruthenian educated in Austro-Hungary, who headed the school for five years, was a learned physician and an experienced educator. He believed in a strict, but benevolent and rational discipline. The students' schedule, including classes taught from nine to twelve and from three to five, was meticulously regulated, quarter-hour by quarter-hour, from 5:30 in the morning when they were to rise and "greet their tutors in a foreign language," until nine o'clock in the evening when after a quarter-hour devoted to prayer, they "retired to their beds for undressing and placing themselves on same." A half-hour, from six-thirty to seven, was reserved in the evening for "agreeable and nobly-jocose exercises, the reading of La Fontaine's fables in the French or the German language," etc.

It would seem, however, that these regulations were not always followed literally, and that amusement was not always restricted to the half-hour from six-thirty to seven, nor to the reading of La Fontaine's fables. Thus, for the month of February 1824, Nikosha was given the grade of 1 in conduct (the grading in Russian schools: the lowest is 1 and the highest and best 5) — "for untidiness, clownery, stubbornness and disobedience." This, however, was an exception rather than the rule.

A passage in Chapter Seven of *Dead Souls* has been identified by Gogol's first biographer, Kulish, as a reminiscence of the Nezhin years and an accurate description of the Nezhin scenery. The passage is introduced at a climactic point of the narration. The town is suddenly roused from its lethargy by the discovery of Chichikov's shadowy dealings and by fantastic rumors of various crimes and conspiracies attributed to him; the local officials are dazed and befuddled:

> For a moment their state was like the state of a schoolboy who was asleep, and into whose nose has been introduced by his mates who rose ahead of him, a twist of paper with snuff in it known as *hussar*. Drawing in unawares all the snuff in one hearty breath of a sleeper, he awakens, jumps up, stares foolishly, his eyes popping, in all directions, and cannot understand where he is, what he is, what has happened to him, and then, after a while, distinguishes the walls lit up by an oblique ray of the sun, the laughter of his mates hiding in corners, and — peeping in through the window — the morning that has arrived, with the awakening forest resounding with thousands of bird voices, and the river now luminous, its glittering loops disappearing here and yon between slender reeds, and scattered all along it, naked youngsters shouting encouragements for a swim — and then only does he realize at last that a hussar has been placed in his nose.

The passage follows the typically Gogolian meandering course — from the situation that occurs in the narration by analogy (simile), to the comic image of the schoolboy awakened by inhaling a dose of snuff; then, within one syntactic unit, the imagery, now endowed with its own dynamics, breaks the link of analogy (the pretect of the simile is abandoned) and moves along a line of the narrator's reminiscence into the pure lyricism, and the irrelevance, of the picture of the morning; then the window of the lyrical reminiscence is shut, the schoolboy with the hussar in his nose (the simile) is brought back, and the narration continues.

Nikosha's letters home during his first years in Nezhin consist for the most part of dutiful inquiries about his parents' health and welfare, and of extremely elaborate salutations (such as "With true respect and devotion I have the honor to be your most humble servant and most obedient son Nikolai Gogol-Yanovski." − October 10, 1822). Between the inquiries and the salutations, or, sometimes in a postscript, one finds some carefully worded request: for books (a Latin grammar and dictionary, a French and a German conversation book, Marmontel's *Conte Moraux* in the Russian translation [December 10, 1821], a *Collection of Exemplary Works in Verse and in Prose*, with portraits of the authors, in six volumes "for we are now studying poetry and parts of aesthetics, and we are in great need of examples." [October 1, 1824]); for money − eight rubles to be paid monthly to the dancing and violin master (". . . I have not yet begun to take dancing lessons, but if you send the money with Fedka (a manservant), then I shall be able to dance perfectly before Christmas." − October 3, 1823); ten rubles badly needed to pay some debts and to buy paints (June 13, 1824); another ten rubles to pay the tailor (". . . you would not believe how dreadful it is to have a creditor. . . ." − March 1825); an unspecified amount to purchase a bow: he received a violin, but no bow, and had no money to buy one (January 22, 1824). There are also requests for such miscellaneous items as blue cloth for a tunic (October 19, 1824); or dried pitted cherries which mother had promised (October 10, 1822); or a warm overcoat and two waistcoats; or picture frames with glass (two measuring 21 inches by 14 each; one 35 by 21, and two smaller ones − 7 inches by 10) for some drawings he had done in pastel and which were doomed to perish if not framed immediately (January 22, 1824); or for a few yards of fine canvas for painting (March 30, 1824).

The approach of vacations, which he spent at home, was always greeted by Nikosha with the greatest joy, expressed regularly in his letters at appropriate seasons. Gradually his childish clichés become more refined and take on a tinge of literary sentimentality. The young *Gefuhlsmensch* appears. Thus, a few days before his voyage to Vasilyevka in June 1824, he wrote:

> I can already see all that is dear to my heart − I see you, I see my dear native country, I see the quiet Psyol, shimmering through a thin veil which I shall cast off (?), enjoying true happiness, forgetting those misfortunes that swiftly fleet by. One happy moment rewards for years of grief! . . .

Nikosha also spent the Christmas holidays at home that year, and it was during those holidays that he saw his father, who had been ailing for some time and had left Vasilyevka for Kibintsy in order to receive medical care. His mother was expecting a child in March; it was therefore decided that Nikosha should stay in Nezhin.

In March 1825, Nikosha wrote to his father asking him to send books to help him while away the lonely holiday (most of the boys would go home), and another yard or two of canvas; and maybe some victuals could also be sent for the holidays; and ten rubles to pay the tailor.

There was no reply to this letter. Then sad news reached Nezhin: Vasili Afanasyevich had died that month.

Chapter VII

FATHER'S DEATH

In her Autobiographical Notes written more than a quarter of a century later, Mariya Gogol recalls vividly her husband's death. Her condition at that time was apparently close to temporary insanity. For days she refused all nourishment; she wanted God, she recalls, to see how she suffered; had He known what her pain would be, so she thought, He would not have inflicted upon her so terrible a punishment. Then gradually she began to realize that it was her duty to spare herself for the sake of her children, and giving in to the exhortations of her old aunt Anna who cared for her, she would force herself to swallow a little tea or a spoonful of soup.

Mariya Ivanovna was thirty-three when she lost her husband. She must have relived in her memory, at that time, the remote days of Vasili's courtship, and of her marriage, and the nineteen years of her married life.

During those nineteen years, Mariya Ivanovna gave birth to twelve children: she had two still-born babies before the birth of Nikolai in 1809; her second son, Ivan, who was born a year later died at the age of nine; between 1811 and her husband's death, she had another eight children: two sons and six daughters; of these eight children, six, including the two boys, died in early infancy. The youngest child, a daughter christened Olga, was born some two weeks before Vasili Afanasyevich's death, when, seriously ill, he had gone to Kibintsy leaving his pregnant wife with the children.

The death of three-year old Tatyana came only two or three months after the death of her father, when Mariya Ivanovna had scarcely begun to recover from the terrible shock she had experienced, and it seems that the events of this period produced a permanent traumatic injury, even though during the following years she showed much courage and stamina in facing a very difficult situation.

The repeated pregnancies of his mother, this childbearing and these early deaths so frequent in his family throughout his childhood and adolescence, these frail and mysterious human existences, beginning precariously and ending early, all this must have left an imprint on Gogol's personality. The death of Vasili Afanasyevich was an event of a different nature: it menaced the very existence of *home*, and Nikosha seemed eager above all to preserve the *status quo* (mother must take place of father), at least for the time being.

Mariya Ivanovna Gogol recalls that her older daughter fell ill with a "nervous fever" when the news of her father's death reached her, while her son Nikolai "wanted to throw himself out of a window on the third floor." Violent sorrow, and violent expression of sorrow, seem to have been a family tradition with the Gogols.

There is no reason to doubt the sincerity or the intensity of Nikosha's grief when the news of his father's death reached him. But in the letter which sixteen-year-old Nikosha wrote to his mother to express this grief, and to comfort her, he sounds somewhat too analytical, too self-centered in observing and in recording his own reactions to the said event.

He announces in his letter that he "took this blow with the firmness of a true Christian." Then he proceeds as follows:

> It is true that at first I was terribly shocked by this news, but I did not permit anyone to notice that I was grieved. Left to myself, however, I surrendered to all the might of overwhelming despair. I even wanted to make an attempt upon my life. But God restrained me from doing this — and toward evening I could observe in myself only sadness, I was no longer shaken by fits of despair, and finally this sadness changed into a scarcely noticeable melancholy mixed with a feeling of reverence for the Almighty. I bless Thee, Sacred Faith! In Thee alone do I find a source of consolation and solace in my affliction.

The letter continues in this rather rhetorically sentimental tone: he has not lost everything — fate has not abandoned him; has it not left him his loving mother? She will now be the only object of his affectionate attachment. To her he will now dedicate his whole life. He proposes to his mother what may be termed a pact of mutual love and support: he will give her solace and joy, he will do for her all that a tender and grateful son can do; and she will take the place of the father and friend he has lost, bring him comfort and peace — she alone can do this. He implores her finally to turn to God, as he did, assuring her that thereby she will lessen her pain.

The letter had two postscripts. In the first, Nikosha inquired about his sisters and about "grandmother" (his mother's aunt) Anna; the second postscript was a request for ten rubles to buy a textbook. The next day more supplications followed that his mother do not abandon herself to grief, and that she spare herself, were it only for the sake of her children.

Later, over a number of years, until he himself succumbed to the destructive forces within him, Gogol addressed to his mother frequent exhortations to resist gloom and despondency, and these appeals sometimes sound as warnings against a sinful rejection of the gift of life and of joy bestowed upon man by his Creator.

For a month Nikosha was without news from home, but finally his mother wrote, relieving his anxiety over her condition. Thus reassured, Nikosha gave vent, in his next letter home, to his joy over the forthcoming reunion; this was in June, and the summer holidays were approaching. Nor did he forget to give detailed instructions as to the time and to various details of the trip: it would be best to send the little yellow carriage for him, and he would like to avoid Kibintsy, for he had no clothes except those he was wearing. There is also this touching note: he thought of bringing his mother a present; but he knows that none would please her better than the gift he will bring: the gift of his heart, all aflame with the most tender filial love.

His mother apparently replied with some appreciative effusion, but, judging by Nikosha's answer, she also alluded to the responsibilities he would have to assume now that his father was no more. Nikosha responded to this invitation somewhat evasively; in an earlier letter he had appealed to her to take the place of his dead father, and now she was turning to him with a similar request. Nikosha would rather place the future of the family in the trust of Providence:

> . . . your words that your life has ended for yourself and for this world, and that, maybe, I shall soon have to take the place of a father for my little sisters, these words lodged sad forebodings in my heart. Why abandon oneself to melancholy reveries? Why raise the awesome curtain of the future? Maybe it has in reserve for us peace and quiet joy, a serene evening and unperturbed family life. Let us rely on the Almighty in whose hand rests our fate.

During the next two years, Nikosha's letters to his mother reflect a certain detachment; they are generally short and many begin with apologies for their scarcity, and end with promises to do better in the future.

Requests for money are frequent. Arrangements had been made for a regular allowance, but it was often delayed and was not sufficient: he needed books, oil paints and brushes, clothes.

The tone of the letters is generally optimistic: repeatedly he assures his mother that his health is excellent and that he is happy and content.

It does not seem that his father's death marked a turning point in Gogol's life, nor that it caused any immediate changes in his character. His personality continued to grow and to take a more definite shape during the last years of his adolescence, gradually becoming more articulate, standing out in clearer relief with its complexity and its contradictions. There was much brooding about his future during those years, much introspection, much questioning of himself, and of his destiny.

When his father died, Nikosha had three more years of school before him. During those years he seems to have been absorbed in the activities and pursuits at school and in the events of school life, showing toward the end, as graduation approached, an increasing impatience to gain freedom to begin the next chapter of his life, which he saw brilliant and fascinating, with its *Wanderjahre* , and achievement and fame. But the *Lehrjahre* had yet to be completed.

Chapter VIII

SCHOOL YEARS CONTINUED

LIBERAL ARTS

(ARCHITECTURE, PAINTING, EMBROIDERY)

Whatever its shortcomings, there was in the Nezhin Gymnasium a certain humanistic atmosphere which favored the development among the students of talent and of interst in the arts and letters. Not all the students were gifted, nor were all the professors competent. It must be noted, however, that among the pupils of the Gymnasium of Gogol's generation several gained prominence, while others, even if their achievements were not outstanding, preserved literary and cultural interests throughout their lives.

Gogol's schoolmate, his junior by one grade, Nestor Kukolnik, a now completely forgotten poet, playwright and novelist, was the author of several rather superficial and bombastic dramas in verse which enjoyed a very great popularity in the 1830's. Platon Lukashevich devoted himself to Slavic philology and folklore; he displayed talent, but unfortunately was led astray by a completely ungovernable imagination. Vasili Lyubich-Romanovich, who served in the Departments of Justice and of Foreign Affairs, was a translator of Byron and Mickiewicz. Peter Redkin became a learned and highly respected jurist who held chairs at the universities of Moscow and St. Petersburg. Constantin Bazili, with whom Gogol maintained friendly relations over a number of years, was Russian Consul in Syria and published several works on Greece and the Orient. Two of Gogol's classmates, Alexander Danilevski and Nikolai Prokopovich, remained his closest friends throughout his life. Neither achieved prominence, but both were active in the field of education and had literary interests. Prokopovich taught Russian literature at the Corps of Cadets in St. Petersburg and published some poetry. Danilevski served as officer in the Guards in his young years and later drifted between the management of his estate and a government career which culminated in a superintendency of schools in his (and Gogol's) native province of Poltava. He was Gogol's companion in many of his travels abroad, his confidant and one of his favorite correspondents. Gogol often urged him to write, failing however, to arouse in his friend any literary ambitions.

In Nezhin the students could satisfy their literary appetites by using the library which had 2,610 volumes in 1822, and over 5,000 in 1830 (approximately one-third of this number in Russian). When the school was founded, its honorary curator, Count Kushelev-Bezborodko, made the generous gift of 1,877 volumes; later it was discovered that, among the books donated by the Count, were several French eighteenth century novels such as *La Belle Allemande* ou *Les Galanteries de Thérèse, Le Paysan Perverti, Les Bijoux Indiscrets, Histoire de la Papesse Jeanne* and a few other specimens of the amiable pornography of the gallant age.

But the school library may not have been quite up to date, and the students had a small library of their own of which Gogol was in charge. The young literati purchased such novelites as the works of Pushkin, or the recent works of Zhukovski, and subscribed to literary magazines and almanacs: Delvig's *Northern Flowers,* Polevoi's *Moscow Telegraph,* Kuchelbecker's *Mnemozina*. This interest in current literature is significant; remote and provincial Nezhin, and also Vasilyevka and Kibintsy, were abreast of the literary life of the time. Thus, in September 1824, Vasili Afanasyevich mentioned in a letter to his son Pushkin's *Eugene Onegin,* and on October 1, Nikosha wrote to his father asking him to send Pushkin's poem (and any other verse he may have). Actually the first chapter of *Onegin* was published, as a separate book, only in February 1825 (some two months earlier a few stanzas had appeared in the *Northern Flowers*); but the news of the forthcoming publication was announced in literary magazines and reached Vasili Afanasyevich who conveyed it to his son in Nezhin.

Pushkin was much admired and avidly read by the literary-minded students in Nezhin. They were not encouraged by the faculty, however, in their interest for new literature. Literature was taught by a Professor Nikolski, a solemn pedant faithful to the principles of classical eloquence and rhetoric as expounded by de La Harpe, Batteux, Sabatier de Castres and other French authorities of the eighteenth century. The outline of Professor Nikolski's course read:

The notion of literature; the origins of the fine arts and of letters, with a reference to the history of Russian literature; on the artistic imitation of nature as the general principle of artistic creation; on the fundamental rules of literary composition, and especially on the perfection of the plan and of the parts of a plan; on expression and the styles with their properties; on the exalted, on intelligence, taste, genius and criticism; with practical exercises in composition and the consideration of the beauty of passages taken from the most estimable authors, if time permits.

A short paper written by Gogol for Professor Nikolski has survived in which he discusses the principles of literary criticism; it reads in part as follows:

The first and most important attribute, without which criticism cannot exist, is impartiality. . . . Criticism must be strict in order to give even greater recognition to the beautiful, for the enlightened author does not seek unreasoning praise and fame, but requires it to be determined by strict intelligence and a correct understanding of his thought, of his creation; it must be decent, excluding all offensive expressions whereby the merits of the criticism are diminished and one is to think that the reviewer was guided by some resentment, animosity or ill will. Consequently the absence of any personality is also essential in criticism.

Professor Nikolski marked the paper "fair."
These uninspired lines undoubtedly reflect the teacher's dogmatic approach to his subject. Even if his influence was resisted by the students, it is probable that some injury was done by the teaching of rigid precepts and by encouraging the building of harmonious and meaningless periods, or the use of rhetorical figures according to the best classical models. The students' turning to contemporary poetry, above all to Pushkin, had precisely the significance of a resistance to obsolete classicism. As for Nikolski, he rejected Pushkin's predecessors, such as Zhukovski or Batyushkov, as "insufficiently classical," and he judged Pushkin himself as trivial and careless, conceding, however, that some of his verse did not lack harmony.
In contrast to Nikolski, the professors of French and German literature, Landragine and Singer, were capable and liberal men who were successful in stimulating the literary interests of the students. Of Singer, it is known that instead of theorizing on the Beautiful and learning the principles of versification, his students read in the original the works of Schiller, Goethe, Wieland, Koerner and Jean-Paul. Gogol apparently acquired a reading knowledge of French, but he seems to have had a peculiar resistance to the German language. In 1827, he acquired the works of Schiller which he ordered from Lemberg (Austria). To pay the price – forty rubles – he had been depriving himself even of essentials, he wrote to his

mother "... in order to satisfy my craving to see and to feel the Beautiful." But he was "more than rewarded by spending several hours daily in the greatest enjoyment." This purchase, however, is evidence of Gogol's passion for books rather than of his proficiency in German: there is a contemporary report that soon after he "saw and felt" the attractive volumes, his enthusiasm subsided, and he abandoned the struggle with the intricacies of German syntax and of the Gothic alphabet.

The students in Nezhin, or at least some of them, were not only lovers of literature: they also tried their hand in various literary genres, and their efforts were circulated in the form of manuscript journals and almanacs. The titles of two of these publications are known: one was called *The Meteor of Literature*, while the other was baptized in a less poetical mood, *Parnassian Manure*. Gogol is reported to have participated in these publishing ventures not only as an author, but also as the cover designer.

Very little has survived of his efforts of these years: a rather clumsy acrostic ridiculing a classmate, a fragment of a piece of poetry about his heart filled with sorrow, and these lines written in 1826 in the album of a fellow-student:

> The light does soon chill in the eyes of a dreamer. The hopes which kindled him he sees unfulfilled, his expectations frustrated, and the flame of rapture flies away from his heart. ... He is in a state of lifelessness. But happy is he when he discovers the value of reminiscence of bygone days, of the days of his happy childhood, where he left the nascent dreams of the future and the devoted hearts of his friends.

In addition to this little masterpiece of melancholy vacuity, young Gogol is said to have produced an historical narrative: *Bratya Tverdislavichi* (The Tverdislavich Brothers, or better: The Sons of Tverdislav), and − this was probably the most important of his efforts − a satirical comedy entitled *Nechto o Nezhine ili Durakam zakon nie pisan* (Something About Nezhin, or Fools Recognize No Laws).

References to his literary efforts are frequent in his letters of the Nezhin period. Shortly after the death of Vasili Afanasyevich, he wrote to his mother that he had been about to send her several of his compositions and also some drawings he had done; but fate had determined otherwise, and he did not know whether he should send them, and whether his mother would be pleased with these first fruits of the care his parents had lavished on him.

In a letter of October 1825, he promises to compensate for a composition, which apparently was lost at home, by a new one which will be much better.

Announcing his return home for Christmas 1826, he wrote: "How many writings and pictures I shall bring you! . . ." And a few days later:

> I think you will be surprised by my progress the evidence of which I will hand over to you personally. You will not recognize my compositions. A complete change has come about in them of late. They are now of a quite particular kind. . . .

Unfortunately, no information is available on the nature of this revolutionary change, nor on the new manner of the young author.

The son of an amateur playwright and actor, Nikosha took an active part in theatricals which flourished in the Nezhin Gymnasium.

The theater is first mentioned in a letter to his parents dated January 22, 1824, in which he asks them to send him "some comedies;" he mentions *Poverty and Nobility* (*Armuth und Edelsinn*, by August von Kotzebue, a German writer of dramas and comedies (1761-1819); *Hatred of Man and Repentance* (*Menschenhass und Reue* , by the same author); *Bogatonov, or a Provincial in the Capital* (by M. N. Zagoskin; first performance in 1817, in St. Petersburg). The letter continues:

> Also, if you can, send me some canvas and other requisites for the theater. The first play we are performing is *Oedipus in Athens* , a tragedy by Ozerov. I trust, dearest father, that you will not deny to me this pleasure and will send me the necessary things. So, if it is possible, arrange to be made and send me several costumes, as many as possible, or even only one, but more would be better, and also a little money. Be so kind and do not reject this request. Everyone here has donated what he could, except me. And I will give you an account of how I performed my part.

His father showed no haste in sending the costumes or the money; on March · 30, Nikosha dispatched a desperate note complaining that he had been left without news from home for nearly three months. But whether Nikosha contributed any costumes or money, *Oedipus in Athens* was performed on the Nezhin stage during Shrovetide of the year 1824, with Constantin Bazili in the title role, Danilevski as Antigone, and Gogol as Creon.

Ozerov's now thoroughly forgotten tragedy, based less on Sophocles than on Jean-François Ducy's tearful *Oedipe à Colone*, which Ozerov further sentimentalized, was first performed in 1804, and for years enthusiastic audiences applauded it, shedding abundant tears. Ozerov's version ends in the triumph of Oedipus and the annihilation of his enemy, villainous Creon (Nikosha Gogol in the Nezhin production), who is defeated by Theseus and finally killed by a thunderbolt.

Theatricals in Nezhin seem to have reached their peak in the spring of 1827, and Nikosha sent detailed and almost identical accounts of the season to his mother and to his friend Vysotski. To the latter he wrote on March 19, 1827:

> For four consecutive days we had theater, and all acted excellently. All of the visitors present, who are men of experience, said that in none of the provincial theaters had they ever seen such a beautiful show. The scenery (there were four changes) was done masterfully, even magnificently. A beautiful landscape on the curtain completed the charming sight. The illumination of the hall was brilliant. The band, too, distinguished itself. There were ten in it, but they pleasantly substituted for a big orchestra, and were placed in the most advantageous and loudest spot. Four overtures by Rossini, two by Mozart, one by Weber, one composed by Sevryugin, and some others, were played [the latter composer was the local music teacher].

It was required of the Nezhin students that they include in their repertoire plays in French and in German, in addition to Russian plays, and Gogol mentions in his account of the season "two French plays, by Molière and Florian, and one German play, by Kotzebue." The Russian plays were Fonvizin's famous *Nedorosl* (The Minor), Knyazhnin's *The Unsuccessful Peacemaker, or I Shall Go Home without Dinner*, a comedy first published in 1790; *Lukavin* , an adaptation by A. Pisarev (five acts in verse) of Sheridan's *School of Scandal* ; finally, a Russian version of another play of the phenomenally prolific and once popular Kotzebue.

Gogol's Chichikov, in *Dead Souls*, strolling in the streets of the provincial town where he had just arrived, tears a bill from a post and puts it in his pocket; in the evening, back in his room at the inn —

> . . . he sat down in front of the table, had a candle brought, took the bill out of his pocket, placed it under the candle, and began to read it squinting a little with his right eye. There wasn't much, however, that was remarkable in the bill: a drama

by Mr. Kotzebue was presented, in which Rolla was played by Mr. Poplevin, Cora by a Miss Zyablova and the remaining characters being even less remarkable, but this notwithstanding he read through them all, reaching even the prices of the parterre seats, and learned that the bill was printed at the official printing office of the *guberniya*; he then turned it over to see whether there wasn't something on the other side, but finding nothing, he rubbed his eyes, folded it carefully, and placed it in the little coffer where it was his custom to place whatever he would chance to come across.

The two characters mentioned by Gogol, Rolla and Cora, appear in Kotzebue's *Die Spanier in Peru, oder Rolla's Tod* (The Spaniards in Peru, or Rolla's Death), a tragedy, and one of the more ambitious of this author's efforts.

In more than one instance reminiscences of the literary repertory of Gogol's young years are introduced, with a note of ridicule, in the provincial world of *Dead Souls*. He was undoubtedly acquainted with the works of Madame de Genlis (his mother wrote of her beloved aunt Anna that her intelligence equalled that of Genlis, but that she had a better heart).

A volume of one of this author's numerous novels accompanied Chichikov in his journeys; once, staying in his room with a cold and not knowing how to occupy his time, "he made several new and detailed lists of all the peasants he had purchased, (and even read an odd volume of the *Duchesse La Vallière* which was hidden away in his traveling bag"). This was apparently the second volume, for Chichikov's belongings, which he carefully arranged in his room at Tentetnikov's, included the second volumes of two different novels. Mme. de Genlis's novel is mentioned once more (this time, however, as *"Countess La Vallière)* when Chichikov recalls that he has not yet finished reading this work due to the pressure of business.

Elsewhere in *Dead Souls*, after the grandiose luncheon he had been offered, and many libations, Chichikov begins to recite to landowner Sobakevich Werther's message to Charlotte (Sobakevich, however, "only blinked his eyes, seated as he was, in an easy-chair, because after the sturgeon he felt an impelling urge to take a nap").

Even Zhukovski's "Lyudmila," the famous graveyard ballad which quite obviously inspired more than one passage of Gogol's own Kuchelgarten, is not spared in *Dead Souls*:

. . . many of them (the local officials) were not without education: the chairman of the Board of Treasury knew by heart Zhukovski's "Lyudmila," still a fresh novelty in those days, and recited with accomplishment a number of passages, but especially "Slumber spread o'er grove and dale," and the word "hark!" — so that one seemed actually to visualize that the dale slumbered; for greater verisimiliturde when reaching this point he would even half-shut his eyes.

These are instances of Gogol's freeing himself, through irony and parody, of the pre-romantic and romantic conventions of his young years. But even in those years, when his prose (epistolary) was inflated with sentimental phraseology, his scenic talent (he and Kukolnik shone on the Nezhin stage) was essentially realistic, at times even rather coarsely realistic, according to the reminiscences of his contemporaries. One of them speaks of his excellent mimicry, of his ability to change his voice and to "reincarnate himself completely in the character he played."

There are several testimonies to the effect that Gogol excelled particularly in rendering old women, such as Prostakova in Fonvizin's *Nedorosl* . "I saw this play," writes Bazili, "both in Moscow and in St. Petersburg, but I remain convinced that no actress has succeeded in rendering the part of Prostakova as well as it was played by sixteen-year-old Gogol."

Gogol was versatile in his artistic interests and pursuits. His interest in painting awoke early in his life, during his school years, and he preserved it throughout life.

In St. Petersburg, he attended classes in painting at the Academy, and there is evidence that he practiced the art of painting in later years, especially in Italy. He had many contacts with painters; except for his Ukrainian stories, painters (Piskaryov in "Nevski Prospect" and Chartkov in "The Portrait") are his only important characters lacking the comic element. Art criticism was the subject of some of his essays, and art appreciation and various discourses on aesthetics are introduced in several instances in his fiction.

Combining the two arts was not exceptional in the first half of the nineteenth century, in Russia or abroad; Zhukovski and Lermontov, among others, and the Ukrainian Taras Shevchenko were proficient in drawing and painting.

Gogol mentions his drawings in pastel colors as early as January 1825; in September 1825, he informs his mother that he had discussed his plans to continue painting in oil with his professor of art, and that the professor promised to supply him with brushes and with some of the paints; he could purchase the others. This professor, Kapiton Pavlov, was fervently devoted to his art and did much to stimulate the interest of his students.

In "A Few Words about Pushkin," one of the essays included in

Arabesques (this essay was probably written in 1832), Gogol has this recollection:

> I always felt a little passion for painting. I thought a good deal of a landscape I had done, with a dead tree spreading in the foreground. I was then living in th ecountry; the connoisseurs, my judges, were our neighbors. One of them, after glancing at the picture, shook his head and said: "A good painter chooses a tall tree, a stout one, with fresh leaves on it, one in full growth, and not one that's dried up."

The anecdote is told to illustrate a point in the argument: the landscape, however, existed; it was seen, in Vasilyevka, by Gogol's biographer Kulish who describes it as follows:

> It was done in sized-color, on a canvas primed with a coating of red paint, 28 inches by 42. It represented a pavilion overlooking a pond, among tall trees, one of them with dead branches. The trees were apparently copied after some model while the arbor was entirely, or in part, the artist's invention. Remarkable in it were latticed, pointed windows, similar to those of the little outhouse which was designed by Gogol. There are such windows even now in Vasilyevka, in the outhouse in the garden.

This landscape, this view of the pond and of the vaguely gothic structure between the trees, and the tree with the dead branches in the foreground, probably done with minute care, perhaps allegorical ("everything is mortal") – all this sounds rather dull and conventional, rather literary, in the mood of Vasili Afanasyevich's reveries, valleys of meditation and nightingales. In his understanding of the arts, Gogol always remained literary and conventional; he was never able to go beyond the worship of the sublime, beyond cloudy verbiage about "deep significances," or "inspired ideas," or "unforgettable expressions," or whatever else the literary mind would produce, in Gogol's own day, apropos of a work of art, something which is both more and less at one and the same time, than what the work of art is in its own terms (and it is not any lack of expert knowledge that matters, it is the lack of a specific emotional response to the specific stimulus of an art).

Gogol was inclined to use the language of the Jena romantics when he dealt with art. He went into the traditional ecstasies before "divine" Raphael. But he hardly knew even the name of Delacroix, or that of Goya, whom Victor Hugo and the French romantics discovered and admired, and whose genius was much closer to his own than the genius of the Italian Renaissance. Chernyshevski said of Gogol that he "read the wrong books." It would be unjust to say that he admired the wrong pictures – some of the pictures he admired were good – but his perception was obscured by preconceived notions, inherited from the romanticists or learned from academic professors. Gogol remained alien to the mainstream of European art. He found in Rome a refuge from the futile agitation of the nineteenth century; in Rome there were the glorious monuments of the past, but there were also the artists who practiced an art that was dull, academic and provincial. Gogol's association with the German Nazarenes in Rome (group of German painters inspired by the idealism of the primitive Italian painters), or with Russian counterparts, the meek followers of a dead tradition, was an impasse typical for Gogol – one of the several into which he was led during his life.

Kulish's description of Gogol's picture mentions the "latticed, pointed windows similar to those of the little outhouse which was designed by Gogol." The history of these windows may be worth telling. Gogol was not only an amateur painter, but also, like his versatile father, an amateur architect. While in Nezhin, he showed the keenest interest in the rebuilding of the family house in Vasilyevka, concerning himself both with the artistic and with the technical aspects of the project.

The rebuilding of the house was first considered in 1826, but the project was carried out only in 1830, when Gogol was in St. Petersburg.

In a letter from Nezhin dated August 20, 1826, Gogol asked his mother to give him detailed information about the Vasilyevka estate.

In particular, keep me informed concerning any buildings, new installations, etc., and if you need a façade or a plan, so please do me a favor and let me know immediately, and of this you may be assured – the façade will be nice, and also, this is important, the expenses will be small. . . .

Further in this letter Nikosha strongly recommends that once the harvest is over, a search be made in Vasilyevka for clay suitable for the manufacture of tile. "A tiled roof," he writes, "needs no repair for fifty years and more, and at the same time the buildings under it will be so pretty. . . ." He also knows a cheap method for preparing plaster which he will soon communicate; he guarantees the durability of the plaster prepared according to this method.

In *Hans Kuchelgarten*, there is this description of a house in a

German village, somewhere near the seashore:

> One sees white looming in the distance, the dwelling
> Of Wilhelm Bauch, the farmer; long ago,
> The pastor's daughter when he married, he built it.
> Gay looking little house! It's painted green,
> And covered with resonant and pretty tiling.

It is not clear why the house, painted green and covered with tile, perhaps white, probably red, "looms *white* in the distance," but the tiles are in the picture in this description of the idyllic dwelling of the German farmer (prosaically named "Belly"), and the house designed by Nikosha was greenish gray with a red roof.

The subject is taken up again in a letter of September 10:

> I have found the plan and the façade for the new house which I designed when dear father was still alive. I am sending them to you; the scale is wrong, and they are imperfectly executed, but they may be useful, as long as there are no others, especially for the exterior decoration. One façade represents the front view of the house, the other the rear. . . .

There are numerous inquiries in the following letters: have his plans been received, and does his mother like them? Has any clay for tile manufacture been discovered? Has the windmill been completed? Is the pavilion for grand-aunt Agafya Matveyevna going to be built in the garden? He has in mind a very elegant façade for this structure.

The rebuilding or renovating projects were not carried out until three years later. Gogol took up the matter once more after his return to St. Petersburg from his dash to Germany, which caused his mother's justified anxiety and anger. Gogol returned to Russia with new ideas about the house in Vasilyevka and offered to draw up plans for alterations which, at a very low cost, would make it look like some houses he had seen in Germany, but exact measurements must be taken and sent to him.

On January 5, 1830, he dispatched to Vasilyevka a plan with minutely detailed instructions. He had thought of a completely new façade, in the new style which he saw in "civilized Europe." But as this would be too expensive, he suggests only alterations which will cost practically nothing. Here are some of his suggestions:

> Once the mezzanine is removed, the four columns spaced out along the broad porch would be ugly and out of proportion; I

decided therefore to place eight columns, arranged in pairs. Through this the porch will become even broader, but it will offer a beautiful sight, as you may see from the enclosed [design of the] façade. These columns are all of the Doric order, with grooves, or flutes, along their full length which also is no small embellishment. For this the old columns could be sawed into two, and the four will give eight; they will not be too short. . . . In the drawing-room and the bedroom, the windows and the glass door will have a gothic aspect: this is now the general taste, and I find that in the country this will be charming. I enclose a separate drawing with explanations. . . .

A facsimile of this drawing has been published. A profile of a Doric column, with its base and the entablature is done with great care and professional skill; there is also a very neat design of the "gothic" glass door between two windows: they are rather narrow, rectilinear, with the top pointed, divided into rather large lozenges and triangles, some left white, others colored either yellow, or a greenish blue. Inscriptions on the drawing comment that colored glass is unusually beautiful and blue glass may be procured from a factory near Nezhin (it is much more expensive in the stores); the lattice separating the panes must not be too thick and must be painted black.

Gogol's projects were carried out, with the "gothic" windows which first appeared in his picture done three or four years earlier, in Nezhin. He saw the new arrangements during his first visit home from St. Petersburg, in July 1832. He was working at that time on a novel based on the history of the Ukraine; in a fragment of this fortunately unfinished gothic novel, a mysterious prisoner is brought by the Poles to a monastery and is thrown into a dungeon, inhabited by spiders, lizards and a giant toad, a cave humid and completely dark. There follows in the fragment this extraordinary study of pure vision, of retinal memory-producing images in the dark:

> With all his senses he sank into the darkness. And then a completely new, strange world began to unfold before him. In the dark there began to appear to him luminous trails — the last reminiscences of the light! These trails combined in many different patterns and hues. For the eye ther is no complete darkness; however tightly you screw it up, it will always present and recreate the colors it has seen. These variegated patterns now took on the aspect of a multi-colored shawl, now of wavy marble; or else that aspect which strikes us with its wonderful quaintness when we examine through the microscope

a particle of an insect's leg or wing. Sometimes the elegant lattice-work of a window – there was none, alas, in his prison – would fantastically gleam for a moment, then it would change to a coffee-brown, then disappear completely, leaving a blackness sprinkled with yellow, or with indefinitely colored speckles.

Once more, having made its way through the labyrinth of reminiscence and creative imagination, the image of the window appears – with its "elegant latticework," and the azure glimmering

Chapter IX

THE SCHOOL YEARS END

LIBERALS AND REACTIONARIES

During Gogol's last two years in Nezhin, the Gymnasium became the scene of incidents and disturbances which culminated in a serious crisis involving both the students and the faculty.

The crisis arose in connection with the change in the administration of the school in the summer of 1826, when Director Orlay left his position and was replaced by an acting director, the professor of mathematics and natural history, Casimir Shapalinski. Before leaving, Orlay appointed as inspector the junior (assistant) professor of law, Nikolai Belousov.

Returning to Nezhin in the fall of 1826, Gogol reported to his mother: ". . . our school is noticeably improving: the food has become excellent, and we owe all this to our new inspector." Two months later he amplified:

> You wish to be informed who is now our director; we do not have a director, and it is desirable that there should not be one at all. Our boarding-school is now on the very best degree of advancement, a degree which Orlay has never been able to attain, and the reason for all this is our present inspector; to him we owe our happiness; food, clothing, the interior arrangement of the rooms, the order that has been established, all this you would find in no other place than our institution. Recommend to everyone to bring their children here: they would not find anything better in the whole of Russia.

The merits of the new inspector are also mentioned in the letters to Vysotski, Gogol's former schoolmate, dated January 17 and March 19, 1827; in the second letter Gogol goes beyond his praises for the students' material welfare:

> We have been provided with all possible entertainment, pleasures and amusements, and for all this we are obligated to

100

our inspector. I do not know whether it is possible to find words of praise worthy of this extraordinary man. He treats us all absolutely as his friends and takes our side against the cavils of the Faculty Council and the faculty pedants. And, I must confess, were it not for him, I should lack the patience to complete the course here, [but] now at least I am able to withstand firmly this cruel ordeal, these last fourteen months.

Gogol's feelings were shared by other students: the young inspector (Belousov was only 28 in 1827) rapidly gained respect and popularity, and Gogol's letter shows that the students not only considered him their friend and champion, but also that they had some awareness of the antagonism between their inspector and the "faculty pedants."

Actually some of Belousov's colleagues were jealous of his popularity, especially the senior professor of law, Mikhail Bilevich, a much older man, who is described in all available reports as a narrow-minded pedant with a limited knowledge of his subject and a total lack of talent. Bilevich's teaching, according to Bazili, consisted of reading a chapter from the textbook, which was then assigned to the class; the students also practiced conducting litigations, and the professor demonstrated some skill in legalistic chicane.

During the three-year feud which Bilevich initiated, and which ended in his complete victory, he had the support, among others, of the professor of Russian literature, Nikolski, and also of the professor of Divinity. Belousov, on the other hand, was supported by Shapalinski, by the German and French professors Singer and Landragine, and by some of the junior members of the staff.

Professor Bilevich commenced open hostilities in May 1827. The battleground he chose was the course in natural law which was taught by his younger colleague.

The doctrine of natural law was judged dangerous by the government and the teaching of the subject in the Gymnasiums was prohibited in 1824. It was continued, however, in the universities. Because of the special status of the Bezborodko Gymnasium, there was some uncertainty in Nezhin as to whether it was permissible to teach the subject. An inquiry was made in St. Petersburg, but no answer came, and it was decided to proceed with the course.

It is not impossible that the fact that natural law was a proscribed subject was known to the students, and that this added a special aureole to Belousov's course.

Judging by the testimony of Nestor Kukolnik, the students felt that in this course some supreme truth, some unique wisdom was

101

concentrated and was revealed to them by the young professor; Belousov inaugurated, in 1826, a preliminary, two-month course, but, writes Kukolnik:

These two months were more important to us than whole years. With extraordinary mastery, Nikolai Grigoryevich [Belousov] presented to us the entire history of philosophy and, at the same time, that of natural law, all in a few lectures, so that every one of us had firmly lodged in his head a well ordered, systematic skeleton of the science of sciences which each of us could invest with a body according to his wishes, his abilities and his scholarship.

Bilevich, in his attack against Belousov used the weapon of denunciation for political subversion. That was a deadly weapon in those days – a year and a half after the Decembrist uprising. The Decembrists' (Dekabristis') movement, the first revolutionary movement of the nineteenth century, was formed after the Napoleonic wars. The movement chiefly comprised aristocratic officers and was aimed at abolishing serfdom and introducing a liberal constitution. On the accession to the throne of Nicholas I in December 1825, the Decembristis carried out a badly organized revolt in St. Petersburg, which led to the hanging of five of them and the banishment to Siberia of several others. Bilevich wrote in his report to the Faculty Council on May 7, 1827:

I likewise deem it my duty, as senior professor of legal science, to say that I have noticed that some students hold principles of liberalism and this, I believe, may derive from which, although it has been prescribed that it be taught according to the system of M. Demartini, junior professor Belousov teaches according to his own notes, following the principles of the philosophy of Kant and of Mr. Schad.

Belousov defended himself vigorously against the accusation of subversion and introduced as evidence the lecture notes of some of his students. Bilevich retorted, however, that these notes had been expurgated and presented notes of other students whose notes had been introduced by either party were questioned, and Kukolnik's, it was discovered, contained passages from such "subversive" works as Voltaire's *Dictionnaire Philosophique*, Rousseau's *Contrat Social*, Kant's *Zum Ewigen Frieden*, Montesquieu's *L'Esprit des Lois*. Kukolnik explained, not too convincingly it must be said, that he had been reading on his own, and had interpolated the incriminating quotations in the course notes. In part, he also stated, he had copied them from a notebook borrowed from Gogol who took the course a year earlier. Gogol was questioned on November 3, 1827, and confirmed this statement.

At one point the Faculty Council found itself engaged in a controversy on whether certain views held by Belousov were in opposition to the teachings of the Orthodox Church, and it was decided to submit the whole matter to the expert judgement of the professor of Divinity, Reverend Pavel Volynski. Father Volynski (he is mentioned, with very little respect, in two of Gogol's letters) was hardly at home in the dispute involving Kant, Rousseau, Locke and a few others. Nevertheless, after due consideration and with the obvious prompting of Bilevich, he pronounced that Belousov's views were, in part at least, irreconcilable with religion.

In May 1828, shortly before Gogol's graduation, Bilevich's effforts resulted in a "confession" by two or three students: their earlier testimonies, they admitted, had been inspired by Belousov, Singer or Landragine; later come Kukolnik's recantation. It also developed that a student had done for Landragine a traslation into French of "verses by Kondrati Ryleyev having reference to an appeal for freedom." Ryleyev, it must be remembered, was hanged as one of the leaders of the Decembrist uprising in July 1826, scarcely a year before the Nezhin affair, and the possession of his poems was at that time a very serious matter indeed.

Belousov, however, was hardly responsible for the presence in Nezhin of such explosive matter; he supervised the students' reading and reported, in October 1826, that "some pupils . . . write verses which do not attest to good morals . . . [they] read books unsuitable for their age, and keep the works of Alexander Pushkin and the like." In this instance Belousov may have condemned Pushkin as licentious, but soon thereafter he reported with alarm the discovery of a copy of Pushkin's incendiary "Ode to Freedom" in the possession of a pupil. These lines of the Ode, which Pushkin wrote when he was eighteen, reflect the doctrine of natural law: "O Rulers! 'Tis from your crowns and thrones that your law comes − not from nature; you stand above the people, but eternal law is above you." Natural law was taught at the Tsarskoye Selo Lyceum by Kunitsyn, a young enthusiast in many ways resembling Belousov.

Even though Belousov confiscated the Pushkin's poem, there is no doubt that in him was alive that spirit of opposition, related to the great rationalist and liberal tradition of the eighteenth century. This tradition had never been completely smothered in Russia, despite all the efforts of the government, despite all the restrictive measures which preceded the tragedy of December 1825 (Decembrists), and the persecutions that followed it.

In 1822, the tsarist government prohibited Freemasonry in Russia because of connections between masonic lodges and secret political societies, and all government servants were required to sign statements to the effect that they did not belong to any secret society and to make known any previous affiliations. Similar declarations were required once more by a rescript issued in April 1826, soon after the Decembrist uprising.

The statements signed by professors Shapalinski and Landragine show that they had both been members of the lodge of the "United Slavs" founded in Kiev in 1818. It may be noted that, also in 1818, a secret society was founded in the Poltava province which in 1823 (that is a year after the masonic lodges became illegal), assumed the name of "The Society of the United Slavs." On the eve of the 1825 uprising, it joined the Southern Society, one of the two major Decembrist organizations. These facts do not prove any revolutionary affiliations of the two men, but they do indicate at least the possibility of contacts with the Decembrist circles; and it does seem that an echo, even if only a faint one, of the defeated Decembrist movement could be heard in Nezhin in Gogol's schooldays.

The situation in Nezhin was apparently judged serious by the government which, in February 1830 (Gogol was no longer in Nezhin at that time), dispatched there a high official from St. Petersburg to supervise the investigation. It was finally closed, and Director Yasnovski, who took over in October 1827, presented a report condemning Shapalinski, Landragine, Singer and Belousov. Yasnovski also stated a few general principles, namely, that "the statutes of His Majesty consider that the essential foundations [of education] are Faith, Piety and the Fear of God, and then only useful sciences and arts."

Soon thereafter the government took action: Shapalinski, Landragine, Singer, Belousov and later Andrushchenko were not only dismissed from the Nezhin Gymnasium, but excluded for ever from the academic profession and placed under police surveillance; the two foreigners were ordered to leave the country.

In addition to the accusation of subversion, Bilevich's denunciation had another aspect, less dramatic, but of interest for the study of Gogol's formative years: Belousov was criticized for relaxing discipline in the Gymnasium and for tolerating various disorders. "Certain educators," he wrote, quoting one of the supervisors, "are in the habit of walking back and forth, in the corridors, arm in arm with pupils and treating them with excessive familiarity."

Belousov's reply was that the disorders originated before he took over as inspector, and that far from relaxing discipline, he had restored it. He wrote:

> For a long time I declined the position offered to me, for I saw how much labor, trouble and worry it would mean considering the utter deprovity of the conditions in the school. But when this man [Orlay] who is honored for his services to out country, began to argue with me, with tears in his eyes, representing to me both the peril menacing the young people, and the deceived hope of their parents, and the threat to our very institution, adding that in me alone did he place his hope, then only did I resolve to take upon myself the heavy burden. The Lord lent me support in my undertaking . . . And at a time when the terrible disorder in the pupils' conduct had been put down; when they not only lost the former habits, but did not even think any more of gadding about in a crowd from one inn to another for drinking bouts; of visiting ill-famed places and causing shameful scandals; when one no longer saw in the museums [dormitories] crowds of cadets who brought all manner of depravity from the outside to these inexperienced children; when instead of firing rockets and shooting, as they used to, in the garden, or strolling in Magerki [a suburb of Nezhin], they were engaged in study, or sought relaxation in respectable and authorized games . . . (at that very time, the period winds up, he was accused, etc. . . .).

One of the incidents brought up by Belousov's critics, it must be explained, was that during his inspectorship, "the firing of rockets had frightened the pregnant wife of one of the professors."

Other incidents were reported by Moiseyev, the former inspector:

> . . . the pupils have begun lately to read unauthorized books in class, and when they are asked questions, it comes out that they are engaged not so much in study, as in learning parts for theatrical performances; that in town they play cards and gamble away their clothes; that they shout and whistle offensively, out of the windows of the school building, at passing noble ladies escorted by officers. . . .

Additional information on the mores in the Gymnasium may be found in the report presented in 1830 by the new director who wrote:

Corporal punishment was applied rarely: in the case of the junior pupils for extreme laziness and dangerous pranks, and in the case of the senior pupils, for nocturnal vagrancy, rioting, gambling and drunkenness.

He also stated that some instructors, who had their living quarters in the school building, gave board and lodging to some fifty students; he insisted that this irregular practice be discontinued, for it was the source of various disorders:

> Especially the young women and wenches hired in large numbers as laundresses are the cause of highly improper occurrences which it is not possible to prevent.

According to the same report, there were instances of disorderly behavior in the school chapel.

Earlier reports denounce Singer and other professors for often being late for their classes, and state that before the professor's arrival some students (Kukolnik is named among others) mount to the chair and deliver speeches on "metaphysics, aesthetics and magnetism, referring in a free and indecent language to relation."

Whether the disorders originated before or during Belousov's inspectorship, it does seem that at one time the students were given excessive freedom which some of them may have misused. But if Belousov's accusers criticized what they calll his "excessive familiarity," Gogol and other students praised him for treating them as his friends.

Gogol preserved his friendship and admiration for Belousov for years after he left school. In 1833, living in St. Petersburg, he wrote to his friend Maksimovich, who was soon thereafter appointed rector of Kiev University:

> If you go to Kiev, look up ex-professor Belousov. This man will be useful to you in many ways, and I do wish you get to know each other.

This was followed up a year later in June 1834:

> And arriving in Kiev you must not fail to meet ex-professor Belousov. He lives in a house he owns in the Podol [a suburb], I believe. Tell him I asked him to make you his friend, like myself. . . .

To a former schoolmate, Tarnovski, he wrote in August of the same year: "I heard that Belousov's situation has improved, and I feel very happy about this."

This faithfulness to Belousov, the "dangerous radical" under police surveillance, is significant. Gogol preserved his memory for years, like all the memories of his young days, and the "ideal educator" in the second volume of *Dead Souls* was unquestionably inspired by the young professor in Nezhin.

The treatment of this image is worth closer consideration.

In the first chapter of the unfinished second volume of *Dead Souls*, Gogol tells the story of the education of a landowner by the name of Tentetnikov, a prototype of Goncharovs' Oblomov:

> As a boy of twelve, quick-witted, with some inclination for brooding, rather frail, he entered a school whose principal at that time was an extraordinary man.

Nikosha Gogol was twelve when he entered the Nezhin Gymnasium, and the "extraordinary" principal — he is given the name of Alexander Petrovich — is in more than one way a reflection of Belousov. Gogol's schoolmate Kukolnik, in his outline of Belousov's biography, insisted on his "fairness, honesty, accessibility, good advice and, in appropriate cases, the necessary encouragement" which the students received from him. This ability to encourage and to inspire confidence is brought out in Gogol's panegyric of Alexander Petrovich:

> An idol of the youth, a marvel among educators, incomparable Alexander Petrovich possessed the gift of intuitive understanding of human nature. How he knew the children! How he could encourage them! There was not an imp among them who having done some mischief would not go to him of his own accord and confess everything. And that was not all: leaving him after a severe reprimand, he would not feel downcast, but heartened; there was something cheering in him, something that said "Forward! Hurry to get back on your feet again even if you have stumbled."

The pupils adored Alexander Petrovich:

> Never do children have such an attachment for their parents. No, not even in the crazy years of crazy infatuations could unslaked passions be so strong as was their love for him. To the grave, to his declining days the grateful pupil, when he raised his glass commemorating the birthday of his wonderful master who had long been resting in his grave, would close his

eyes and would shed tears for him.

The course which Belousov taught in Nezhin (this marvelous course, this foundation of all learning, the "science of sciences" in the words of Kukolnik) is also reflected in the story of Tentetnikov and of the unequalled Alexander Petrovich who gave a special course for a few select students (a different abridged program was judged sufficient for the mediocre); Tentetnikov was eager to be part of this elite:

> . . . the fervent heart of the ambitious boy kept throbbing at the mere thought that he would at last be admitted to this class . . .

And in the earlier version: ". . . he was distinguished by a transfer to this superior class as one of the very best . . ." According to Danilevski, Gogol, before the end of his course at Nezhin, was "remarked and began to be distinguished by Professor Belousov whom, in his turn, he respected and loved."

Gogol remains rather vague when he attempts to describe what was actually taught to the privileged few. A difficult problem faced Gogol at this point: a statement of the ideas which Belousov professed would be barred by the censor: and even regardless of the censor, the Gogol of the second volume of *Dead Souls* had traveled a long way from the ideas which may have aroused his enthusiasm in the Nezhin days. What survived was the pure and noble image, perhaps somewhat dimmed by time, of the inspiring teacher, the admired Older Friend of his schooldays. But the content of his teaching could not be rendered in *Dead Souls*, and a substitute had to be found.

So we are told of Alexander Petrovich's teaching that "among the sciences those only were chosen which are capable of making a citizen of his country out of a man," and that he instructed his select pupils in the "science of life," endeavoring above all to stimulate their ambitions and to train their characters and their will-power.

The purpose of the great pedagogue, in this somewhat anticlimactic presentation, was in the final account to prepare ideal government servants:

> The lectures consisted mostly of telling the youths about what awaited them in their future, and he could survey the entire horizon of their careers in such a manner that, while still on their school benches, in their minds and their souls they already lived there — at the place of their service.

This is clearly a reflection of Gogol's own thinking of the 1840's, with its emphasis on the "useful" and on "duty," with its tritely conservative Utopia: a monarchy which is almost a theocracy, served by perfect public officials, and resting upon a perfect landed gentry owning perfect serfs. Education in this scheme could hardly be more than instruction in the "science of life" and training of character.

The true story of Belousov's fall could no more be told in *Dead Souls* than the substance of his teaching. But Gogol may have felt the need to give some account of his experience, and, on the other hand, in *Dead Souls* it was necessary that Alexander Petrovich disappear: if Tentetnikov were permitted to take the course in the "science of life," then his failure in life would be difficult to explain: it would also be a failure for the miraculous pedagogue.

Gogol chose a simple solution: at the very moment when young Tentetnikov, triumphantly admitted to the senior year, was about to be given his share of supreme wisdom, Alexander Petrovich suddenly fell ill and died.

All went wrong after the death of Alexander Petrovich and the arrival of the new principal. The parallel here is obvious: Belousov was dismissed later, but in the fall of 1827, when Gogol began his last year, the new principal, Yasnovski, arrived, and the Shapalinski-Belousov regime came to an end. Yasnovski was later to report, with a note of resentment, that the pupils who had known that period referred to it as the "golden age."

Belousov, it will be remembered, was attacked for his teaching of subversive views and also, as inspector of the students, he was made responsible for their improper behavior. In *Dead Souls* both these aspects are reflected.

Alexander Petrovich (like Belousov) was a liberal educator, and was little concerned with the pupils' external discipline:

Never did he mention good conduct to them. He would say: "Brains and nothing else is what I demand. He who is concerned with being intelligent has no time for pranks; prankishness will have to disappear of itself." And so it was pranks ceased by themselves.

And in the earlier version:

The crowd of his pupils was so frolicsome, bold and sprightly that it may have appeared to one an unruly community of freegooters; this, however, would have been a wrong judgement . . .

Further Alexander Petrovich's views in matters of discipline are explained as follows:

> Often he would not seek to restrain prankishness, seeing in it the early development of the traits of character, and would say that pranks are useful for him as a rash is for a physician — in order to ascertain what is concealed within a man.

This was certainly the "golden age" for the pupils. But everything changed with the arrival of the new principal, one Fyodor Ivanovich. He insisted on order and discipline, stating the very first day that intelligence and accomplishment meant nothing to him and that he would consider only good conduct. But, strangely enough, good conduct was precisely what Fyodor Ivanovich did not obtain. Discipline based on coercion generated vice, however successfully it put an end to innocent pranks:

> Everything was shipshape in the daytime, and the boys marched in pairs, but orgies started at night . . . Depravity developed which was by no means childlike . . . Andrei Ivanovich [Tentetnikov] in *Dead Souls* was of a quiet disposition. He was not allured by the nocturnal orgies of his comrades who had availed themselves of a certain lady under the very windows of the director's apartment, nor did he follow the others in profaning what is sacred, which they did for the only reason that the priest happened to be none too intelligent.

A few additional details may be found in the earlier version:

> He did not participae in the nocturnal orgies with his comrades who, despite the strictest surveillance, availed themselves of a mistress on the side — one for eight of them — nor did he take part in their other pranks which did not stop before sacrilege and mockery over religion itself for the only reason that the director demanded frequent attendance at church services.

These passages corroborate the earlier quoted reports on the depravity of the students, and it is likely that Gogol was a witness, if not a participant (he was of a "quiet disposition"), of some rather crude debauch in which his less inhibited schoolmates indulged. One may also note that in both the passages quoted, sexual depravity is mentioned side by side with sacrilege and religious profanation.

Another detail is worth mentioning: in the Tentetnikov story the new principal "had the boys seated at a table, for the sake of better

110

appearance, according to their height and not their intelligence, so that the blockheads got the best morsels, and the intelligent the scrapings. All this caused murmuring. . . ."

The matter of how the boys should be seated for their meals was considered in Nezhin in the early days. In September 1823, the honorary curator, Count Kushelev-Bezborodo, visiting the school, suggested to Director Orlay that the boys be seated in the refectory according to their accomplishment and conduct, but it developed that Orlay had just issued a similar order himself. We do not know whether Yasnovski, the new director, actually changed this arrangement, but it may be conjectured that he did. The small boy – and the most brilliant one – who suffered from the new arrangement could obviously be none other than Gogol himself (there is no mention of Tentetnikov being small), and the identification of smallness with intelligence, and of high stature and strength with stupidity, seems to bring back a compensated inferiority dating from the author's childhood. The passage about the refectory was omitted by Gogol in the later version.

The new regime instituted by Alexander Petrovich's successor not only damaged the morals of the students but also the teaching which became lifeless and purposeless. He invited several new professors who had

> . . . new views and new angles and standpoints. They showered their audience with hosts of new terms and expressions; they displayed in their expositions both logical consistency and adherence to new discoveries, as well as the fervor of their science.

And further:

> What subjects and courses did he [Tentetnikov] not take! Medicine, philosophy, even law, and a universal history of mankind so formidable in scope that all the professor had been able to cover in three years was the introduction and the development of the municipal community in some German cities or other . . .

The formidable history course which does not go very far beyond the introduction may well be an ironical reference to Gogol's own venture in history teaching. It must be noted, however, that Gogol insists on the modernism (the "new views," the "new angles and standpoints") of the professors who taught all these lifeless and useless courses.

Young Tentetnikov feels lost and despondent after the death of Alexander Petrovich. Belousov was dismissed only in 1830, but Gogol began his senior year in the fall of 1827, under the new regime: the "golden age" was over.

In Gogol's letters dating from his last year in Nezhin, no direct references are to be found to the events which agitated the school, and in which he became directly involved when he was called to testify in November 1827. But one often hears a note of disappointment in his studies and of intense boredom. To his second cousin Pavel Kosyarovski, he wrote:

> Now I am in my last year . . . but there is practically nothing to do. The past year was the most vigorous for me, I shall never forget it, there was plenty to toil for! Now a lot of free time is left after the studies, and I occupy my leisure by reading the *Bibliothèque des Dames*. It is a very excellent publication; there are in all two hundred volumes.

And a few months later to his mother:

> I will only say that one ought to be surprised that I learned so much in this stupid institution . . . I did not want to alarm you by informing you of this, since I knew that you were not in a position to give me a better education . . . Besides incompetent instructors and the greatest neglect, they do not teach languages at all here . . . If I know anything at all, I owe it to no one but myself.

The complaints about language teaching were hardly justified; the truth was that Nikosha had fallen far behind most of his classmates, and in modern languages had not been transferred to the senior division. He was obviously preparing an excuse for his lack of proficiency in French and German. And generally, the once-exalted gymnasium had become a "stupid institution" with "incompetent instructors." Belousov who had singled himout and whom he adored was no longer his teacher. The new principal was in command; "Alexander Petrovich" was dead.

The last of the schoolyears finally came to an end. In June 1828, Nikosha Gogol graduated, with a not too brilliant record, and set out on the last of his many trips from Nezhin to Vasilyevka where he was to spend the summer before leaving his native Ukraine for St. Petersburg.

The opening lines of the "Chapter from an Historical Novel," published by Gogol in 1831, present a lonely horseman journeying along a difficult and unfamiliar road. He is a Polish emissary sent on a secret errand. After a long and tiresome ride across the steppe, as darkness descends, he enters the forest —

Unclad by pitiless autumn, the trees could be seen through like a sieve, and seemed to tremble in the evening chill. Yellow leaves, like scraps of food and pieces of shattered dishes — the remains of a recent feast — were untidily strewn around, and their rustle alone, as it moved about the wood, betrayed the presence of our rider. Through the bared summits of the trees the sky loomed dark; a sharp wind rising in the field rushed with doleful wails into the thick of the forest. The itinerant, lost in thought, stopped his mount undecided on what course to take, for the road had now vanished completely and there was nothing before him but the bristling forest — and uncertainty; but suddenly a loud *tsob! tsob!* ["gee up!" of the Ukrainian peasant when driving oxen] struck his ear, a heavily laden cart creaked and a pair of oxen appeared from behind the trees.

From the old peasant driving the cart the traveler learns that the bridges over the Sula, which lies ahead of him, have been destroyed. In the very first line of the fragment we are told that the emissary had crossed the borderline between the districts of Piryatin and Lubny. The road passing through Piryatin and Lubny, then across the Sula, is the road that Gogol traveled on his way home to Vasilyevka from Nezhin. Shortly before the last of these journeys, he wrote to his mother:

The main thing for me is to have a spacious carriage, and it needn't be anything better than the one in which I returned last year to Nezhin. It was that immense calash in which the Kibintsy butlers used to drive. I think it will be large enough for my belongings. At the same time it is very light, made as it is of wicker, and also it isn't jolty . . .

On the eve of one of his earlier trips home he asked for some books "because the journey will be so terribly boring." One easily imagines Nikosha in the immense wicher calash on the long and weary journey across the steppe and the woods; and the mysterious rider making his way through the forest may well have been imagined by him during his journey, in a reverie, when it got too dark to read one of the books he had taken along with him in the carriage.

The "Chapter" was a fragment of that unfinished historical novel, of which the hero was to be Hetman Ostranitsa who fought a mighty battle with the Poles, in the seventeenth century; the home of Vasili and Mariya Gogol-Yanovski was quite near the old battlefield, at the point where the Goltva falls into the Psyol.

Chapter X

THE FUTURE

THE CRAVING FOR GREATNESS

AND THE FEAR OF OBSCURITY

The young listeners of Alexander Petrovich's inspired lectures, "while still on their school benches, were transported in their minds and souls to the future place of their service." So was Tentetnikov, even though he did not take Alexander Petrovich's course:

> As the time for graduation approached, his heart throbbed; he said to himself: "This is not life yet, this is merely preparation for life; real life is service: it is there that great deeds are accomplished."

This is clearly autobiographical in intention: in his *Avtorskaya ispoved* (The Author's Confession), which belongs to the same period as the second volume of *Dead Souls*, Gogol wrote of his young years:

> I am unable to say positively whether authorship was truly my vocation. I know only that in those years when I began to think about my future (and I began to think about my future early, at a time when other boys thought of nothing but play), the idea of being a writer never came to my mind, although it always seemed to me that I would be a man of renown, that a broad field of action awaits me, and even that I would accomplish something for the common good. I simply thought that I would advance in service and that all this would be achieved through serving the government. That is why the eagerness to serve was so strong in me in my young days. It was everlastingly present in my mind, preceding all other concerns and occupations.

To the picture given in the *Confession,* and reflected in the Tentetnikov chapter of *Dead Souls,* it must be added, however, that there were practical reasons for Gogol's decision to go to Petersburg and to enter government service. For a young man of the landowning gentry the choice was limited in those days: it was a choice between staying at home and becoming a country squire, or taking service in the army or in the government. The liberal professions were practically non-existent at that time, and trade would not even be considered in a family belonging to the gentry and not to the merchant class.

Gogol's frail constitution excluded an army career (it had been considered at one time for his father); the choice was consequently between Vasilyevka and government service, and government service meant St. Petersburg, for the capital offered far greater opportunities for a successful career.

Going to the northern capital was by no means unusual, although for a Ukrainian it was almost expatriation. Many of Gogol's schoolmates preceded or followed him there forming that little colony to which Gogol himself belonged during his first years in Petersburg, even if he rapidly succeeded in broadening the circle of his friends and connections in the capital.

Furthermore, the economic conditions in those days stimulated the trend away from the parental estates and toward the government offices of the capital. In the early 1820's a serious depression began which affected the market prices of wheat, the staple product of Ukrainian agriculture. Ukrainian export by way of the Black Sea, mainly through the port of Odessa, which early in the century had reached important figures, was reduced to almost nothing as a result of international developments; a slump of export and then of domestic prices of wheat followed. The trend was not reversed for many years: the recovery began only in the late 1830's. The depression coincided consequently with Gogol's schoolyears in Nezhin (1821-1828) and with his Petersburg period which ended in 1836 when he left Russia.

For the middle and the small landowner such as the Gogols, these years were years of constant struggle with financial difficulties. It is understandable that their sons were expected to seek an independent income rather than to live on the dwindling income of the family estates.

In Gogol's case the very fact that he was sent to an expensive school seems to indicate the choice that was made for him by his parents. A country squire would not need so many years of expensive schooling. Gogol was granted a scholarship beginning July 1, 1822, but 1,000 rubles were paid for his first year, and 166 rubles due for May and June, 1822, were paid only in January 1827. The highest salary Gogol earned in government services was 750 rubles a year.

In Gogol's correspondence the first reference to St. Petersburg is made in a letter to his schoolmate and lifelong friend Alexander Danilevski in August 1825: "I am now enlightened with new knowledge, with new information about our beloved St. Peter." It was in the company of Danilevski that three years later he set out for St. Petersburg.

His future life in the capital becomes a leitmotif in Gogol's letter in 1827. In January of that year he wrote to Vysotski, a schoolmate who had graduated in 1826:

> You are already living in St. Petersburg, you are enjoying life; with avid haste you partake of the pleasures, but I am not to see you before another year and a half, and this one and a half years stretches out before me like ages.

And in February, to his mother:

> If I think of anything now, it is of my future life. Sleeping or waking, I see Petersburg and together with it service in the government.

In March, he asked Vysotski for detailed information on life in the capital, on cost of living, the salaries, the working hours. And in June: could Vysotski order a frock-coat at the very best tailor's in the capital for him? He would prefer a blue coat with metal buttons: he has many black ones (an obvious lie) and is tired of them.

But if he was preoccupied with such practical matters as the cost of living, or with such frivolous ones as the buttons on his future frock-coat, he certainly gave serious thought to the problem of his future destiny: his destiny had to be one of greatness, and his life would be devoted to a high ideal. In March 1827, he announced to his mother his resolve to "undertake a task important and noble — for the good of the country, for the happiness of the citizens, for the benefit of his fellow men . . .

This is given a fuller expression in a letter to "uncle" (second cousin) Peter Kosyarovski to whom he revealed his plans with great solemnity, and under the seal of secrecy (in a letter dated October 3, 1827):

> My lot is perhaps to spend my whole life in St. Petersburg; this, at any rate, is the aim I traced for myself long ago. Since then a long time has passed. Almost since my age of ignorance, I burned with unquenchable eagerness to make my life to serve

117

for the good of the country. I yearned to do something useful, be it even in a small way.

But how could he best serve his country?

In my mind I went over all the offices, all the stations in the government, and I made my choice. It is Justice. I saw clearly that here was the most work to be done, that only here could I be of service, only here can I be truly useful to mankind. Injustice, this greatest of the world's afflictions, tore my heart asunder. I swore not to waste a single minute of my brief life without doing good. For two years I have been constantly studying the laws of other nations and natural law, the foundation of them all, and now I am studying the laws of our country.

The influence of Belousov is obvious in the reference to natural law as the foundation of all positive law; but the "two years" of "constant" legal studies is clearly an overstatement.

It is strange, on the other hand, that Gogol found it necessary to envelop the news in a shroud of mystery. He had not yet confided it to anyone. He writes: "even mother who wanted to know about my intentions could not say yet with certainty what path I chose to take; I cannot yet reveal some of my reasons." That Nikosha would take government service in Petersburg was no news, and it is difficult to see what was so daring in the choice of the Department of Justice rather than of some other department. This choice was by no means unreasonable: the department had been administered by Troshchinski, the "benefactor" of the family, and his recommendation would be particularly effective in this branch of government.

The example of the former Minister, on the other hand, may have combined with Professor Belousov's lectures to inspire the laudable intention to serve mankind by fighting for a better administration of justice. It is not impossible that Gogol had knowledge of the imperial rescript entrusting Troshchinski with the noble task of protecting the weak and of eradicating corruption. Nor is it unlikely that Nikosha considered the fact that Troshchinski's reward for serving the cause of justice was not only universal esteem, but also the thousands of serfs and acres of land which had been granted him by the monarchs he had served. Both the exalted lines of Gogol's letter to Uncle Kosyarovski and the earlier quoted passage from the *Confession* about government service seem to lead to the glorious image of his Excellency Dmitri

Prokofyevich Troshchinski.

Passages from young Gogol's letters, proclaiming his intention to devote his life to the good of his country and to that of mankind in general, have been piously quoted in support of the "Citizen-Writer" theory: he burned with civic ardor as an adolescent, and later, with the same ardor, he used his mighty satirical talent to castigate evil, weeping in secret over existing conditions which he endeavored to improve (and it must be said that Gogol contributed as much as belinski to this interpretation). But a closer examination of Gogol's early letters reveals a different aspect of his personality which cannot be neglected.

During the last years of the Nezhin period, Vysotski seems to have been the "select soul" with whom Gogol could communicate. In a letter to him of March 1827, Nikosha complained of his loneliness among other people; the superior being lived in complete isolation:

Much time has passed since the day of our separation; the years of the ebullient age have been cooled by the continuously changing inconstancy of the fate in the present. Gradually I grew colder, losing the ability to meet warmly oncoming events. Without joy and without grief, in deep thought did I stand over the road of life, silently inquiring into the future. From the moment of your absentation, an emptiness lodged itself in my soul, some kind of a feeling of lifelessness. And now you have freed me from my deadly slumber. Now I am the one I was before: gay, devoted to you, cold in appearance, but in my heart all afire with feelings of friendship.

Another letter to Vysotski followed on June 26, 1827, with more effusive assurances of friendship and this picture of loneliness and dejection:

Isolating myself completely from all, finding no one with whom I could blend my enduring thoughts, to whom I could confide my meditations, I have become an orphan and a stranger in deserted Nezhin. I am a foreigner who wandered into a strange country seeking for what can be found in the homland alone, and the secrets of my heart — bursting forth on my face, thirsting for expression — sink sadly into its [the heart's?] depth, where reigns the same silence of death.

And further in the same letter:

How painful it is so be buried together with creatures of mean obscurity in a silence of death! You know all our e x i s t e r s

119

[Gogol coined the word used in the original], all those who have populated Nezhin. They have quashed under the crust of their earthliness, of their contemptible smugness, the high destination of man. And between these existers I have to crawl. . . . I do not exclude our beloved preceptors. Only among my fellow-students, but very few of them, do I chance sometimes upon one to whom I can say something.

The inflated phraseology, the often obscure metaphors and the awry syntax of the passage are typical; and as it continues, an image gets out of control shifting from the visual to the auditory:

Now you can see me like in a mirror. Have pity on me! Perhaps a tear of sympathy reflected in your eyes will be audible to me.

The "audible tear" is no more than a slip, yet it is characteristic of Gogol's syncretic, non-differentiating thought and style. It is an important feature of his art that ideas are allowed to become sounds, sounds wander into the realm of the visual, and images dissolve in rhythm or ideation.

In the letter to Vysotski, the melancholy confession of the lonely soul is followed by some two pages of rather coarse caricatures of the Nezhin "existers;" one or two examples will illustrate the aggressive, almost sadistic, humor of these caricatures:

We are now in communication with Odessa by means of a steamboat . . . This steamboat sails monthly from here with cucumbers and pickles, and returns stuffed with olives, tobacco and halva [an oriental delicacy] . . . During its seventh expedition, the steamboat took on board Myshkovski [a supervisor discharged for drunkenness], and in his stead disembarked, to be overseer, the director's housekeeper, a fathom and a half tall, who caused to tremble all the domesticity of the Prince Bezborodko Gymnasium of Higher Learning, until Bodyan [a retired soldier serving as watchman] demonstrated that a Russian soldier does not fear the devil himself, and in the glorious battle of the Shursha [?], twisted her front jaws [sic] to her occiput.

Of a schoolmate, whom Nikosha supplied with a whole series of nicknames, he tells Vysotski that after leaving school he returned unexpectedly:

He had made his application for joining the dragoons; but his judicious father, learning of this, decorated his rear façade with his own paternal hand, the blows numbering 150, and Little Baron, thus renovated, appeared here again, rejoicing over his rejuvenation.

Then once more, after the long gallery of grotesques:

I do not know whether my expectations will come true and I shall really live in this heavenly place [St. Petersburg], or whether fate's inexorable spinning wheel will toss me, together with some rabble [a terrifying thought!], into the backwater of non-existence, and will assign to me in the world the dark quarters of oblivion.

The dread of obscurity, of a life spent among the "existers" is also expressed in the letter to Kosyarovski quoted below:

Cold sweat broke out on my face at the thought that perhaps my lot was to perish in dust, without making my name by any admirable deed — to live in this world, and not to make my existence — this was dreadful to me.

Then, after the announcement of his choice of the judiciary branch of government for the arena of his future endeavors:

Will my lofty intentions come true? Or will Obscurity envelop them in its somber cloud? Over these years I kept buried within myself these long nourished thoughts. Distrustful of all, reticent, I confided to none my secret ideas . . . I do not know why I let out my secret now . . . [but] a feeling has entered my chest that you will not deem a miserable daydreamer one who for three years has unflinchingly held to one single purpose and whom mockery or allusions will only strengthen in the design he conceived.

One does not need too much critical sense to perceive that the eagerness to accomplish great things for the benefit of mankind, even if it were sincere, was not a primary impulse, but that it was derived from a yearning for a great destiny, a yearning to rise high above the common people and their commonplace existences, and from the dread — its counterpart — that he would not be able to rise above the "exister," or that his superiority would not be recognized. Gogol wrote to Kosyarovski that "cold sweat broke out on my face at the thought that perhaps my lot was to perish in dust . . ." This feeling is not one of a humanitarian idealist.

121

That the craving for greatness was Gogol's primary impulse does not exclude an ethical ideal; but the realization of the ethical ideal was in conflict with his contempt for average humanity. And it was this contempt, his aggressive humor, his aggressive and distortive mimicry — not the ethical ideal — that were the true sources of his art which he tried to justify by attributing to it *ex post facto* moralistic purpose.

In Gogol's letters of the years 1827-1828, beside his plan to take government service in St. Petersburg (and to accomplish great things in government service), there appears an alternative plan. It is first revealed in his letter to Vysotski of June 26, 1827:

You have wasted no time in announcing in my behalf my approval of your plans to go abroad. Look out that later we have no regret! Maybe I will find life in Petersburg so pleasant that I will hesitate and will recall the saying: don't go overseas looking for what can be found nearer. But so be it; you made the promise, and I have to forgive your rashness. But when is it that this will happen? I have another year to spend here, then a year, I'd say, in Petersburg; but anyhow, I will not stay there without you: wherever you go I'll follow you.

The plans for a voyage abroad are mentioned again, more than one year later, in a letter to Kosyarovski:

I am going to Petersburg in the early winter, that is definite. From there God only knows where I may go. It may well happen that it will be to foreign lands, and that one will not hear from me for several years. And, I must confess, I have little desire ever to return home, especially since I witnessed, more than once, how our extraordinary mother struggles and torments herself sometimes for a mere kopek, how these worries murderously ruin her health, and all this only to provide us with the necessary and to satisfy even our fancies.

Nikosha, in other terms, was so concerned with his mother's worries and difficulties that he decided to leave the country. However, he provided for his mother's security:

I renounce my inheritance and I am now engaged in writing a deed by which part of the estate bequeathed to me . . . is transferred to my mother for lifetime possession . . .

The estate was the property of Gogol's paternal grandmother, Tatyana Semyonovna Gogol-Yanovskaya, who died in 1827 leaving one half of the property to her grandson Nikolai, the other half to be shared between his sisters; Mariya Ivanovna was made guardian of her children, but owned no property. The deed mentioned by Gogol was not executed, and obviously, it would have been nothing but a vain gesture if it had. Nikosha repeated the gesture a few months later in Petersburg, when he appropriated 1,450 rubles his mother sent him to pay interest on a mortgage. The deed, he then discovered, would cost 300 rubles, so he sent a power of attorney instead, which would permit his mother to dispose of his half of the estate. It is clear that "disposing" of the estate would have meant financial ruin for his mother and sisters.

The voyage abroad is brought up once more in a letter to Mariya Ivanovna from Petersburg, dated May 22, 1829:

I had a wonderful opportunity to go to foreign countries. The journey, ordinarily entailing very great expense, would have cost me nothing, everything would have been paid for me . . . But imagine my misfortune, it just had to happen. My generous friend, who was to provide me with this, suddenly died, and his plans and my expectations were shattered.

Gogol's biographers have not been able to identify this generous and mysterious friend and he may well have been the product of Gogol's imagination. In general, hardly anything is known about Gogol's plans, and whether the "generous friend" existed or not. According to Danilevski's story (reported by Shenrok) Gogol considered at one time going to America where he would begin a new life of unremitting activity and work.

There is an unreal, a dreamlike quality in these plans for a journey abroad; but the strangest thing about them is that they did materialize.

In May 1829, five months after arriving in St. Petersburg, Gogol published a long narrative poem, or "idyll in pictures," as it was subtitled: *Hans Küchelgarten*. Concealing his identity under the pen name "V. Alov," Gogol introduced his poem as the work of an eighteen-year-old youth, written in 1827, two years prior to the publication. It is generally believed that the work was antedated, but there is no agreement on the time when it had actually been written. But whether it was completed or only begun before Gogol left the Ukraine — or entirely written in Petersburg, between January and May 1829 — the poem, in its content and its phraseology, is clearly a product of the Nezhin years.

The dependence of *Küchelgarten* on a variety of literary sources has been pointed out many times. The poem does produce the general impression of an often rather awkward potpourri of motifs and images of the romantic repertory. One also feels the effort to imitate the more sober style of Pushkin, especially in the less "visionary" and "graveyard" passages. The poem was largely imitative, but the very fact that Gogol leaned so heavily on literary sources in this early work shows the importance for him of the literary and cultural fund he accumulated in his young years. Apart from borrowings and influences, the poem abounds in literary and scholarly references; Hans's library, for example, includes the works of Plato, Schiller, Petrarch, Tieck, Aristophanes and Winckelman (the latter rhymed with Russianized *Aristofan*, both names stressed on the last syllable); a chapter devoted to the "land of classical and beautiful creations, of glorious deeds and Liberty the home," mentions the eloquence of Aeschiles, Sophocles's poetry, the elegance of the Parthenon, the paintings of Parrhasios and Zeuxis, Phidias's Minerva.

This, to be sure, is no evidence of vast erudition: one can mention Plato or Sophocles, Goethe or Winckelmann without reading their works. But whatever the extent and the thoroughness of Gogol's knowledge, the fact remains that his first work had its roots in the world of ideas and of art, of classical antiquity and of the poetry of his own age. The Gogol who made his first, furtive appearance on the literary scene with his *Hans Küchelgarten* was not the provincial who had brought to the capital some amusing anecdotes and colorful folk tales, or the candid observer of human nature with an innate gift for caricature.

Essentially literary was Gogol's choice of a German hero and German scenery; in the epilogue of the poem he signs "his" Germany – "the land of lofty thoughts, the land of aery visions" of which the great Goethe, he believed, was the guardian-angel.

The hypothesis advanced by Desnitski that the name of Gogol's hero was suggested by the name of Wilhelm Küchelbecker is very convincing. He also indicates Kuchelbecker's "fragment from a Journey to Germany" as a possible source of Gogol's inspiration. He finally makes the useful reminder that Pushkin's Lenski was in many ways a portrayal of his Lyceum friend, the future Decembrist. Gogol was unquestionably familiar with Eugene Onegin, and Gogol's German romantic hero may be connected with Lenski directly. It seems possible that Pushkin's ironic portrayal of a Germinized – if not German – romantic influenced Gogol in his depiction of the romantic's defeat. Pushkin mocked romantic vagueness in his Lenski who "sang separation and grief, and *something*, and *misty distance* . . .;" the elegy attributed to Lenski is followed by the

124

comment: "thus he wrote, *obscurely* and *limply* (this we call romanticism, although I do not see any romanticism here at all . . .) . . .;" in his characterization of Hans, Gogol something;" "in his reveries he heard someone;" and "what he strove for in his obscure thoughts, what he desired and longed for . . . in his passionate soul . . . – that he was unable to understand." The vague yearning for a vague ideal is finally condemned in Gogol's poem.

Gogol's hero and his story belong to a well established literary tradition: young Hans is an exalted day-dreamer discontented with his environment which he leaves for distant lands in the hope of finding life made of beauty, freedom and glory. The "suffocating environment," however, a village called Lunendorf, near the Baltic seaport of Wismar, seems to be a perfectly delightful place, so that it is rather difficult to feel any sympathy for the hero's torments (the borrowings from J.H. Voss's *Luise* appear in these descriptions of country life in Germany; Voss's idyll was available in Nezhin in a Russian translation). Hans, moreover, is loved by charming Luisa, the granddaughter of the local pastor. But all this is vain: even Luisa's innocent passion and beauty fail to retain him. He leaves, knapsack on his back and a staff in his hand, to reappear, in a later chapter, in Athens (a vision of luxuriant India is also introduced in the poem, but only a vision: the romantic pilgrim does not actually visit this remote country). Hand finds, however, nothing but disappointment in his journeys (a desolate picture of the dust-covered ruins of "real" Athens is contrasted with a glorious vision of ancient Greece). After some two years of this pursuit of a vague and elusive ideal, Hans returns to Lunendorf where he finds peace and happiness with Fraulein Luisa who becomes Frau Küchelgarten.

The poem clearly opposes the romantic and the idyllic elements, and it ends with the surrender of the romantic hero to the idyll. Love, it may be noted, is placed in the realm of the idyll (of the prosaic world which the hero had attempted to escape), and shortly before Hans sets out for Athens, the grandfather of his future bride, and her mother, exchange a few sly – and prophetic – remarks to the effect that the cure for Hans's pallor and *Sehnsucht* might well be holy matrimony.

Hans's motives and his ideals are vague; but two themes may be distinguished in his yearning for the romantic "something:" one is beauty. At one point the reader is allowed to peer into the hero's dreams which "hitherto have been a puzzle." This introduces Hans's vision of the glorious beauties of ancient Greece. Hans's journey is consequently an aesthetic pilgrimage: the mysterious call he hears is the call of Beauty, the romanticist's Divinity. The theme of absolute beauty is not further developed in the poem; divine beauty – of which the Poet, the son of Heaven, is the priest – is the central theme of Küchelbecker's poem "The Poets," in which the poets descend upon Earth and save mankind by reconciling it with beauty. Certain images, and lines, in Gogol's poem sound like reminiscences of Küchelbecker's "The Poets."

But there is another voice urging Hans on his venture: it is the fear of perishing in the obscurity of a life without glory, the fear of oblivion. Could he "condemn himself to be the victim of Obscurity? While alive, to be dead for the world?" How could his "soul in love with glory" be content with nonentity, with the non-existence of everyday life? And could it be that his "existence will not leave a mark?"

Here Hans is particularly close to the author who expressed, sometimes in the very words he lent to his hero, this dread of being buried alive in obscurity and oblivion and not leaving "a mark" of his existence. But having shown his defeated hero trudging along wearily on his homeward journey, the author disassociated himself from him in an interpolated "Meditation" which may be freely rendered as follows:

> Blessed is that divine hour,
> When in his age of self-cognizance,
> In the age of vigor and strength,
> He who has been chosen by heaven
> Comprehends the supreme aim of existence;
> When it is not of reverie the empty shadow,
> And not the glittering tinsel of fame
> That trouble him night and day
> Luring him into the world noisy and turbulent,
> But when it is thought alone, firm and bright,
> That holds him in its grasp and stirs in him
> The yearning for good and welldoing,
> And teaches him to perform great labors.
> For their sake he will not spare his very life.
> In vain will resound the mad cries of the mob:
> He remains firm amidst these living debris.
> He hears only the distant murmur
> Of posterity's blessings.

This is a condemnation of Hans who lets himself be lured into the world by vague reveries and by the tinsel of fame. If he was defeated, it was because he lacked an ideal; and the firmness and courage of a true hero. The "Meditation" continues:

If deceptive fantasies
Disturb one with the craving for a brilliant destiny,
But his soul is not armed with a will of iron,
And he does not have the strength to stand up in the turmoil,
Is it not better then that quietly and peacefully
He travel the field of life,
And be content with a modest family,
Remaining deaf to the clamor of the world?

This solution was the best for Hans Küchelgarten, not for Nikolai Gogol; for clearly, Gogol saw himself endowed with that firmness and vigor which Hans lacked; the great Thought would inspire and guide him in his great labors, for it is not the tinsel of fame that he pursues, it is the ideal of good. But after the condemnation of purposeless reveries and of a futile and egotistic pursuit of fame, after the proclamation of the moral and altruistic ideal, there come in the "Meditation" the lines about the hero's standing alone amidst the shouting mob. The true hero serves mankind, but mankind is the insanely shouting mob, the living debris, and only future generations – humanity in the distance – will understand him.

The parallelism between Gogol's poem and his letters, especially those of the year 1827, is obvious, and it has been pointed out more than once; there are actually a few textual coincidences. This fact alone, however, would not prove the validity of either the poem or the letters as biographical and psychological evidence. Both have a pronounced literary flavor, and it may be asked whether young Gogol was not merely following the same literary models in his epistolary writings and in his poetical narrative. And finally: much in the letters as well as in the poem is typically adolescent, and especially typical for a literary-minded adolescent of the 1820's. There is here, in other terms, largely a pattern, rather than the expression of an individuality.

Yet the evidence derived from Hans Küchelgarten and from Gogol's letters cannot be dismissed, for the main motifs expressed in the pompous and often helpless language of the adolescent, can be traced throughout Gogol's life. They are his feeling of being chosen for a great destiny, for a great accomplishment of universal significance; his feeling of aloneness among men, his contempt for the "existers" and his fear of the "mob." Such was the urge which made him lead a life of a homeless wanderer, and unlike Hans, to shun until the end the "idyll" of a home and a family. The image of

127

the ascetic prophet, serving humanity and dominating it, willing to sacrifice himself for a humanity he despises, was born during Gogol's adolescence; it receded during his years of intense creative activity, but only to return with great and destructive power in his later years.

The poem undoubtedly expresses a permanent, and a very important component of Gogol's personality. But does it also have a more concrete autobiographical significance? If Gogol did not return to the idyll of his own home, was he at least tempted to return? Vasili Gippius formulated his fundamental interpretation of Gogol's dualism in connection with *Hans Küchelgarten*:

> Poetic imagery, to be sure, is not to be taken as evidence . . . but on the other hand, it cannot be accidental, and we are entitled to say that the idealization of the farmstead near Wismar, or, what is the same, of the farmstead near Dikanka, was one of the possibilities which presented itself to Gogol's consciousness. Gogol had deep roots in the tradition, in the milieu, in the soil, and his attempts to escape from them alternated with their attractive power in an ever renewed conflict. To a great extent this determined his personal drama.

It does not seem that this equation of Lunendorf with Dikanda, or of Hans Küchelgarten's dilemma with Gogol's, should be accepted without serious reservations. The "farmstead near Wismar," was a reality, in terms of the poem of course, as well as young Luisa: the idyllic delights were offered to Hans as the price for the repudiation of his romantic ideal. Hans could live on the farmstead idealized for him by Gogol. But Gogol would have had to live in real Vasilyevka if he had renounced his quest, not in the "idealized farmstead near Dikanka" which appears in his fiction. The "idyll," a reality in terms of Hans's conflict, was, in Gogol's own dilemma, only a nostalgic dream of a life of peace and contentment which belonged to the past.

Gogol's attachment to his native Ukraine is unquestionable; it was sentimental and, one might say, physiological, associated as it was with warmth and sunshine, with a blue sky and abundant food. Life in Vasilyevka, however, was another matter. It was, in the first place, a life full of concern over the management of the estate in a time of economic depression, and Gogol was well aware of the problems and difficulties which had to be faced: he even mentioned his mother's plight as one of his reasons for leaving the Ukraine. From St. Petersburg, placing himself in the position of an expert adviser, he expressed more than once his concern over the situation of the Ukrainian landowners. Thus, in a letter of April 16, 1831, he wrote:

I am extremely curious to know the conditions of our countrymen; the continuous ruins of their estates affect me very much. Often, during moments of leisure, I ponder over remedies that might be found to help them out of their predicament, and if eventually I succeed in doing something for our common good, I shall deem myself the happiest of men.

Actualy, he suggested a diagnosis in his letter which implied the remedy:

Our landed proprietors for the most part are contaminated with some kind of oriental magnificence: they keep swarms of flunkeys, they buy things when domestic products could perfectly well be used instead . . .

This preaching of simple life, of reverting to the patriarchal self-sufficient economy in which money — this source of all evils — plays no part, was to be developed and magnified later; Gogol was unquestionably more imaginative as writer of fiction than as economist. And after years of meditation over the problems of the land- and serf-owning class, he offered advice, in his *Correspondence with Friends*, which added little to what he wrote to his mother when he was twenty-one.

He seems, however, to have taken a more realistic and businesslike view of the situation when he visited the Ukraine in the summer of 1832, after three and a half years in the capital; in a letter from Vasilyevka to Ivan Ivanovich Dmitriyev, a retired statesman and, in his days, a poet of great reputation (the letter calls him the "Patriarch of Russian Poetry"), Gogol gave the following account of the situation he had found at home:

What is there, one may ask, that this country lacks? . . . Grain, fruit, all kinds of vegetables are in abundance. But the people are poor, the estates are ruined, arrears cannot be collected. The cause of all this is inadequate transportation. It has plunged the inhabitants into slumber and indolence. The landowners see now themselves that with raising crops and distilling alone there can be no appreciable increase of income. They begin to understand that it is time to start factories, but capital is lacking . . . [and] they hound hares for nothing better to do. I admit that I was pained seeing the condition of my mother's estate. With but another thousand [rubles], it could

129

bring an income six times what it is now within three years. Money, however, is altogether a rarity here. But I suppose I am wearying you with these statistics . . .

The letter mentions "factories," a year after her son's visit, Mariya Ivanovna started a tannery and a shoe factory in Vasilyevka. Gogol's warnings were not heeded, and the venture very nearly brought about the complete ruin of the family. The problem of factories in the country estates is amply discussed in the second volume of *Dead Souls*, in the conversations between Chichikov and Kostanzhoglo.

Gogol also deplores in this letter the "slumber and indolence" in which this "slumber and indolence" are poeticized, and a year later the "Quarrel," in which they are caricatured. The idyll depicted in the first of these stories clearly belongs to the past; the story of the quietly waning existences and of the quiet end of the "Ukrainian Philemon and Baucis," is the story of a species almost completely extinct and of a disappearing way of life. The author, moreover, places himself outside of the vanishing idyllic world of the "Old-Time Squires:" "I like to descend sometimes for a moment into the sphere of this life . . .;" and further, he remarks that if he recalls his visit to the old people with such delight, it is "perhaps because that is always dear to our heart from what we are separated." He also uses a significant term — "lowly bucolic" — to describe the patriarchal life of the old squires.

But did his home offer Gogol an idyll even imperfect or a "lowly bucolic" life? Before leaving the Ukraine, Nikosha spent two very pleasant summers at home, in the company of his second cousins, Peter, Paul and Barbara Kosyarovski. Nikosha occupied with the two young men an attic which he calls, in his letters to them, "our lofty dwelling." In the fall of 1828, he was alone in Vasilyevka; his gay companions were gone, and in a few months he was to leave for St. Petersburg; on September 2, he wrote to his cousin Paul:

Imagine that alone, with no comrades, I am bored in Vasilyevka. I am in a kind of apathy and for a moment only will my thoughts be brought into motion by the memory of our blessed jolly trinity which lived jointly, in good health and cheer, in the lofty dwelling. But now it is gloomy and deserted, there is neither a chair nor a table, and even the shaky floor itself has been taken apart to make tents when the fair was being set up. Only Darling has remained faithful to his old shelter and to avenge his having often been chased from the place, he snores there unremittingly. As for me, I moved with

Syuska to the warmest room, next to grandmother's, and set up a screen to separate myself from her because the exhalations of the older female and the uncouth maiden; her attendants, resting in the hallway, send a deathly reek through my half-open door. For the rest my quarters are not as bad as all that.

This picture may serve as an epilogue to the Vasilyevka "idyll," and as a farewell to home, to the old, broken down house, and to its many inhabitants. It was not this reality that could attract Gogol, but he did carry away from home his dream of sunshine, warmth and satiety, and also some of the poetry of his country. Later he enriched his knowledge of Ukrainian folklore, and produced some Ukrainian legends himself. In a sense, the Ukraine was Gogol's Greece as well as his Lunendorf.

Chapter XI

ST. PETERSBURG

(POEMS, VOYAGES, GOVERNMENT SERVICE)

During his schoolyears in Nezhin, Gogol conceived a bright image of St. Petersburg – a typical instance of his love for the unknown and the distant, and of imagination preceding experience. In March 1827, he wrote to Vysotski:

Often, in the midst of my occupation . . . my thoughts leap to Petersburg: I sit with you in your room, I stroll with you along the boulevards, I gaze admiringly at the Neva and the sea.

He concludes his long letter with a note of irony apparently aimed at his own enthusiasm:

How many houses there are in Petersburg, how many monuments, illuminations, fires, floods, celebrations – and the vistas from Vasili Island!

And again, in June 1827:

Mentally I am already in Petersburg, in a gay little room, its windows opening on the Neva, for I always had the thought of finding such a place for myself.

Gogol's first impressions of the Russian capital – this could have been easily foreseen – were disappointing; about a week after his arrival he wrote to his mother:

Petersburg appeared to me quite different from what I thought, I imagined it much more beautiful, more magnificent, and the rumors which some spread about it are false.

He was immediately faced with serious practical problems; everything was terribly expensive in the capital, especially food, and the apartment alone, which he shared with Danilevski (two small rooms with kitchen privileges, but with no view of the Neva) cost eighty rubles a month, only water and firewood included.

Three months later, on April 30, 1829, followed a letter with a detailed, carefully composed description of the city; it is introduced by the remark that "Petersburg is quite unlike other European capitals, or Moscow." Gogol had seen no other European capital, nor had he visited Moscow. The remark is followed my these considerations of the analytically-minded observer:

Every capital in general is characterized by its people who cast upon it the imprint of nationality, but Petersburg has no character: the foreigners who have made their home here are acclimatized and in no way look like foreigners, while the Russians have received a foreign tinge and are neither one thing nor the other. An extraordinary silence reigns here, no spirit shines in the people, there is nothing but government servants and functionaries, all discussing their departments and committees; everything is repressed, everything mires in paltry, meaningless labors in which their sterile lives are wasted.

At this point a concrete image is introduced:

It is really amusing to encounter them on the boulevards or the sidewalks; they are so absorbed in their thoughts that when you overtake one of them, you may hear him swear or talk to himself, and some enhance this with gestures or by waving their arms about.

He admits that Petersburg is "large enough" (the population of the city by 1830 had reached 450,000), and proceeds to describe the houses which are large, but not particularly tall, mostly three or four stories high, with numerous signboards on many of them:

The house in which I dwell contains two tailors, one *marchande de modes*, a cobbler, a stocking manufacturer, a mender of broken china, a shrinker and dyer, a confectioner, a grocer, a store where winter clothes are preserved, a tobacconist and, finally, a licensed midwife. Naturally, the house is all patched over withgilt signboards. I live on the fourth floor. . . .

Gogol also observed the elegant crowd of the capital:

There are many promenades in Petersburg. In winter all the idlers stroll from twelve till two (the functionaries are busy at that time) along the Nevski Prospect. In spring, if this season can be termed spring, for no verdure has yet clad the trees, they take their walks in Ekaterinenhoff, in the Summer Garden, and the Adimiralty Boulevard. All these promenades, however, are unbearable, particularly the one to Ekaterinenhoff on the first of May [Gogol had not yet spent this day in the capital]. The whole pleasure consists in the promenaders mounting into their carriages which stretch out in a file more than ten versts long, following one another so closely that the snouts of the horses of a carriage bestow friendly kisses on the tall, richly liveried footmen of the carriage in front. These carriages are continuously ranged by police officers and sometimes are halted for hours for the sake of order. . . . Once I had directed my humble steps thither, but enveloped in a cloud of dust and half suffocated in the crush, I turned back. At this time Petersburg is about to be deserted: all leave for out of town residences and the country for the spring and the summer. The nights now last no more than an hour, and in summer there is no night at all, only an interval between sunset and sunrise in which the evening twilight merges with the twilight of dawn, and it is like neither evening nor morning. But cnough about Petersburg for this time.

Obviously the letter was not a spontaneous account of first impressions, but another one of those "compositions" he offered to his admiring mother. It is significant that in more than one instance he uses "knowledge" rather than actual impressions, as in the references to foreign capitals, to Moscow, or to the summer nights in Petersburg: the letter was written in April, and he had arrived in the capital three months before.

Some six months later, in an essay entitled "Petersburg Notes for 1836," Gogol expressed essentially the same judgement about the northern capital of the Russian Empire. The article begins in a humorous vein:

But really, where has it been flung, the Russian capital – to the very edge of the world! The Russians are a strange people: they had their capital in Kiev – it was too warm, there wasn't enough cold; the Russian capital moved to Moscow – but no, here too it wasn't cold enough: the Lord sent us to Petersburg!

Then, after the facetious parallel between the old and the new capital:

It is difficult to grasp the general expression of Petersburg. There is something in it that reminds one of a European-American colony: as little true nationality, as much

134

foreign mixture which has not yet merged into a solid mass. How many in it are the different nationalities, how many different classes of society. This society is completely separated: there are aristocrats, the government employees, the tradesmen, the British, the Germans, the merchants — all form completely separated circles . . . Each of these classes, if you look closer, consists of a multitude of smaller circles, which also keep apart from one another. Take for example, the government employees. The young assistant heads of offices form a circle of their own, into which an office head will never descend. And an office head raises his coiffure a little higher in the presence of a copying clerk. German tradesmen and German employees also form two separate circles. The teachers form their circle, the actors theirs; even the littérateur, who is still an ambiguous and altogether doubtful character, stands completely apart. In a word it is as though a formidable stage-coach had stopped before a tavern, and the passengers, who had sat each one huddled up separately, now all entered into the guest room simply because there is no other place for them to go.

In the 1840's the writers of the so-called "natural" school (who believed and whom Belinski believed to be the followers of Gogol), Vladimir Dal among others, a famous lexicographer and a writer as talentless as he was prolific, applied themselves to produce drab "physiological" studies of the mores of the circles mentioned by Gogol. The "sociological" passage quoted, however, is from one of Gogol's articles, not from his fiction. In his fiction he used images and symbols which he had to discover in the reality of the big city, or to invent. He also found some help, in solving the problem of a poetic interpretation of the big city in the work of E.T.A. Hoffmann or of Jules Janin.

Gogol's "Petersburg Notes" appeared on the pages of the *Contemporary,* in the first issue of Pushkin's magazine published after his death. The manuscript of a polimical essay was found in Pushkin's papers. It was directed against Radishchev's *Journey from Petersburg to Moscow* (the censor did not pass the article, apparently because even an attack upon Radishchev, a writer and thinker, generally regarded as founder of the revolutionary tradition in Russia, seemed dangerous). There was a chapter on Moscow in Pushkin's essay which was closely reminiscent of Gogol's characterization of the old capital in his "Notes:"

By the way: I found in my papers a curious comparison between the two capitals. It was written by one of my friends

135

(Pushkin), a great melancholiac, who has his light moments of gaiety at times.

Gogol arrived in Petersburg in the last days of December 1828, equipped with letters of introduction to one or two bureaucrats in high position, obligingly provided by Troshchinski. An offer of a position, however, is first mentioned in a letter of May 22 to his mother — five months after his arrival:

And so I am staying in Petersburg. I am offered a position with a salary of 1,000 rubles a year. But for a price hardly sufficient to pay the yearly rent and the food, do I have to sell my health and my precious time? . . . To have not more than two hours free a day, and the rest of the time not to move away from the desk, copying old rubbish and nonsense of the office chiefs . . . So here I stand meditating, on the path of my life, awaiting the outcome of certain of my expectations. Perhaps in a few days a more profitable and noble position will become open, but I must frankly say — if there too one has to spend so much time in stupid occupations, then — no, and I thank you humbly.

A request for money followed: three hundred rubles, most urgently needed by him.

Before Nikosha had had any experience in government service, his lofty ideal collapsed: one did not strive for the benefit of mankind in the Government offices; "one copied old rubbish all day long, and two hours a day was all the leisure one had." But what use did he intend to make of his time which he was unwilling to sell for a miserable thousand rubles a year?

Even if he did not know whether "authorship was truly my vocation," Gogol (anonymously) published his first printed work in the March issue of the *Syn otechestva* (The Son of the Fatherland), a very conservative magazine: a short poem entitled "Italy." It was, consequently, not more than six weeks after his arrival in the capital that Gogol submitted his poem to the magazine.

On April 30, he asked his mother for information on Ukrainian popular traditions and beliefs, descriptions of old national costumes, etc., that is, quite obviously, for material which he planned to use, and did use in the *Evening on a Farmstead Near Dikanka*. In the same letter he asked Mariya Ivanovna to send him two of his father's comedies: "There is a general interest in everything Little-Russian here, and I will see whether one of them could not be presented in the theater." Actually Gogol used the plays as material for his stories, and the plan to produce them was very probably a pretext. "The Fair of Sorochintsy" utilizes many of the situations of Vasili Gogol's comedy *The Simpleton*.

But Gogol had a ready manuscript, and he decided to publish it although it had nothing to do with things Little-Russian: it was the manuscript of his *Hans Küchelgarten*, the poem about the poet's destiny. He may have been encouraged to do this by the fact that *The Son of the Fatherland* had accepted his "Italy," an indifferent but rather correct piece of poetry. This encouragement proved fatal.

Hans Küchelgarten was passed by the censor on May 7, 1829, and was published toward the end of June. Gogol obviously placed great hopes on this work: the words in his letter of May 22 to his mother, quoted above, about "awaiting the outcome of certain of [his] expectations" were obviously a reference to *Küchelgarten* ; the context — the mention of the job with the niggardly salary of a thousand rubles a year — betrays his hope that a literary success would permit him to evade the necessity of sacrificing his time and his energy to the drudgery of office work. The retail price of *Hans Küchelgarten* was five rubles. Since the printing of the little volume cost Gogol 300 rubles, the sale of some four or five hundred copies would have brought more than a year's salary, and it seems likely that Gogol made some similar calculation.

Unfortunately, however, *Hans Küchelgarten* was not a success. Two influential journals, *The Moscow Telegraph*, in June, and *The Northern Bee*, in July, published reviews which were as brief as they were annihilating. "V. Alov," alias Gogol, thereupon withdrew the copies of his poem from the bookstores and burned them.

The poem was a journey to Germany on the wings of Pegasus; a few days after the burning, Gogol boarded in St. Petersburg the steamboat leaving for the German seaport of Lubeck. Upon reaching Lubeck he wrote a letter dated August 13, 1829, to his mother:

> Six days I sailed by sea: this happened because during all this time we had unfavorable wind. Only now, when I found myself amidst boundless waters, did I realize what the separation from you meant to me, my inestimable, dear mother; in those momentous and dreadful hours of my life, when I fled from myself, when I endeavored to forget all that surrounded me, the thought of what I was doing to you weighed on my soul like a heavy stone, and it was in vain that I sought to persuade myself that I was compelled to obey the will of Him who governs us from above.

In a letter he wrote before leaving Petersburg, on July 24, 1829, he explained his sudden departure by a passionate love for some inaccessible, divine, or angelic creature. A journey abroad was the only escape from the infernal torments he suffered. A week later, in the letter quoted above, he gave the reason for his choice of Lubeck: he had a bad rash on his face and hands, and the doctors recommended a watering cure in Travemunde near Lubeck.

Despite most biographies, the two letters do not seem to give contradictory motives for Gogol's journey. The consuming passion was to explain his journey abroad, and the rash was the choice of Travemunde near Lubech where he planned to spend only two weeks. It may be remarked, however, that, in the first place, Travemunde is a seaside resort where no mineral waters for medicinal use had ever been known to exist. In the second place, a subsequent letter, dated September 24, 1829, describes the disease from which he sought a cure in Travemunde no longer as a "rash," but as a "pain in the chest such that I could hardly breathe . . ."

It is generally believed (but by no means established) that Gogol's passion for the angelic creature, and the angelic creature herself, were invented by him for the benefit of his mother, as an excuse for his voyage and for his misappropriation of the money she sent him to pay the interest on a mortgage. The real motive, it is held, was the failure of *Hans Küchelgarten.*

The connection between this failure and the trip to Lubeck is very likely. Gogol's departure, however, should not be interpreted as a flight before the critics who ridiculed his effort. Gogol was struggling to preserve his freedom, and the publication of the poem was a first effort to escape the servitude of a clerical job. When the high hopes he had placed on the poem failed, he reverted to the old plan of a journey abroad, or even of expatriation. One will recall his correspondence with Vysotski, the letter to Kosyarovski saying that it was very likely that he would go to foreign lands for several years and the letter to his mother from Petersburg about the death of the mysterious friend who was going to take him abroad.

He might have abandoned the plan had his poem been a success, but it was not, and at the very moment of the *Küchelgarten* debacle the journey became possible thanks to the 1,450 rubles sent by Mariya Ivanovna.

Vasili Gippius writes on the connection between *Küchelgarten* and Gogol's journey:

It is, of course, impossible to think that Gogol simply repeated in life what he had depicted in his poem — especially since he was able to take a detached view of his hero, and since he put into his very dreams a content which may not be clear to us,

138

but which was concrete and practical, something that was lacking in the case of Hans.

That Gogol should not be identified with Hans Küchelgarten is perfectly true, yet he did "repeat in life what he had depicted in his poem." The similarity between Gogol's journey and the journey of his hero could not be a coincidence. The poem, and the early plans for a journey to foreign countries, and the trip to Lubeck, and the expatriation seven years later – all this stemmed from the same source concealed in the deeper strata of Gogol's personality.

Gogol, to be sure, was not Küchelgarten, nor did he identify himself with his hero whom he brought back, in his poem, to the idyll of family happiness. Gogol himself was to continue on his lonely journey – toward the supreme accomplishment or the supreme sacrifice. This image of the lonely wanderer presented itself to him with the insistence of a compulsion: it was a dream that had to be enacted. In 1829, he soon abandoned the journey, but this was only a postponement.

In his *Confession* Gogol stated that "the plan and the purpose of my journey were quite unclear." It does seem, however, that he had some vague intention of pursuing his literary work. He added the following postscript to his letter, dated July 24, 1829, to his mother, which announced his departure:

Offering you my heartfelt and inexpressible thanks for your precious information about Little-Russians, I ask you insistently not to fail to write such letters to me in the future. In the quiet of solitude I am preparing a reserve which I will not offer to the world before working it properly, [for] I do not like to hurry, and still less to be superficial. I also ask you, kind and incomparable mother, to write as clearly as possible proper names and generally all Little-Russian appellations. My work, if it is ever published, will be in a foreign tongue, and I need exactness all the more, in order not to distort by inaccurate renderings the important national names.

Gogol felt the need to add an apology: he could not fail to realize that the news of his departure would cause great anxiety in Vasilyevka, and with his characteristic preoccupation to justify himself, at least in his own eyes, by offering compensations (one may recall the power of attorney), he proposed this "deal" to his mother:

In exchange [for information on the Ukraine] I shall describe to you the way of life and the occupations of the good Germans, the modern spirit, the strangeness and the charm of what hitherto I have not seen and everything that will produce a strong impression on me.

His mother, it seems, was not particularly anxious to have first-hand information on German customs: Nikosha was ordered to return without delay.

Mariya Ivanovna wrote to her cousin Kosyarovski: "I ordered him to return to Petersburg and to take a job . . . and he replied that, pleasant as it was for him there, and [although] the air is healthier than in Petersburg, . . . but if I so order him, then he will return without fail and take the job . . ."

Returning to Petersburg on September 22, Gogol made an unsuccessful attempt to find employment as an actor, and resumed his search for a job in one of the government offices. In November, that is, a full year after he left the Ukraine, he was finally appointed to a clerical position in the Department of Government Properties and Public Buildings, with a salary − after a period of probation − of thirty rubles a month. Before the end of February, however, he resigned, and the next month he found another job, with the Department of Domains. In July a vacance occurred for the position of "Assistant Chief of the First Bureau of the Second Division," and the head of the Division proposed for this position the "official of the fourteenth class Gogol-Yanovski," his salary to be raised from 600 to 750 rubles a year; he wrote in his proposal for advancement:

To the aforesaid I have the honor to add that, although this official has been in service for not more than four months, but having received a good education and giving evidence of proper diligence, he is able to expedite these duties usefully.

The promotion was granted, and Gogol held his new position until February 1831. Even before he took a job he had discovered that nothing but drudgery was to be expected from a position in one of the departments; and it was difficult even to earn a livelihood, let alone to attain prominence or fame. He had to apply repeatedly to Mariya Ivanovna for subsidies, and once she pointed out to him that there were people who make fortunes in government service merely through endeavor and perseverance (his own, apparently, were questioned). He knew of such cases himself, he replied in a letter dated June 30, 1830, but when did they occur? Could his mother

Troshchinski's brilliant career, in other terms, could not be duplicated: the golden age of the bureaucrat, the reign of Catherine "of blessed memory," belonged to the past. Gogol continues his letter with this rhetorical question: "Then, you will ask, are there no advantages in government service?" The answer is that such advantages exist. After thirty-five years of service, advancement and a pension await him who has a solid mind, an unbending willpower and perseverance, and enough courage not to "shudder befor the steep, almost endlessly tall and slippery ladder" he has to climb.

Like Gogol, Tentetnikov in *Dead Souls*, arrived in the capital full of hopes for a brilliant future and of exalted notions about service in the government; and like Gogol, he was soon disappointed:

With much difficulty and with the help of his uncle's connections he finally obtained a job in one of the departments. When he was led into a magnificent chamber filled with light, looking with its parquet floor and its lacquered desks, as if the highest dignitaries sat there deliberating over the destinies of the Empire, when he saw the legions of handsome gentlemen, busy writing, their heads askance, and producing a rustling noise with their quills, and when he was himself seated at one of the desks and requested to copy some paper which, as it happened, was of rather trifling importance (the proceedings which had been carried on for six months actually concerned three rubles), a very strange sensation seized the inexperienced youth; it was as if he had been transferred for some misdemeanor from the higher grade to a lowere one; and it appeared to him that the gentlemen sitting all round him looked exactly like schoolboys. To complete the similarity, some of them were reading the translation of some silly foreign novel hidden between the large sheets of the file before them with which they pretended to be occupied, starting each time their chief would make an appearance. It all seemed so strange to him, his former occupations so much more important than the present, the preparation for service so much better than service itself. He regretted his school. And suddenly he saw Alexander Petrovich, just as if he were before him, and he very nearly burst into tears.

He regained control of himself, however, and "resolved to serve, following the example of the others," and

soon Tentetnikov became accustomed to his work, except that it was not his primary concern and purpose as he had at first expected, but something secondary. It served him as a time regulator, making him treasure every spare minute.

But although Tentetnikov had thus become reconciled to his work, he developed a strong dislike — a "nervous aversion" — for his chief, and after an incident which he actually provoked, he resigned and withdrew to his estate. To his uncle, the influential bureaucrat who acted as his guardian, Tentetnikov explained that he had another, and a more important service to perform: he had the responsibility of caring for the three hundred serfs "entrusted" to him and of improving their lot. He told his uncle:

> If I . . . present to the state three hundred well-behaved, sober, hard-working subjects — will my service be any worse than the service of some chief of a division? . . .

Gogol himself served in the Department of Domains under V.I. Panayev, whom he described in a letter dated June 3, 1830, to his mother as "an excellent man for whom I feel genuine respect." Vladimir Panayev was a successful bureaucrat and a sentimental poet who published a volume of *Idylls* in 1820. Pushkin called him, in a letter to his brother dated December 4, 1824, "the idyllic collegiate assessor."

Contrasting bureaucratic work with the effective management of their estates, which he considered the primary responsibility and duty of the landowning gentry, was a favorite idea with Gogol, expressed with particular insistence in his later works, such as the second volume of *Dead Souls*, or the *Correspondence* . He interpreted ownership of land and of serfs as a sacred trust — sacred in the most literal sense — for which the owner is accountable to God and to the government of his country. Gogol severely condemned those who abandoned their land to join the ranks of the ever expanding bureaucracy. A fragment from the second volume of *Dead Souls* (probably a speech of the Governor-General) contains these lines:

> They would all live at the expense of the public treasury, would make, out of [government] service, lucrative positions for themselves, would change the state into an almshouse which they expect to feed them all! . . . This rush to join the ranks of the officials and the administrators! . . . But let us consider: who then will remain in the ranks of the administered? And will the governed have the means to support the host of those

142

who govern them? The country is being depleted of manpower. The soil is not cultivated. Russia continues in its primitive state of wasteland.

But even much earlier, in "The Old-time Squires," Gogol pronounced this vigorous indictment – not yet of bureaucracy, or "statism," as we would now say – but of his countrymen who seek their fortune in Petersburg:

> . . . those mean Little–Russians, those upstairs – the peddlers and wood–tar boilers who, forcing their way upwards like locusts, invade courts and government offices, who rob their own countrymen of their last kopeck, inundate Petersburg with pettifoggers, gain a capital at the end and gravely add the letter *v* to their name ending in *o* (*o*, often *-enko* is a typical ending for Ukrainian family names; *ov* is typically Great–Russian).

The story of the "Old-time Squires" was begun after Gogol's visit home in the summer of 1832. By that time he had resigned his position in one of the government offices; he was no longer one of those Ukrainians who abandon their native land and "invade like locusts" the imperial capital. Unlike Tentetnikov, however, he did not return to the earth to perform his sacred duty of landowner; he stayed in the capital as teacher of history and as a man of letters.

In February 1831, Gogol resigned his position with the Department of Domains. Government service, as in the case of Tentetnikov, had not been "his primary concern and purpose," as he had expected, "but something secondary." His primary concern and purpose was literature. By the time of his resignation, Gogol had published, in addition to the poem "Italy" and *Hans Küchelgarten*, a story entitled "Bisavryuk, or the Eve of John the Baptist" (in the February–March, 1830, issue of *Otechestvennye zapiski*); a "Chapter from an Historical Novel" (*The Northern Flowers*, January 1831); another fragment from an unfinished novel, entitled "The Tutor," and an essay, "A Few Ideas on the Teaching of Geography to Children" (both in the *Literary Gazette*, January 1831). Another essay, "Woman" (in the second January issue of the *Literary Gazette* and *The Northern Flowers*, and a literary almanac, were published by Delvig's death in 1831, the *Gazette* was edited by Orest Somov, a Ukrainian by birth and the author of a number of tales based on the folklore and popular beliefs of the Ukraine which preceded, by a year or two, Gogol's own *Evenings on a Farmstead near Dikanka*.

Toward the end of 1830, Gogol was introduced (possibly by Somov) to Zhukovski who recommended him to Pletnyov, the future rector of St. Petersburg University. Pletnyov mentioned Gogol in a letter to Pushkin, then in Moscow. Pushkin's reply contains his first, and quite laconic, reference to the young author: "I will say nothing of Gogol because I haven't read him yet for lack of time. I put this off till Tsarskoye Selo." (He was planning to spend the summer there.) Step by step, Gogol continued to approach the meeting with Pushkin; it took place in Pletnyov's house, on May 20, 1831.

A few months earlier, in December 1830, Pushkin's *Boris Godounov* had appeared. Gogol hastened to express his enthusiasm in an essay written in dialogue form and introduced by the following scene:

The bookstore glistened on the second floor of **** Street; the lamps reflected their warm light on the books piled up into high walls, and illuminated brightly and sharply the titles of the blue ones and the red ones, with their gilt edges, of the dust-covered and the buried, of the mighty and the impotent work of man. The crowd was growing thicker and larger. The thunder of the thoroughfare and of the carriages echoed in a clattering of the large windows, and, so it seemed, the lamps, the books, the people – everything was seized by a slight tremor which redoubled the brightness of the picture. The clerks bustled about.

"A fine piece! An excellent piece!" one could hear from all sides.

"Well, my good fellow, have you read *Boris Godounov*? You haven't? Then you haven't read anything that is really good," a coffee-colored overcoat muttered to a square figure who was completely out of breath.

"And what do you say about Pushkin?" said a newly-made hussar cornet, quickly turning around to a neighbor who, with great impatience, was cutting the last pages.

"Yes, some passages are astounding! . . ."

"And his expertness, above all his expertness; just look, just look how skillfully he, you know . . ." prattled a stout little cube, turning his hand before his jolly little eyes, the fingers slightly bent, as if he held in them a ripe, translucid apple.

"Yes, it has considerable merit, considerable merit!" repeated a gaunt connoisseur, dispatching a full half-ounce of snuff into his Roman snuff-depository . . .

"And is this composition actually written with feeling?" stammered a young Senate clerk as he entered with an air of humility.

144

"Why, surely it's with feeling!" retorted the bookseller with a murderous glance at his threadbare overcoat; "if it weren't with feeling, they wouldn't have snatched away four hundred copies within two hours!" . . .

Two friends, answering to the names of Helladius and Pollior emerge from the crowd — "literally and figuratively" — leave the store and, in the moonlit street, pronounce a few ecstatic monologues about Pushkin and his new work. The following lines may serve as a sample:

Great one! When I open thy divine creation, when thy immortal verse thunders and rushes toward me the lightning of fiery sounds, a sacred chill spreads along my veins, and my soul trembles in terror; God has been called forth from his limitless abode . . . and what then? If the sky, and the rays of the sun and the flames devouring the entrails of this earth, and endless air enveloping the world, and the angels, and the blazing planets were turned into words and letters — even then I should be unable to express with them one-tenth of the wondrous things that are happening in the bosom of *invisible me.*

Gogol submitted his manuscript to Pletnyov, but it did not see the light before the year 1881; Pletnyov was known as quite a sagacious critic. Much of the excellent descriptive part of the essay, however, reappeared in Gogol's Petersburg stories. The adoration of Pushkin, like so many other traits of Gogol's young years, is reflected in the Tentetnikov chapter of *Dead Souls*; Tentetnikov has overcome his crisis of nostalgia and has resigned himself, at least for the time being, to the tedium of his work:

Is there a place where joy cannot be found? It is alive even in Petersburg, in spite of the city's austere and somber appearance. A vicious thirty-degree frost crackles in the streets; the offspring of the north, the fiendish blizzard, winds sweeping over the sidewalks, blinding the eyes, powdering fur collars, the mustaches of the humans and the muzzles of shaggy heads; but a friendly gleam comes through the criss-cross flying snowflakes, from a window somewhere up on the fourth floor. In a cozy room lit by modest stearin candles, to the murmur of the samovar, a conversation goes on that warms the heart and the soul, a bright page of an inspired Russian poet is read, one of those whom God has bestowed upon his Russia, and the innocent heart of a youth throbs with such fiery exultation which one would not find even under southern skies.

The meetings with friends, the evenings spent around a samovar in hearty discussions about literature and art are autobiographical; they are reminiscences of Gogol's early years in St. Petersburg. The young collegiate registrar and littérateur found still another outlet for his aesthetic cravings, another remedy against the tedium of office work and the austerity of the northern capital. In June 1830, he described his day in a letter to his mother:

> Every morning, at nine o'clock, I go to my work where I stay until three o'clock; at half past three I have dinner, and after dinner, at five, I go to a class at the Art Academy to study painting which I feel completely unable to give up . . . Thanks to my connections with artists, and even some famous ones, I enjoy opportunities and advantages which are inaccessible for many. Even apart from their talents, I cannot help admiring them for their characters and their manners; what men! Once you get to know them, you cannot part from them for the rest of your days; what modesty, combined with the greatest talent! And they do not even mention ranks, although some of them are state councilors . . .

"An artist is a stranger in the St. Petersburg world," writes Gogol in "Nevski Prospect;" he "no more belongs to the citizenry of St. Petersburg, than a face we see in a dream is part of the material world" —

> A Petersburg artist! An artist in the land of snows, an artist in the land of the Finns, where everything is wet, flat, smooth, wan, grey, misty. These artists are the opposite of Italian artists — proud and fiery like Italy and her skies; they, on the contrary, are for the most part good-natured people, meek, shy, easy-going, quietly loving their art, drinking tea with a couple of friends in a small room, discussing unassumingly their favorite subject, never concerned with the superfluous . . . They will paint the perspective of a room with all kinds of artistic rubbish found in it: plaster casts of hands and feet which their age and dust have turned coffee-colored; a couple of broken easels; an overturned palette; and a friend playing a guitar, and the walls all stained with paint, a glimpse of the pale Neva with wretched fishermen in red shirts. Nearly always their palette is greyish and dull — marked forever with the imprint of the north.

Two of Gogol's earlier Petersburg stories, "The Portrait" and

Nevski Prospect," are stories about artists; "The Madman's Diary," the third of the stories included in the *Arabesques*, is the story of a petty official — a titular councilor like the hero of the later "Overcoat," Akaki Akakiyevich Bashmachkin (Gogol himself, a collegiate assessor, outranked his two characters: titular councilor was a rank of the ninth class, collegiate assessor of the eighth). The unfinished comedy *Vladimir of the Third Class* dealt with higher bureaucracy; but the highest rank among the characters in the Petersburg stories was held by Major Kovalyov's nose which paraded as a state councilor.

Gogol's career in the government ended early in 1831, after some fourteen months; he attended classes at the Academy for some two months, in the spring and early summer of 1830. It was consequently during the early part of his Petersburg period that he was in contact with the world of theofficialdom and, for a short while, with that of the artists.

The passages from the second volume of *Dead Souls* concerning Tentetnikov's brief career in the Petersburg bureaus and his life in the capital undoubtedly come closest to autobiography — and artistically they are the least interesting of the different reflections of the capital in Gogol's work. It is significant that Gogol treated his Petersburg years in a relatively objective, or "true to life" manner, when they had become an old memory: at least twelve years separated him from his experiences in the government offices when he wrote the Tentetnikov chapter.

But observation plays but a minor part in the stories about Petersburg, actually written in Petersburg (and also the subsequent "Overcoat" written abroad).

The Petersburg stories were immediately preceded by the *Evenings* and, as it has been pointed out earlier, Gogol continued to develop Ukrainian themes during the period when he also worked on his Petersburg stories. There are many points of contact between the two cycles. Thus, for example, the typically Ukrainian theme of the hidden treasure and of the curse that gold brings with it, as in "The Eve of St. John the Baptist," appears in "The Portrait," one of the stories of the Petersburg cycle. "The Portrait" is linked, on the other hand, to "The Terrible Vengeance" by the image of the Great Evil-Doer, the usurer Petromikhali in "The Portrait," and the Sorcerer in "The Terrible Vengeance." There is also a similarity in the structure of the two stories: both fall into two pars, the second part — or developed epilogue — being a narration which takes the reader into the past and reveals the origins of the curse and of the supernatural forces shown in action in the first part which is the story proper. The death of the painter Chartkov in "The Portrait," it may be added, is reminiscent of the death of the seminary student Khoma in "Viy." Both die in a paroxysm of horror; Chartkov is placed in the world of insanity, Khoma in the world of folk demonology; but in Chartkov's hallucinations and in the horrible spectacle of the demons invading the church in "Viy," the unbearable paroxysm and death are brought about by staring eyes – endlessly multiplied eyes of the portrait gazing from all sides at Chartkov, and the eyes of the monster Viy who kills Khoma by fixing his glance on him.

To these analogies in structure and motifs an example of stylistic similarity may be added. Gogol uses, in his descriptions of Ukrainian nature, a highly emotional style, with a strongly marked cadence and with frequent exclamatory and interrogatory sentences addressed to the reader. Thus, the opening lines of the "Fair of Sorochintsy:"

How luxuriant, how enrapturing is a summer day in Little-Russia! How agonizingly hot are those hours when noonday glitters in a sultry silence, and the blue limitless ocean – a voluptuous cupola stopping over the earth – seems to be sleeping, overcome by languor, embracing and pressing the loved one in his aery embrace! Not a cloud on it. Not a word does one hear in the field.

And in "May Night," the beginning of a long passage:

Do you know Ukrainian nights? O, you do not know Ukrainian nights! Look: from the middle of the sky gazes the moon. The boundless vault of heaven has expanded and spread out still wider. It is gleaming and breathing. A silvery light is over the earth; and the wondrous air is cool and dense, and full of languor, and waves pass through this ocean of fragrances. Divine night! Rapturous night!

This lyrically dithrambic style is parodied in the "Quarrel:"

A wonderful city, Mirgorod! All the buildings in it! And covered with straw, and with reed, and even with timber; there's a street to the right and a street to the left, and everywhere beautiful fences; hop twines about them, clay pots hang on them, sunflowers show their yellow heads, the poppies gleam red, and here and there you glimpse a bulky pumpkin . . . What luxury! A fence is always adorned with objects which make it even more picturesque: a skirt stretched on it, or a

148

shirt, or a pair of trousers. Thievery or larceny is known in Mirgorod, and therefore everyone hangs on it whatever he thinks fit. If you approach the square, you will surely pause for a while to admire the vista: there is a puddle in it, a marvelous puddle! Nowhere else will you have seen one like it! It covers almost the entire square. Beautiful puddle! The houses, the larger and the smaller ones, which from afar one might mistake for haystacks, crowd around it and admire its beauty.

In "Nevski Prospect" the description of the capital's main artery begins in a cadenced and hyperbolic style very close to the nature descriptions of the Ukrainian stories. The lyrical style of the *Dikanka* stories is not caricatured as in the "Quarrel," but it is tingled with irony:

> There is nothing finer than the Nevski Prospect, not in Petersburg at any rate; the Prospect means everything to it. What is there that could add brilliance to this street — this adornment of our capital! I am certain that not one of its pale, office-working inhabitants would trade the Nevski for all the blessings in the world. Not only he whose age does not exceed twenty-five and who boasts a splendid moustache and an amazingly tailored frock-coat, but even those with a few white hairs sprouting on the chin and the head as smooth and glossy as silverware — even they are enraptured by the Nevski Prospect. And the ladies! O, the ladies find even greater delight in the Nevski . . . All-powerful Nevski Prospect! The only diversion of St. Petersburg where promenades are scanty. How spotlessly clean its sidewalks are swept — and, heavens, how many feet leave their marks on them! The unwieldy, mud-covered boot of an ex-serviceman, under whose weight the very granite seems to crack; and — light as mist — the miniature shoe of a young lady who turns her pretty little head towards the glittering store windows, like a sunflower turning to the sun; and the rattling sabre of a lieutenant filled with hope and expectation which traces a sharp scratch — everything etches its mark on the sidewalk, with the power of strength or the power of weakness. What a rapid phantasmagoria is performed on it within one single day! How many transformations it undergoes within twenty-four hours!

These "transformations," the succession of pictures of the Nevski in the morning, at noon, in the late afternoon, etc., have a close parallel in the pictures of the Dnieper in "The Terrible Vengeance" (sunny day, summer night, storm). An essential difference between the descriptions of nature in the Ukrainian stories and the Petersburg imagery, is that nature is felt by Gogol as an absolute reality and unity – a unity often expressed in animistic metaphors. The city, on the contrary, with its multitude of people and objects, lacks this unity (metonymy, rather than metaphor, is used to render its endless fragmentation), as it lacks the divine realness of nature: the city is a mirage, a phantasmagoria. Behind the turmoil and the futile agitation there is nothingness. And in the man-made world of the city man is hopelessly alone.

The theme of loneliness and of the void gaping through the mirage of the city are perhaps the main themes of Gogol's Petersburg stories. These stories, however, vary considerably in their style and in their treatment of the thematic material of the big city. They follow, then abandon different literary models belonging to different trends of the later romanticism. One may mention among the more important and the more obvious influences that of E.T.A. Hoffmann, of Jules Janin (*L'Ane Mort et la Femme Guillotinée*), of Charles Maturin (*Melmoth the Wanderer*), of Thomas de Quincey (*Confessions of an English Opium Eater*). These influences have been amply studied and discussed. In connection with these influences, it seems useful to make but one remark here concerning Gogol's general attitude toward the romanticist's antinomy between dream and reality.

This antinomy, "the eternal discord between dream and substantiality," as the artist Piskaryov in "Nevski Prospect" puts it, is the basic theme of this story and of the "Madman's Diary" (which, in Belinski's words, "in truthfulness and depth is worthy of the brush of Shakespeare . . ."). What is, however, the content and the quality of the "dreams" opposed to reality in the two stories? The "Madman's Diary" is one of Gogol's most brilliant achievements (whether or not it is "worthy of the brush of Shakespeare"); it is remarkable, however, that contrasting with the originality and the fantasy displayed in the details, the "dream" itself – the insane office clerk believing that he is a king – is a banal (intentionally banal) clinical case of megalomania. The impoverished psyche of clerk Poprishchin produces a grotesque, and he is pathetic in the "grandeur" of his insanity.

One may have expected more from Piskaryov in "Nevski Prospect:" Piskaryov is an artist, and he becomes an opium eater in the hope of escaping the unbearable reality of his love for a vulgar prostitute. Unlike Hoffmann or de Quincey, however, Gogol does not allow his hero to escape by creating a world of beauty and freedom which eclipses reality. Piskaryov's dreams are fantasies of wish fulfillment: the prostitute appears to him as a young lady of high society, then, in another dream, as his modest and virtuous spouse (reminiscent of Küchelgarten's Luisa). This is correcting reality, not abandoning contemptible reality for the superior world of fantasy. Piskaryov, moreover, reverts to reality in his vain attempt to convince the prostitute to abandon her degrading existence and to become his wife. This is an important deviation from the romantic tradition: the dream world in Gogol's stories is a narrow alley, an impasse, not a substitute preferred to reality.

The inability of Gogol's characters to find an escape in the subjective world seems to reflect a significant aspect of his own personality; he isolated himself from reality in the last period of his life, but this isolation was not the poet's escape into a world of his creation; it was an abandonment of the aesthetic for the ethical ideal, and it was the end of the artist.

The theme of loneliness and some of the elements of the imagery of the Petersburg stories appear in Gogol's early letter to his mother in which a first, and perhaps unconscious attempt is made to isolate significant images: such are, in the letter, the muttering clerk met in the street, or the glittering signboards. Some of the less specific descriptions of the "brilliant" capital with its thundering streets, its elegant crowd, etc., on the other hand, are clearly developments of the *a priori* picture of Petersburg conceived in Nezhin.

Yet in the very early Petersburg fragments Gogol leans on literary models in his search for a poetic interpretation of the city. Hoffmann's influence has been shown in these fragments, written between 1830 and 1832, in which first appear the motifs of the lone wanderer through the city, and of the phantasmagoria (the street lamps and the shadows on the walls) of the city at night.

> It was long after midnight. A lonely lantern capriciously illuminated the street throwing a glitter, somehow frightening, onto the stone houses, while the wooden houses were left in darkness; their grey became completely black.

This is developed into a more complete picture in another fragment:

> A street lamp was expiring in one of the remote lanes of Vasili island. Only the white stone houses could be distinguished here and there. The wooden ones appeared black and merged with the dense mass of darkness overhanging them. How frightening it is when the stone-paved sidewalk comes to an end and is replaced by one of boards, when even the boards vanish, when

everything senses the midnight hour, when the far-distant guard is asleep, when the cats, the senseless cats, alone, wake and serenade in unison! But man knows that they will not signal to him and will not sympathize with his misfortune if suddenly some rascals attack him, leaping out of this dark lane which extends toward him its somber embrace.

The writer was groping for form and expression, experimenting with literary styles of urbanistic romanticism, combining experience with literary models, to arrive at the imagery of "Nevski Prospect," of "Notes of a Madman," of the later "Overcoat."

The streetlamp motif is further developed in "Nevski Prospect:"

But as soon as dusk descends upon the houses and the streets, and the guard, covering himself with some matting, climbs his ladder to light the street lamp, and from low shop windows peep those prints which dare not show themselves in daylight, stir, This is the time full of mystery when the street lamps invest everything with their strange and alluring light. You will meet a great many young men, for the most part bachelors, in warm coats or cloaks. At this time one senses the presence of some purpose, or rather of something resembling a purpose. It is something completely unaccountable; everyone accelerates his steps, and they become altogether very uneven. Long shadows flicker over the walls and the pavement, their heads very nearly reaching the Police Bridge.

The motif is given particular significance in the concluding paragraph of the story:

Away, for God's sake, away from the street lamp! And quick; pas it, as quickly as only you can. You are lucky if you get away with a mere spatter of its reeky oil on your dandy frock-coat. But aside from the street lamp, everything breathes deceit. It lies always, the Nevski Prospect, but most of all at that time when the night in a thick mass comes to rest upon it and marks out the white and the pale yellow walls of the houses, when the whole city becomes thunder and glitter, and scores of carriages come rolling down the bridges, and the outriders shout and jolt on their horses, and when the demon himself sets the street lamps burning for the only purpose of making everything appear in a wrong light.

The demon of the big city is the demon of delusion, the night is his realm, the false light of the street lamp is the poison he instills into human souls, awakening desires that lead them to their perdition. A picture of Petersburg appears in one of the *Dikanka* stories, "Christmas Eve," in which a petty demon obligingly carries blacksmith Vakula to the capital. The description is very close to "Nevski Prospect" (and this shows how artificial it is to separate the Petersburg tales from the Ukrainian):

> God Almighty! What tumult, thunder, glitter; on either side pile up walls four stories high; the clatter of the horses' hooves, the rattling of the wheels resounded thunderously and echoed on all four sides; houses grew, as if rising out of the earth at every step; the bridges trembled; carriages flew by; coachmen and outriders shouted; the snow whizzed under the thousands of sleds which came dashing from all parts; the pedestrians prssed close to the houses studded with lampions, and their huge shadows flickered along the walls, their heads reaching the chimneys and the roofs.

The motif of fast motion and tumult filling the street is used in an altered form in "Nevski Prospect" to render the intense emotion experienced by Piskaryov, the young artist, who follows, timid and entranced, a mysterious beauty. She suddenly turns around, and it seems to him that a furtive smile appeared on her lips; but he cannot believe his eyes: "It was the street lamp with its deceitful light that produced this illusion . . ." – once more, the "demon's street light" –

> But his breath was taken away, a vague tremor seized him, his feelings were all aflame and some kind of a mist overcast everything before his eyes. The sidewalk dashed along under him, the carriages with their galloping horses seemed motionless, the bridge stretched out and threatened to break over its arch, a horse was standing its roof downward, a sentry-box reeled toward him, and the guard's halberd, together with the gilt letters of a signboard and the scissors painted on it, seemed to glitter on his very eyelashes.

The elements used in other descriptions are reversed here to convey intense emotional shock: motion becomes immobility (the carriages and the horses); the static sets into swift motion (the pavement, the sentry-box); the distant becomes close (the glittering letters, the halberd); the house stands upside down. The scenery "as seen by . . ." is treated as a projection of emotion.

The illusion of the static in motion already occurs in "Christmas Eve;" it is experienced by the blacksmith riding in a swift carriage:

it seemed to him that "on either side four-storied houses were running toward him, and the pavement rolled on, thundering under the horses' hooves."

In this instance the fantastic vision is justified by an optical illusion; in "Nevski Prospect" it is justified by an emotional state.

The motifs of the early fragment, "A lantern was expiring . . ." (walking at night from the center toward the outskirts of the city, a guard sleeping in his far distant sentry box, fear of an attack) are developed in the robbery scene of "The Overcoat."

The woman met in the street is the central theme in "Nevski Prospect;" on a reduced scale (a woman passing by, a furtive glance). And, treated humorously, the motif also appears in "The Overcoat." Returning home after the party, wearing his new garment (he will be robbed of it a few minutes later) —

> Akaki Akakiyevich walked along in a very happy mood and all of a sudden, for some unknown reason, he even very nearly ran a few steps after some lady who passed by like a streak of lightning, and every part of whose body was animated with most unusual mobility. He brought himself, however, to a stop at once, and went on at his former slow pace, himself wondering at his completely unaccountable nimbleness.

In *Dead Souls* the story is told by the postmaster, of Captain Kopeikin, the invalid who came to Petersburg in the vain hope of obtaining a pension; he spends a sizable portion of his savings on a meal in an expensive tavern, and goes for a stroll in the Nevski:

> On the sidewalk he sees a graceful Englishwoman walking along, just like a swan as one might say, if you can picture it. Our Kopeikin — his blood, you know, began running fast in him — made a few hops — thud, thud, thud, with his wooden peg, right after her, then: "Now there," he thought, "that's for later on, when I get my pension; but for the present I seem to be getting too sprightly."

Poprishchin, in "The Madman's Diary," censures the office clerks for their flirtatious disposition, though with a note of envious admiration:

> There was nobody in the streets; only plain women, their heads covered with the hems of their clothes, and merchants, in Russian garb carrying umbrellas, and coachmen were in sight. As for the gentry, there was only our kind, the functionary, trudging along. I saw him at the street-crossing. And when I

saw him, at once I said to myself: hey, my good friend, that's not to the office you're going! You are hurrying after that one over there, the one that's running ahead of you, and you are peering at her feet. What rascals they are, our kin, the functionaries! By God, he won't yield to any army officer: just let one wearing a bonnet pass by, and he will tag on immediately.

Poprishchin, however, is also distracted from going to the office: he hears two little dogs engaged in a lively conversation and decides to follow them and their mistresses:

Let's go, I said to myself, after this little mongrel, and I'll find out all about her, and what she has on her mind. I opened my umbrella and set out after the two ladies. We crossed the Gorokhovaya, turned into the Meshchanskaya, thence to the Stolyarnaya, and finally to the Kukushkin Bridge and stopped before a large house. I know this house, I said to myself. This is Zverkov's house. What a colossus! And all the different kinds of people that live in it: how many cooks, how many Poles! And our breed, the functionaries, like dogs, sitting one on top of another. I have an acquaintance living there who plays the trumpet very well. The ladies mounted to the fifth floor. Very well, I thought: I won't go in now, I'll take note of the place . . .

Paranoic Poprishchin's ever recurring "I said to myself" reminds one of the muttering clerks in Gogol's letter; the talking dogs, however, are reminiscent of E.T.A. Hoffmann's "Kater Murr." But the Zverkov house near Kukushkin [Cuckoo's] Bridge is autobiographical: Gogol lived there, and so did, at another time, his friend Danilevski whom he often visited. In a letter to his mother dated November 12, 1829, Gogol gives the address: "near Kukushkin Bridge, in the Zverkov house, room №16."

Gogol is almost uniformly bitter and sarcastic in his treatment of the big city. He refused to see its beauty which Pushkin sang in *The Bronze Horseman*; in an extensive essay on "Architecture of Our Time," he does not mention the splendid monuments he could admire every day, but instead, he goes into exstasies over the Cologne Cathedral which he had not seen. In his "Petersburg Notes," however, he seemed to discover the poetic qualities of the capital in which he was living, of the city which he called, in his prayer to the year 1834,

a heap of houses cast one on top another, with its thundering fashions, of parades, government employees, wild northern nights, glitter and base colorlessness.

In the "Notes" he wrote:

The break-up of the Neva came early. The ice, undisturbed by the wind, could thaw almost entirely before the break-up, and floated friable, falling apart by itself . . . The capital suddenly changed. The spire of Sts. Peter and Paul, and the Fortress, and Vasili Island, and the Viborg suburb, and the English Quay — everything took on a picturesque look. The first steamer sailed in, pouring forth its smoke. The first boats with officials, soldiers, old nurses, English office-clerks shuttled across to Vasili Island. I cannot remember ever seeing such clear and radiant weather. When I entered the Admiralty Boulevard — this was the eve of Easter Sunday — when by the Admiralty Boulevard I reached the piers in front of which glisten two jasper vases, when the Neva opened before me, when the rosy hue of the sky became clouded by a bluish mist coming from the Viborg suburb, and the buildings of the Petersburg suburb clad themselves in a color close to purple, concealing their unseemly appearance; when the churches, all their prominences evened out by the uniformly colored mist, looked as if they were painted or pasted on a rose-colored fabric; and in this purply-blue haze alone glittered the spire of Peter and Paul, reflected in the limitless mirror of the Neva — then it seemed to me that I had come to some other city where I had been before, where I knew everything, which has something that Petersburg does not have . . . And there's a boatman I know, but haven't seen for six months, bobbing up and down in his skiff near the bank, and familiar speeches are heard, and the water, and the summer which never were in Petersburg . . . I ardently love the spring. Even here, in the wild north, it is mine. It seems to me that no one in the whole world loves it as much as I do. With it, my young years come back to me; with it, my past is more than a remembrance: it is before my eyes and it fills my eyes with tears. I was so enraptured by the clear, radiant Easter Sunday, that I did not notice the huge fair of Admiralty Square. From afar I only saw the swing carry a husky fellow up into the air. He was holding hands with a young lady wearing a very smart little hat; and a signboard caught my eye on a corner showbooth, on which an enormous red-headed devil holding an axe in his hand was painted. And that was all I saw.

In this haze, in this rosy mist, on a warm spring day, the

156

northern city became acceptable to Gogol – for it was not itself. But he remained a stranger in the capital. He was to discover his second homeland in Rome, with its blue sky, its sunshine, its eternal beauty, and above all, its timelessness and stagnation: it was the best place in the world to be alone.

Chapter XII

TEACHING HISTORY

(HENRY HALLAM AND WALTER SCOTT)

In February 1831, after some fourteen months in government offices, Gogol became a teacher of history. Thanks to Pletnyov's recommendation, he was appointed to teach this subject at the Patriotic Institute in St. Petersburg, an institution for young ladies under the personal patronage of the Empress.

Without undue haste, on April 16, he announced to his mother:

> The Empress ordered me to give lectures at the Institute for Young Ladies of the Nobility which is under her authority.

The Empress, needless to say, did not have the remotest notion of Mr. Gogol-Yanovski whose appointment required her signature.

The letter continued:

> But you mustn't think that this means much. The whole advantage is that now I am a little better known, that little by little my lectures make people speak about me, and above all, that I have much more time: instead of the torture of sitting the whole morning, instead of 42 hours a week, I am now busy only six hours, while the salary is even a little better; instead of the stupid, absurd work, the futility of which I always hated, my present occupations are an inexpressible delight for the soul . . . But meanwhile those occupations which will bring me even greater renown are performed by me in the quiet, in my solitary little room: I have much time for them now.

One may doubt whether the young instructor's "lectures made people speak about" him; and the appointment did not "mean much" in the sense at least that Gogol's initial salary was very modest indeed: four hundred rubles a year. After his first year, however, beginning with January 1832, Gogol was promoted to a senior instructorship, and his salary was raised to 1200 rubles.

Gogol spoke very highly of the Institute, and showed some pride in his connection with it. In October 1831, he wrote to his mother:

I cannot admire enough the way things are ordered here. The pupils here receive instruction in everything they need, from household management to foreign languages and proper behavior in society, and when they leave the Institute, they are quite unlike those frivolous, empty-headed young girls that other institutes produce . . . Two of the local institutes, the Patriotic and the Catherine, are the very best. And that is, you may be assured, where my little sisters will be placed. I have always carried out my plans, even if it took me long to do so, and I am firmly convinced that with God's help, this time I shall also be successful.

He was successful: in the fall of 1832, after spending the summer in Vasilyevka, he brought with him to Petersburg his sisters Anna and Elisaveta, aged twelve and eleven, and placed them in the Institute. To pay for their tuition and board, Gogol abandoned his salary and lived, during the year 1833, on the income from his literary work. In 1834, the girls were granted a scholarship, and the payment of his salary was resumed. It may be noted in this connection that Gogol made his last request to his mother for financial support in April 1831; a year later he sent home 500 rubles, and he often sent presents to his mother and sisters: dresses, shoes, handbags, etc.

This was a period of success: the two parts of the *Evenings* appeared in September 1831, and in March 1832; they were very well received.

Then another dream came true. Gogol spent the summer of 1831 in Pavlovsk, an elegant resort near the capital, living as tutor with a wealthy family of the Petersburg aristocracy. Pushkin and Zhukovski lived in nearby Tsarskoye Selo, and Gogol often visited them, for by now he had been admitted to their small circle. He did some advertising of his friendship with these great men. Thus, although he lived in Pavlovsk, he instructed his mother in a casual postscript, repeated in two letters, to write to him "care of Pushkin, in Tsarskoye Selo." To his friend Danilevski who was then serving in the Caucasus, he wrote:

I spent the whole summer in Pavlovsk and in Tsarskoye Selo . . . Nearly every evening we would get together: Zhukovski, Pushkin and I. O, if you only knew what delightful things come from the pen of these men.

This is followed by an account of the newest efforts of the two celebrated poets, among them Pushkin's *Domik v Kolomne* (A LIttle House in Kolomna), actually written in October of the previous year, but published only in 1833. The frequency of the meetings of the trio was probably exaggerated, were it only because of Gogol's duties as tutor (his pupil was a mentally deficient child) which he forgot to mention in the letter.

A few letters were exchanged between Pushkin and Gogol when Gogol returned to Petersburg in August; they were friendly in tone, but in one of his, Gogol called Pushkin's wife "Nadezhda," instead of "Natalya" — a mistake which a daily visitor would be unlikely to make and which Pushkin corrected in his reply ("Your Nadezhda Nikolayevna, i.e. my Natalya Nikolayevna, thanks you for your remembrance and sends you her cordial greetings").

In September Gogol sent Zhukovski a letter which sounds like a humorous parody of the exalted style of some of his own writings. There was, that summer, a cholera epidemic in Petersburg. Gogol wrote to his mother that the malady was successfully treated with warm milk, and also with egg-white mixed with olive oil; people with a strong constitution, especially peasants, responded well to hot water with salt. The capital was in quarantine, and Gogol was separated from his two famous friends who stayed in the country. He yearned to join them:

O, with what delight would I wipe off the dust from your boots with my hair, and lie down at the feet of your poetic excellency and catch with an avid ear the sweet nectar coming from your lips, concocted by the gods themselves of numberless witches, devils and all that is dear to your heart . . . It seems to me that now the tremendous edifice of poetry purely Russian is being erected . . . Glorious is your lot, Great Architect! What a paradise you are preparing for true Christians! And how terrifying will be the hell awaiting the pagans, the renegades and other rabble: they do not understand you, they do not know how to pray. When will I too join in this marvelous tale? . . . But it is soon midnight, and I am afraid to miss the mail. Farewell! And forgive me this messy letter! The divine art of writing has not been given to me.

It is true that language for Gogol was a difficult medium, but he achieved great things when he could mold his hyperboles and his imagery, his incongurities and his awkward syntax, his Ukrainian dialecticisms and his sweeping rhetoric into an artistic form.

With his letter Gogol sent Zhukovski several copies of the first volume of the *Evenings*: one for himself, one for Pushkin, one, "with a sentimental inscription," for Alexandra Rossette (later Mme. Smirnova), a famous beauty, a friend of Pushkin and of other celebrities of the time and a maid of honor of the Empress. Many years later, in his period of pious moralizing, Gogol maintained with Alexandra Smirnova-Rossette a spiritual intimacy of sorts; in general his preaching was most favorably received by aging ladies of high society.

During the following year, 1833, Gogol showed some signs of depression and disappointment; the creative surge of the previous years had subsided, and a feeling of aloneness and homesickness began to weigh upon him. He had accomplished much in the capital, but he was still a stranger in the big and indifferent northern city. At that time a university was being organized in Kiev, and Gogol made desperate efforts to be appointed there as professor of history, the subject he had taught for three years at the Patriotic Institute.

At the approach of the year 1834, possibly on New Year's Eve, Gogol wrote a prayer, or an incantation, in which he besought the coming year to reveal to him his destiny (this was one of his intimate writings, not intended for publication):

Mysterious, inexplicable 1834! Where shall I mark thee with great labors? Will it be amidst this heap of dwellings thrown one on top another, of thundering streets, of seething mercantilism − this shapeless heap of fashions, parades, officials, wild norther nights, glitter and mean colorlessness? Or in beautiful, ancient Kiev, my promised one, crowned with fruit-rich gardens, girdled with my southern beautiful, wondrous sky, with nights full of rapture, where the hill rises, its gracefully precipitous flanks all strewn with bushes, and beneath, bathing it, my pure one, my swift one, my Dnieper. − Will it be there?

In his efforts to obtain the position in Kiev, Gogol had the support of several of his influential friends. Pushkin was one of them. Pushkin knew the Minister of Public Education, who was also President of the Academy, Sergei Uvarov, a mediocre Littérateur and an amateur philologist, remembered mainly as the author of the celebrated slogan on "Autocracy, Orthodoxy and Nationality," which so happily summarized the guiding principles of the reign of Nicholas I.

On December 23, 1833, Gogol wrote to Pushkin:

If you only knew how sorry I was that instead of you I found only the note you left on my desk. Had I returned but a minute

161

earlier, I would have seen you. I intended to go to see you the very next day; but everything, it seems conspires to go counter to my wishes: a cold has now joined itself to my hemorrhoidal blessings, and I have a whole bundle of kerchiefs around my neck and they look like a horse's collar. Everything shows that illness will keep me locked up for the rest of the week. I made up my mind, however, to waste no time – and to jot my ideas and the teaching plan down on paper instead of an oral presentation. Were Uvarov of the kind of which there are so many in high position, I would not venture to submit my application and my ideas to him . . . But Uvarov is a master hand. His cursive remarks so full of intelligence and the profound ideas in his Note on the Life of Goethe made me appreciate him even more. And I shall not even mention his thoughts on the subject of hexameters which evidence his philosophical understanding of the language and the perspicacity of his mind. I am convinced that he will accomplish more here than Guizot in France. It is my positive belief that were I only given the opportunity to read my Plan, then, in the eyes of Uvarov I would be distinguished from the troop of sluggish professors who crowd our universities.

Gogol's flattering opinion of the Minister was of course intended to be conveyed to him. Pushkin apparently acquitted himself of his mission with some measure of success: the "Plan" which Gogol mentions in his letter to Pushkin and which was to bring his talents to the attention of the Minister appeared on the pages of the official *Journal of the Ministry of Public Education* in its issue for February 1834, under the title "A Plan for the Teaching of World History." In this article (later reprinted in *Arabesques*), Gogol set forth a number of sound ideas; then, mindful of his purpose, he concluded with some self-advertising and an eloquent statement of loyalty and patriotism:

> . . . he who has a deep understanding of history's grandeur will see that it [the Plan] is not the product of some momentary fantasy, but the fruit of long reflection and experience; that not an epithet, not a single word, has been used here for the sake of embellishment or tawdry brilliance – they are all the result of prolonged reading of the annals of the world; that the writing of a general, a complete outling of the history of all humanity – even if only a brief one – is possible only for him who has studied and understood all the fine and intricate threads of history, and that nothing but love for learning – which is my delight – has urged me to set forth my ideas; that

162

my goal is to shape the hearts of young listeners using that substantial experience which history, understood in its true grandeur, has to ofer; to make them firm, virile in their rules so that no giddy fanaticism, no momentary agitation may shake them; to make them humble, compliant, noble, useful, indispensable supporters of their Great Monarch; that in fortune of misfortune, they may never betray their duty, their faith, their noble honor and their oath – to be faithful to their Fatherland and their Emperor.

But after Gogol had expressed such commendable feelings in the pages of the *Journal* of the Ministry, matters made no further headway; the appointment to Kiev was not forthcoming. In May, Gogol turned once more to Pushkin, asking him to tell the Minister that he had visited Gogol and had found him more dead than alive, and that his physicians placed their only hope in his leaving the capital for the south without delay. Gogol's letter, dated May 13, 1834, continued

And when you will have advised him that I may well breathe my last within a month's time, you could let the conversation shift to some other matter, such as the weather, or something similar.

Pushkin replied the same day, with his customary diligence:

Today I'll go to Uvarov and edify him; *à propos* the *Telegraph*'s demise [the Moscow Telegraph which had been suppresed by the censors], I shall mention yours. Therefrom I shall imperceptibly and adroitly pass to immortality – which awaits him. I hope we'll settle it.

Gogol finally failed in his efforts to obtain an appointment to Kiev; but instead, in July 1834, he was made Adjunct Professor of History at the University of St. Petersburg. Mariya Ivanovna was informed of this in a very casual tone:

You complain that I do not keep you posted on my work and other matters. But what could I say, you know very well where I am. However, I cast off extra burdens and gave up other occupations. Now I am only a professor of the university here, and I have no other duties for I have neither the desire nor the time for any.

This letter, dated August 1, apparently caused some commotion in Vasilyevka and aroused a good deal of curiosity. A request came for more details. In his reply, after discussing certain problems of domestic finances, Gogol wrote in that irritated tone which often sounded in his letters home in those years:

You wish to know in what field I am a professor in the university here. I teach the history of the Middle Ages. You have not yet calmed your passion for ranks, and you believe that I must certainly have received a higher rank. Absolutely not: I am what I was formerly, i.e. a collegiate assessor, and nothing more. If there were some substantial advantage for me in a rank, I surely would not have neglected the occasion; I am not so stupid as to overlook this. But my circumstances and my situation are such . . . But how could I make you understand? We will not understand each other and will only be wasting paper uselessly. Let's leave the ranks alone. I love you, I love you as a rare and exemplary mother – so what else can you want?

In September the newly appointed adjunct-professor (and still a mere collegiate assessor) inaugurated his course in the history of the Middle Ages; he showed himself an ardent medievalist, in the best romantic tradition. His opening lecture ended with the following peroration:

The Middle Ages end in an event truly grandiose – a universal explosion lifting into the air everything and turning into nothingness all those terrible powers that held them in a despotic embrace. The power of the Pope was shaken and fell; the power of ignorance was shaken; the wealth and the world trade of Venice were shaken; and when the universal chaos and upheaval cleared away, then – in amazement – one could behold: monarchs holding their scepters with a mighty hand; ships rushing on, in ever broader swings, past the Mediterranean sea, along the waves of the boundless ocean; in the hands of the Europeans – fire replacing impotent arms; printed sheets flying to the four corners of the Earth – and all this was the result of the Middle Ages . . . The human mind, shut in behind a thick layer, could not break loose unless it gathered all its efforts, all that was contained in it. And that is perhaps the reason why no century has produced such tremendous discoveries as the fifteenth – the century which so brilliantly concludes the Middle Ages – an age majestic as a colossal gothic cathedral; dark and somber like its repeatedly intersected vaults; variegated like its multicolored windows and the masses of ornament that adorn it; lofty and impetuous like its pillars and its walls which soar into the sky and end in a spire looming in the clouds.

The text of the lecture, slightly retouched, was also given space in the pages of the official *Journal* of the Ministry, as well as a third essay devoted to the history of the Ukraine. The three essays were later reprinted in the *Arabesques* with three more pieces on historical subjects published in this volume for the first time.

There is in these writings a good deal of sublime grandiloquence and of nebulous bombast compensating at times for scarcity of information. But both the erudition and the style of the young historian must be judged by the standards and the tastes of his time. And for all their romantic transports, for all their hyperbolic imagery, Gogol's essays in many instances offer views and interpretations which are sufficiently substantiated and which lack neither originality nor genuine insight. Gogol was a dilettante, but not an ignoramus. His preparation for the chair of history was of course inadequate. But during his occupancy of this chair he worked diligently and read widely, especially works on medieval history, as is attested by the extensive notes, bibliographies and outlines of lectures found among his papers.

Gogol's failure in his academic career was not due primarily to the scarcity of his knowledge, but rather to his loss of interest in the teaching profession, and also to the peculiar organization of his mind. Even if he "dramatized" history deliberately, even if he created images which were intended to illustrate his exposition, these images, once called into being, would enact dramas of their own which neither the curriculum nor the young Adjunct Professor himself had foreseen. Gogol's mind was not made for systematic thinking based on organized data. Rather than submit to discipline, it would escape into sublime rhetoric and nebulous metaphor, or else it would produce an abundance of concrete images, and these images would break loose, overthrowing the barriers of a scholarly dissertation, seeking greater freedom of motion, striving for a more complete incarnation. It was a problem of literary genre; this freedom and this concreteness were out of place in the lecture or the essay; their proper place was in fiction.

In September 1828 (some three months before Gogol set out from Vasilyevka for St. Petersburg) the *Edinburgh Review* published a critical essay on Henry Hallam's *Constitutional History of England* (this work was listed in Gogol's "Bibliography of the Middle Ages"). The author, Thomas Babington Macaulay, set down in this essay his views on the relations between historiography and historical fiction.

> History, at least in its state of ideal perfection, is a compound of poetry and philosophy. It impresses general truths on the mind by a vivid representation of particular characters and incidents. But in fact the two hostile elements of which it consists have never been known to form a perfect amalgamation; and at length in our own time they have been completely professedly separated.

Gogol did not find the secret of "perfect amalgamation;" his "vivid representations" refused to serve the purpose of "impressing general truths;" and "poetry," if it is to remain poetry, can hardly be an ingredient entering into a "compound."

Macaulay writes further in his essay:

> Of the two kinds of composition into which history has been divided, the one may be compared to a map, the other to a painted landscape. The picture, though it places the country before us, does not enable us to ascertain with accuracy the dimensions, the distances and the angles. The map is not a work of imitative art. It presents no scene to the imagination; but it gives us exact information . . . and is a more useful companion to the traveler of the general than the painted landscape could be [at this point the metaphor expands, as it would, perhaps with a little more fantasy, in one of Gogol's *Arabesques* essays], though it were the grandest that ever Rosa peopled with outlaws, or the sweetest over which Claude ever poured the mellow effulgence of a setting sun.

Gogol was not capable of giving much "exact information" useful to travelers or to generals, or even to his own students. For while attempting to draw a map, to use Macaulay's simile, he would often visualize a "landscape" so vividly that "the dimensions, the distances and the angles" would be distorted if not entirely lost.

In his "View of the Formation of Little Russia" Gogol states his belief in the determinative influence of the geographic factor in history.

This he tries to demonstrate later in his essay, but he begins with the following description:

> This land, which later received the name of the Ukraine, extends to the north no farther than the fiftieth parallel; it is even rather than hilly. Small elevations are frequent, but there is not a sinle mountain chain. Its northern part is intermingled

with forests which earlier gave shelter to whole bands of bears and of wild boars; the southern part is open, it is all prairie land, seething with fertility, though seldom sown with grain. The mighty virgin soil produced of its own will innumerable varieties of grass. The steppes swarmed with herds of antelope, of deer and wild horses. From north to south passes the great Dnieper tangled in the branches of its tributaries. Its right bank is hilly and offers vistas at once charming and daring; its left bank is all meadowland, with groves scattered over it, often flooded with its waters. Twelve cataracts — rocks rising from its bottom — obstruct its course not far from its mouth making navigation extremely dangerous. In the vicinity of the rapids used to live a kind of wild goat, the sugak, with white glossy horns and a soft, silky skin. The waters of the Dnieper were higher before, and its overflow was wider, submerging more of the meadowland. When the waters begin to subside, the view is amazing: all the elevated spots emerge and seem to be innumerable green islands amidst an ocean of water without horizon.

The picture of the subsiding flood and the emerging islands hardly adds anything to the attempted demonstration of the formative influence of the geographic factor; a landscape in the literal sense, it is also a landscape in the figurative sense given to the word in Macaulay's essay. And the *sugak* with its white glossy horns and its silky skin is obviously an intruder. His intrusion signifies the protest of concrete and poetic vision against scholarly generalization.

Macaulay is ready to admit that "amalgamation" is impossible; but if there must be separation he would rather have it complete. He condemns the practice of a writer producing first a history, then a novel, as was done by M. Sismondi in France. "We manage these things better in England," remarks Macaulay, "Sir Walter Scott gives us a novel; Mr. Hallam a critical and argumentative history . . ."

The curious thing with Gogol was that, while he entered the path of Walter Scott in working on *Taras Bulba*, he chose the disguise of a Ukrainian Henry Hallam. *Taras Bulba* — a work of fiction — became a reality; the multi-volume histories, the writing of which Gogol widely advertised, remained a myth.

The first of Gogol's vast projects originated in connection with his teaching at the Patriotic Institute. In February 1833, Gogol wrote to Mikhail Pogodin, Professor of Russian History at Moscow University (Gogol met Pogodin during his visit to Moscow in the summer of 1832, and they soon became friends):

I will send you or bring you something which is entirely my own that I am preparing for print. It will be a world history and world geography in three, if not in two, volumes under the title *The Earth and the People*.

Some three weeks later Gogol wrote once more to Pogodin:

I do not know why but I felt completely despondent . . . the galley proof dropped from my hands and I had the printing discontinued . . . Scarcely do I begin and do I accomplish something in history — and immediately I see my shortcomings: now I will regret that I did not conceive on a broader, more grandiose scale, now a completely new system will arise overthrowing the old one . . . The devil may now take my labor, what I have jotted down on paper — until another, more peaceful time . . .

A new plan appears toward the end of the year 1833: Gogol will write a history of the Ukraine: this plan is first mentioned in a letter dated November 9, to his friend Maksimovich (p. 161), later Rector of the University of Kiev, a diligent collector and editor of Ukrainian folklore:

I set to work on a history of our poor Ukraine, our one and only. Nothing can give peace like history. My thoughts begin to flow quieter and are more orderly. It seems to me that I shall write it, that I shall say much that before me has not been said.

In his letter to Pushkin of December 23, 1833 (quoted on pages 161-162) anticipating his appointment to Kiev, Gogol wrote enthusiastically about what he would accomplish once in the ancient southern capital:

There I will finish the history of the Ukraine and of Southern Russia and will write a world history which as yet does not exist in proper form either in Russia or even in Europe.

Further, he adds:

I want to share with you my joy in a discovery I made: I got hold of a chronicle of the Ukraine — its end and its beginning are missing — written, as all its features show, at the end of the 17th century.

168

On January 11, 1834, Gogol gave Pogodin this optimistic account of the progress of his work:

I am now completely immersed in history, Little Russian and world history; both are beginning to make headway. This communicates to me calm and equanimity with regard to everyday concerns, for otherwise I have been infuriated by what has been happening. Ho, brother! How many ideas I have now! And what vast ones! And so full and so fresh! I feel I shall do something that will not be "General" in General History. My Little Russian history is going to be wild to the extreme — but then how could it be anything but that. I am criticized for its style being altogether too fiery, unhistorically glowing and vivid; but then what is the use of a history if it is boring! . . .

The same month, January 1834, an announcement appeared in several periodicals under this heading: "New books — on the publication of a History of Little Russian Cossacks by N. Gogol (author of *Evenings on a Farmstead near Dikanka*)." Stating that there existed as yet no complete and satisfactory history of Little Russia, the author of the *Evenings* declared: "I have resolved to take this labor upon myself . . ." Further, he continues:

For nearly five years I have been collecting with great care material related to the history of that region. Half of my history is nearly completed, but I delay the publication of the first volumes suspecting the existence of many sources that may be unknown to me and which without doubt are preserved in private hands . . .

The announcement ended in an urgent appeal to send such materials to Nikolai Vasilyevich Gogol in St. Petersburg.

On February 12, 1834, Gogol gave more news on the History of the Ukraine to his friend Maksimovich:

I am writing the entire history of Little Russia from the beginning to the end. It will be either in six small or in four large volumes.

The two statements combined, if one took them literally, would signify that by January 1834, Gogol had completed, or all but completed, two large or three small volumes of a history of the Ukraine; but it would be a fatal mistake ever to take Gogol literally.

The public was finally allowed a glimpse of the monumental

history: in the April 1834 issue of the *Journal of the Ministry of Public Education* (IV, Section II, pp. 1-15), appeared "Excerpt from a History of Little Russia. Volume I, Book I, Chapter I" (with the passage on the flooded meadowland and the *sugak*).

Gogol soon found cause to complain of self-appointed experts who had judged his essay hastily, forgetting that "another eighty chapters" would follow. But no other chapter was ever added to the first chapter of the first book of the first volume.

On August 23, 1834, Gogol wrote to Maksimovich: "My history is undergoing a terrible reshuffling: in the first part a whole half is entirely new." This is the last known reference to the History of Little Russia – in four large, or in six small volumes.

The abandoned project was immediately followed by another one, Gogol wrote to Pogodin on November 2, 1834: "I am planning to shoot off a history of the Middle Ages, the more so that such ideas about it are swarming in my mind . . . but I'll begin writing it not sooner than a year from now;" then again, January 22, 1835: "I think also of tackling a medieval history in, say, eight or nine volumes, if the Lord helps me;" and the same day to Maksimovich: "I am writing a history of the Middle Ages which, I think, will consist of eight, if not of nine volumes."

It is generally believed that Gogol began *Taras Bulba* toward the end of 1833 – at the time when he first mentioned his plans of a "History of the Ukraine." The first draft of *Taras Bulba* was reworked during the second half of 1834; in August 1834, Gogol advised Maksimovich that his "History" was undergoing a "complete reshuffling." Gogol's *Mirgorod*, with *Taras Bulba*, was passed by the censor on December 29, 1834: *Taras Bulba*, therefore, was completed some time before this date, and it is quite likely that the first reference to the "History of the Middle Ages," in November 1824, coincided with the completion of Gogol's historical romance.

Thus, chronologically, Gogol's announcements about the "History of the Ukraine" coincide with the writing of *Taras Bulba* – which he never once mentioned in his correspondence: he was a Walter Scott pretending to be a Henry Hallam.

"History of the Middle Ages" ("in eight or nine volumes") also had a counterpart in imaginative writing: some time after announcing it Gogol began working on a drama based on the life of King Alfred the Great.

In both instances Gogol actually wrote and published an essay, and the two essays were presented as "introductions" to monumental Histories – one of the Ukraine, the other of the Middle Ages.

It is difficult to say whether Gogol's announcements were

deliberately misrepresentations, or merely fantasies; possibly, to some extent at least, he deceived himself while trying to deceive others. The inevitable exposure did not seem to preoccupy him at all: his fallacies afforded him a temporary protection, and that was all he needed. In the case of *Taras Bulba*, which was to remain a secret until it was completed, it was necessary to have an excuse for requesting materials and information; the "History" provided him with such an excuse. For despite the lack of historicity in his historical fiction, Gogol needed and used for it, in his own peculiar way, a considerable amount of source material; he was not content with borrowing a character or a dramatic situation from history — and with using imagination for the rest. He had to be supplied with material in abundance — but he used it precisely as material: selecting, reworking, shaping it according to his needs.

In the case of "Alfred," the unfinished historical drama, it has been shown that Gogol used as source Henry Hallam's *View of the State of Europe During the Middle Ages.*

A more recent study made it evident that Gogol used at least two other sources: Augustin Thierry's *Histoire de la Conquête de l'Angleterre par les Normands* and another French work: an antiquated history of England by de Rapin Thoyras, written in the first quarter of the eighteenth century.

In the spring of 1835, Gogol went to Vasilyevka for his summer vacation. On May 24, he wrote to his friend Prokopovich in Petersburg:

> Here is something I must ask you to do for me: Will you be so kind as to go to my apartment and address yourself to Matryona in order to gain access to the books, and take there the history of England by the Abbé de Thoyras, in Russian, one volume containing parts 1 and 2. It is in a leather binding, and please send it to me as soon as possible. I need it badly. In case you cannot find it for some reason of other, get it from Smirdin's and send it to me at once. And something else: go over to Rospini's and buy three thermometers — 2 for the room and one of the kind that are intended to be placed outside . . . Wrap them in cotton-wool, pack them in a wooden box and send them to me together with the book.

Gogol drew from Thoyras a number of details and also the story, referred to in Act I, of the nuns of Coldingham who, at the approach of the Danes, disfigured themselves by cutting off their noses in order to save their honor; this deterred the Danes from attempts on their chastity, but instead they set fire to the nunnery, and the noseless nuns perished in the flames. Gogol, apparently, realized that the work of Thoyras was obsolete and not entirely reliable: as Alekseyev points out, the work is not included in Gogol's "Bibliography of the Middle Ages." Gogol applied different criteria to his sources according to the purpose they were to serve.

Studying Ukrainian sources (ostensibly for his History, but actually for *Taras Bulba*), Gogol became disappointed with the "chronicles" (or rather eighteenth century compilations) and turned to Ukrainian folklore: in the Ukrainian *dumy*, full of color and drama, of popular memories and emotions – he found something more real and meaningful than in the factual accounts of the chronicles. Gogol wrote enthusiastically about folksongs to Maksimovich who had acquired a new collection of them: "My joy! My life! Songs! How I love you! What are all the stale annals in which I am now rummaging compared to these resonant, living annals!"

He expressed similar feelings in his correspondence with Izmail Sreznevski, later a leading Slavic philologist, who in 1833 began the publication of a collection of materials on Ukrainian history and folklore. Sreznevski responded to Gogol's advertisement by an offer of assistance and several letters were exchanged between them.

On March 6, 1834, Gogol wrote to Sreznevski, congratulating him on the "treasures unearthed" and published by him, especially the songs:

> If our land did not have such a wealth of songs, I would not have comprehended . . . its past, or else my History would be completely different from what I intend to make it. The songs incted me to read eagerly all the chronicles, all the scraps of any kind of rubbish.

And further:

> . . . every sound of a song tells me more vividly of bygone days than our limp and brief chronicles – if only one may term chronicles not contemporary records but later extracts begun at a time when memory had yielded to oblivion.

He made an exception for Koniski "who has sharp physiognomy and character . . . and knew what he was writing about . . ." But when in his reply Sreznevski expressed some reservations as to his trustworthiness, Gogol hastened to agree: "I also often disbelieve Koniski, but it was not his merits as a chronicler that I had in mind . . ."

In April 1834, Gogol published an article on Ukrainian songs which was later reprinted in the *Arabesques* — where it found its place beside the other dithyrambic pieces glorifying the Middle Ages, Cossack bravery, Pushkin, the Cologne Cathedral, a trio of German historians, sculpture, architecture and music, and a horribly operatic painting representing "The Last Days of Pompei."

The *Arabesques* included also "The Portrait," "Nevski Prospect" and "Madman's Diary." These stories were completed not later than November 10, 1834, when the volume was passed by the censor. *Mirgorod* was passed on December 29 of the same year.

Gogol spent the next summer in Vasilyevka and returned to Petersburg in the fall of 1835 for his last semester at the University.

On December 6, 1835, he wrote to Pogodin:

> We spat at each other, I and the university, and in a month I am again a free Cossack. Unrecognized I mounted the chair, unrecognized I am leaving it. But in these one and a half years — the years of my infamy, for the general opinion is that I had no business going into this — in these one and a half years I gained much that I can add to the treasury of my soul. 'Tis no longer the childish thoughts, nor the limited sphere of my former knowledge, but lofty ideas, full of truth and awesome grandeur that agitate me . . . Peace to my narrow quarters, so close to the attic! No one knows you. Once more I let you sink into the depths of my soul, until a new awakening, when you will surge with greater power, and they will not dare resist me, the shameless impudence of the learned ignoramuses, the learned and the illiterate mob, the ever assenting public, etc., etc. I say this to you alone; I would say it to no one else; they would call me a mere braggart . . .

Further in his letter he announced the completion of the *Inspector*. Gogol was now giving himself to his art entirely. He was conscious of his creative power, and he proclaimed it with defiance; he sounded a challenge. But actually he was engaging in a fight against himself, and he carried on this fight until his inevitable defeat.

173

Chapter XIII

THE INSPECTOR

(THE AUTHOR AND HIS AUDIENCE)

Gogol left Russia six months after he parted with the University to become a "free Cossack," as he wrote to Pogodin. He was not maintained on the faculty by reason of a reform of higher education. The reason is stated in the certificate delivered to Gogol which commends him for his character and his ability. Once more, seven years after the "Kuchelgarten Journey," he boarded the steamboat for Lubeck and Hamburg. But this pilgrimage was a long one: exept for two winters in Russia (1839–1840 and 1841–1842), Gogol spent the next twelve years abroad.

His expatriation followed the production of the *Inspector*. The play, first performed in the Mariinsky Theater in St. Petersburg on April 19, 1836, met with success, if not with unanimous approval. Gogol complained, however, with a gradually increasing bitterness, of what he believed to be a general hostility. In a letter to the actor Shchepkin, in Moscow, dated April 29, he wrote:

I am sending you the *Inspector* . . . I was going to . . . bring it myself and read it, to prevent erroneous ideas being formed in advance about some of the characters . . . But now that I got to know the theatrical administration here, I am so disgusted with the theater that the mere thought of the pleasures awaiting me in the Moscow theater are enough to stop me from going to Moscow . . . I had enough! Do whatever you want with my play, I am not going to bother about it . . . The effect it produced was considerable, and loud. All are against me. The bureaucrats — the aging and the respectable ones — shout that there is nothing sacred for me if I dare speak in this way about public officials. The police are against me, the merchants are against me, the littérateurs are against me. They abuse me and they go to see the play; for the fourth performance the tickets are sold out. Were it not for the high intervention of the

174

Emperor, my play would never have seen the stage . . . Now I
see what it means to be a comic writer. The least sign of truth
– and they rise against you, not one man, but entire classes . . .
It hurts one to see people against one, when one loves them
with a brotherly love . . .

Despite the urging of his friends, incluling Pushkin, who was in
Moscow at that time, Gogol refused to go there to supervise the
production. However, in a letter to Shchepkin dated May 10, he did
send the following detailed instructions on the costumes and
make-up of Bobchinski and Dobchinski:

The one who has light hair must wear a dark frock-coat, and
the dark one, that is Bobchinski a light coat. And dark trousers
for both. In general, avoid overdoing it. But little paunches
they must both have absolutely – and pointed ones, like
pregnant women.

The same day, however, writing to Pogodin, he renewed his
complaints and announced that he was leaving Russia; what grieved
him especially in his compatriots "whom he loved with his whole
heart" was to see how falsely, in what wrong way they understand
everything:

. . . the particular is taken for the general, an accident for the
rule . . . . You bring on the stage two or three scoundrels –
and a thousand honest people are angered and say: "We are not
scoundrels". But never mind them! . . . If I am going abroad, it
is not because I am unable to stand all these vexations, I want
to improve my health, to get some relaxation, some distraction,
and then, having chosen a permanent abode, to think over my
future labors thoroughly [this letter is dated May 15, 1836].

When Pogodin pointed out to him with good reason, it would
seem, that all his complaints were altogether ridiculous, and that he
should rejoice, for the hostile reactions were proof that he had hit
the target, Gogol replied with increasing bitterness and this time
with a touch of errationality:

I am not disturbed by the abuse of my literary enemies, the
venal talents; what grieves me is this universal ignorance wich
actuates the capital; it is to see that the most trifling opinion of
a writer whom they themselves have vilified and have spat
upon, at the same time produces such an effect upon them and
deceives them. It grieves me to see the pitiful position which is

still that of the author with us. All are against him, and there are none of comparable power to take his side. "He is a firebrand! He is a rebel!" And who says this? This is said to me by statesmen, by men in high position, by men of experience . . . What would cause loud laughter and sympathy in enlightened men, that rouses the bile of ignorance; and this ignorance is general.

This was a paradoxical situation indeed — at least if one is to accept Gogol's own later statements, or Belinski's interpretation — the "satirist," and "castigator of social evils" went into all this commotion because some people, or even many people, were hurt, and especially because the public generalized what he had in mind, protested the "social satirist," were only exeptions, particular cases — "two or three scoundrels."

That "all were against him" was a manifest exaggeration, if not a morbid delusion: Gogol had many friends, some of thcm influential. If he was alarmed by what hc had heard from "statesmen" and "men in high position," he should have found sufficient reassurance in the favorable attitude of the Emperor who attended the premiére and applauded with some ostenation.

There are some documents to support the story of Nicholas I's personal intervention with the censorship in favor of Gogol's play. The documents seem to indicate that the play was approved rapidly and without particular difficulty. Nicholas's favorable attitude is confirmed by the fact that some ten days after the premiére, the Minister of the Imperial Court, acting upon personal orders of the Emperor, gave instructions that "an object of the value of 800 rubles" (probably a watch) be delivered to him for remittance to Gogol.

Objectively, there was little to justify Gogol's reactions; but he did experience a shock which set into motion certain psychic mechanisms: the shock reawakened the old dream, the *Kuchelgadrten* fantasy of the lone wanderer. At the same time, if the production of his comedy caused these painful reactions, it also made possible the realization of the dream — like Mariya Ivanovna's 1450 rubles seven years earlier. Gogol received for his play, by order of the Director of the Imperial Theaters, the sum of 2,500 rubles. For Gogol this was a very large sum, considering that in government service he earned 750 rubles, and at the Patriotic Institute, 1,200 rubles per annum.

And another of the *Kuchelgarten* motifs was reactivated by the performance of the *Inspector*. Gogol stated repeatedly that if he suffered from the public reaction, it was because of his brotherly love for his countrymen. This does not sound too convincing. One hears clearly in his letters the old theme of contempt for the "existers" or for the "mob." Here, too, Gogol seems to be enacting the *Kuchelgarten* situation of the "chosen one," alone amidst the "wildly shouting mob."

A few months after his escape from the "shouting mob," he wrote to Pogodin (from Geneva on September 22, 1836):

> . . . There is in Russia such a fine collection of vile mugs that I could no longer bear to look at them. Even now I feel like spitting whenever I think of them. . . .

And in one of the early drafts of *Dead Souls,* written during the same period: "I do not want to see the physiognomies at which one ought to spit. . . ." He was "vilified and spat upon," he wants to "spit at the vile mugs. . . ."

Gogol's attitude toward the "mob" — his contempt which, when manifested, aroused hostility — explains in part at least the shock he experienced when his play was produced. There certainly were unfavorable reactions, there were those who took offense, and there were also those who judged his play a vulgar farce. But even more important was the experience of the public performance itself: it was a direct exposure to the "mob", to the anonymous multitude judging him, discussing him, speaking about him. This was a situation far more dramatic and explosive than the impersonal relationship between the author and his invisible reader.

Gogol's dread of exposure before the multitude is apparent in his *Confession;* very significantly he opposes such an exposure to relations with individuals:

> . . . it is enough to acquire a certain equanimity of character and tolerance in dealing with people to make them overlook your faults. But when you expose yourself before people you do not know, before the whole world . . . your every action, everything you do is taken apart thread by thread . . . and rebukes are showered upon you from all sides . . . and they will deal blows, whether deliberately or not. . . .

Individuals, in other terms, can be controlled, but the multitude, the "mob," cannot: the "mob" attacks and destroys a man if he has imprudently attracted its attention. In the opening lines of the *Confession* he recalls how the critics attacked him for his *Correspondence with Friends:*

177

Every word was analyzed with suspicion and distrust . . . Upon the body of a live man a dreadful dissection, a minute analysis, was performed, which would cause even one endowed with a strong constitution to break out in a cold sweat.

The attacks of the critics were felt as a physical aggression: "they" tried to penetrate the innermost recesses of his being, to dissect his live body and lay bare his entrails. The crisis caused by the *Inspector* was less acute than the crisis causes in later years by the *Correspondence.* But even the unfavorable reactions to his comedy were perceived by Gogol as an act of violence of the angered mob, of the infuriated "existers."

Gogol did not speak of himself, in connection with the *Inspector* or with *Dead Souls,* as of a satirical writer: he used the term "comic" writer to which he soon added "contemporary." Thus, in a letter dated April 29, 1836, he wrote to Shchepkin: "Now I see what it means to be a comic writer", and to Pogodin: "A contemporary writer, a comic writer, a writer of manners has to be far away from his native land." These letters followed the performance of the *Inspector.* In the *Confession* one reads: "The further I advanced, the more I felt the desire to be a contemporary writer."

Actually the *Inspector* or *Dead Souls* were no more "contemporary" than several of the works that preceded them; for example "The Portrait" or "Nevski Prospect." But in some way they did differ from his earlier work; whether or not they were intended as social satire, they had an impact which the earlier works lacked. They were extraordinary because they presented images, however distorted, of ordinary people leading ordinary existences, and disturbed in their ordinary existence by violent intrusions engineered by the author. "Existers" had appeared before in Gogol's stories, in the "Quarrel" for example, but they were tinged with Ukrainian *couleur locale,* they were slightly exotic "existers," and they were too far away to complain about their grotesque portraitures.

Later Gogol described the inception of the *Inspector* and of *Dead Souls* as a turning point in his development. He decided at the time of their inception, or so he stated later, to become a writer with a serious purpose. He also associated this deep change in his creative development with Pushkin: Pushkin urged him to write an important work and "gave" him the plots of both the *Inspector* and *Dead Souls.*

In a later chapter an attempt will be made to show the psychological significance of the connection made by Gogol between Pushkin and these two works: at this point it seems useful to present the more important facts concerning the problem of Pushkin's participation in their inception.

Of particular interest is Gogol's letter of October 7, 1835, to Pushkin (who was then at his estate of Mikhailovskoye); it contains the following passage:

I began to write *Dead Souls.* The plot is stretching out into a very long novel, and I think it will be very funny. But now I stopped at the third chapter. I am looking for a nice pettifogger with whom I could become closely acquainted. I would like to show in this novel all of Russia, even if from one side. Do me a favor, give me some kind of a topic, even only some anecdote. My hand trembles to write a comedy in the meanwhile. If this didn't happen, I would be wasting my time, and I wouldn't know what to do with my circumstances. Outside of my foul university salary of 600 rubles, I have no job now. Do me the favor, give me a plot, and we'll have a five act comedy before you know it, and I swear, it will be funnier than the dickens. In God's name, please. Both my mind and my stomach hunger.

This is the first known mention of *Dead Souls;* as for the *Inspector,* it is believed that Pushkin answered Gogol's supplication by "giving" him the anecdote which he used as the plot of his comedy. There is, however, a chronological difficulty: Pushkin left Petersburg for his estate on September 7, and returned on October 23; it may be held certain that he did not send the plot by mail, so that the "donation" could only have taken place after Pushkin's return on October 23. The date of the completion of the comedy is established by Gogol's letter to Pogodin of December 6, 1835, in which, after announcing that he had left his position at the University, he continued:

Now I am out in the fresh air. One needs such a refreshment in life like flowers need rain, or one who has spent a long time sitting in his study needs to take a walk. Let us laugh now, let us laugh more! Long live the Comedy! One I finally made up my mind to give to the theater . . . Tell . . . my good Shchepkin there are ten parts for him in the comedy; let him take whichever he wants, or even play all of them at once. I am very sorry I didn't have anything ready for his benefit. I was so preoccupied all this time that I hardly managed to finish this play the day before yesterday.

The "day before yesterday" was December 4, which would mean

179

a truly extraordinary feat, that the five-act comedy was written in a little more than a month; but Gogol found it necessary to give an excuse – his "preoccupations" – for not finishing the play earlier!

A piece of evidence in support of the story of "donation" is a note written in his hand, discovered relatively recently, which reads:

> Crispin arrives at a fair in a provincial town – he is mistaken for (an ambassador?). The governor is an honest fool. – The governor's wife coquets with him – Crispin seeks to marry the daughter.

These lines, it is held, were written in 1833 or 1834, and it is known that they refer to a real occurrence ("Crispin" is identified as Pavel Svinyin, a journalist and publisher, known for his extraordinary mendacity). It is also known that Pushkin himself was once, during his travels, mistaken for an important official traveling incognito, and treated accordingly. Generally, such mistakes and comical situations arising from them, provided the material for many anecdotes current at that time, whether or not based on real occurrences.

No less important is it that the situation had been used in literature. Very close to Gogol's *Inspector* was a comedy by Kvitko-Osnovyanenko, a Ukrainian like himself, *Priyezzhi iz stolitsy, ili Sumatokha v uyezdnom gorode* (A Visitor from the Capital, or Commotion in a Provincial Town): the comedy, written in 1827, remained unpublished until 1840, but it is very likly that Gogol knew it in the manuscript. The problem of Gogol's indebtedness to Pushkin for the plot of *Inspector-General,* as well as the relation of this plot to contemporary anecdotes and to literary antecedents, has been the object of a considerable number of studies.

Contemporary critics, whether favorable or unfavorable to Gogol's comedy, were almost unanimous in pointing out that it was based on a current anecdote. Senkovski, the influential publisher and critic of *Biblioteca dlya chteniya* in a sharply hostile review, also recalled a short story by Alexander Veltman, published in the magazine "Provintsialnye aktyory" (Provincial Actors), which actually is quite closely related to Gogol's comedy. Senkovski wrote:

> Having shown all that would be worth good comedy from the point of view of genuine humor . . . we must unfortunately say that Mr. Gogol's *Inspector-General* is far from deserving the name of comedy . . . Mr. Gogol does not have an idea. His work does not even have for its object social manners, and without this there can be no true comedy: his topic is an

anecdote; an old one, known to everyone, printed a thousand times, told and used in various ways . . . about how in a small provincial town, where petty administrative disorders and abuses linger — as is customary for all ages and peoples — the officials mistake someone for an important person from the capital, are frightened, begin to bustle, to hide their sins, and then it turns out that all this was nonsense, a mistake, a false scare . . . It [the anecdote] was even once told by Mr. Veltman in the *Biblioteka*. Dramatic compositions of this kind, as long as there was any respect for the meaning of words, were not called "comedies," but *pièces anecdotiques.* . . .

In a very favorable critique, by Vasili Androsov, the following remark was made:

We will readily agree with certain critics that this is by no means a new story, whether in comedy or in real life. People have made so many errors, and about so many things, that it would be very difficult to find a new error out of which something new could be derived in a comedy.

Of particular interest is the article by Prince Vyazemski, because he was one of Pushkin's closest friends, and because it was printed in Pushkin's *Contemporary* (Vol. II, July 1836), to which Gogol himself was a very active contributor. Answering the critics who claimed that the comedy lacked credibility, Vyazemski wrote:

In one of our provinces, and not too remote, an incident like the one described in the *Inspector* actually occurred. Owing to a similarety of names, a young traveler was mistaken for a well-known public official. All the local authorities, in great commotion, arrived to present themselves before the young man. We do not know whether he happened at that time to be in need of money, like the luckless gambler Khlestakov, but it is likly that lenders could have been found.

One may quote finally Gogol himself who seems to echo Vyazemski in his "Teatralny razyezd" (Leaving the Theater). In this dramatized commentary to his play the author overhears the remarks made by the spectators as they leave the theater, among them the following:

A *Voice in the Crowd:* All this is rubbish! Where could such a thing happen? Such a thing could happen only in the Chukotski island.

181

Another Voice": Really? Well, this is exactly what happened in my own little town. I suspect that the author must have heard of it, if he hadn't been there himself.

All these comments reflect what was obviously the general feeling: that Gogol's comedy was based on an anecdote commonly known, and even hackneyed in the opinion of the less favorable critics. Whether Gogol heard the anecdote from Pushkin or from someone else, or had borrowed it from a literary source, is of little importance, and Gogol's debt toward Pushkin, even if Pushkin did suggest that he use the anecdote, was very small indeed. The real problem is psychological: it is the problem of why Gogol found it necessary, ten years after Pushkin's death, to proclaim that he was obligated to him for the plots of his two major works: the *Inspector* and *Dead Souls.*

There is insufficient evidence either to prove or to disprove Gogol's account, in his *Confession,* of the genesis of *Dead Souls;* according to *Confession,* Pushkin urged Gogol to undertake a large work, and —

> . . . he gave me his own plot of which he wanted to make something like a poem himself, and which, in his own words, he would not have given to anyone else. This was the plot of *Dead Souls* (The idea of the *Inspector* also belongs to him) . . . Pushkin found that the plot of *Dead Souls* was good for me in that it gave me complete freedom to travel together with my hero across the whole of Russia and to present a multitude of most diverse characters.

A discrepancy appears at this point. If it was Pushkin who convinced Gogol that he must write a large work, and who "gave" him the plot of *Dead Souls,* pointing out the opportunity this plot offered of the hero's traveling throughout Russia, then it would be difficult to explain Gogol's announcing to Pushkin, in October 1835, that "the plot is stretching out into a very long novel". And it would be even more difficult to account for his announcing that he "would like to show in this novel all of Russia . . ." — for was this not precisely what Pushkin had suggested?

Another question may be asked: Pushkin gave Gogol "his own plot. . . ." But what is to be understood by "plot" — a general plan, or merely Chichikov's scheme (buying up "dead souls" from the landowners) — the pretext for the different episodes of which the novel consists?

The words attributed to Pushkin — that the advantage of the plot

182

was that "it gave an opportunity to travel together with my hero across the whole of Russia and to present a multitude of most diverse characters" — indicate that if Pushkin did "give" Gogol anything, it was only the fraudulent scheme, the pretext for Chichikov's journeys, that is, in the final analysis, another "anecdote". And, like the anecdote which became the plot of the *Inspector*, it was not original: several accounts are known of fraudulent operations with "dead souls."

In fiction, such an operation is described in a "long short story" by Vladimir Dal:

> During that year Vasili Ivanovich did only one sensible thing: he bought in the province up to two hundred dead souls, that is such as appeared as being in existence according to the last census of the population, but which were no more; for these deceased Vasili Ivanovich paid five to ten rubles a piece, had them registered in due form as settled on a tiny plot of marshy land he purchased for some 500 rubles, then mortgaged this property, for which he had all the documents required by law, with the Custody Council at the regular rate of 200 rubles the soul, and carried away 40,00 rubles, leaving it to the Council to take care of the swamp and of the deceased.

It has not been possible to establish the exact date of the publication of this story; it seems certain, however, that it was published before *Dead Souls*, but not early enough to have suggested his plot to Gogol. Whatever internal evidence is worth, it seems obvious that Dal would not have introduced the anecdote in his story after the publication of *Dead Souls*, especially since the episode, told for its own sake, is in no way connected with the action of the story.

There are also indications that Gogol's plot originated in the Ukraine. A story told by a distant relative of the Gogols is particularly convincing. According to this story, when landowners owning less than fifty "souls" were prohibited from distilling alcohol, a neighbor of the Gogols, one Pivinski, conceived the idea of buying "dead souls" in order to make up the required number. According to this testimony, Gogol visited the resourceful Pivinski whose scheme, moreover, was known to the entire district. Gogol may have seen Pivinski during the summers of 1832 or 1835 which he spent in Vasilyevka. There is much in *Dead Souls* that leads to the Ukraine and to Gogol's journeys between Petersburg, Moscow and Vasilyevka in the course of those summers.

The return trip in the fall of 1832 was particularly long owing to repeated breakdowns of the carriage. One of these mishaps immobilized Gogol for a "full week in . . . tedious and unbearable Kursk." It was during this involuntary stop in Kursk that Gogol gained whatever knowledge he had of the Russian provincial town.

Dead Souls opens, one may recall in this connection, with Chichikov's driving into the town of N. N., an event which causes two peasants standing in front of the pot-house to exchange the following comments:

> "See there," said one of them to the other, "that there wheel, what do you think, would that wheel make it, supposing, to Moscow, or wouldn't it?
> "'Twould make it," answered the other.
> "'Twould make it to Kazan, though — what do you say?"
> "No, not to Kazan, that it wouldn't," answered the other. And with the conversation ended.

The first draft of Gogol's "Petersburg Notes for 1836" (probably written soon after his return from the trip home in the summer of 1835), contains the following passage:

> "My! Look where it has been flung, the Russian capital! To the land of the Finn, to the very edge of the world!" I said to myself, turning back when low and even Petersburg had sunk below the horizon, and there they go, darting by, on either side of the road, mounds, charred stumps of pines, young fir sticking up in any odd way, over some sort of grayish-green ground. Like an arrow the higway flies trough this limitless expanse — an expanse of dried swamps. Tighter I wrap myself in my traveling cloak, and shut my eyes: enough of them, of these vistas! They are so many in Russia, that it's really too much.

In *Dead Souls,* Chichikov leaves the town — with his double, the author — who often reveals himself when his hero dozes off in his carriage:

> Now the cobbled street has come to an end, and the barrier and the town are behind, and now there's nothing, and again the road. And again on either side of the highway they go, darting by, mileposts, stationmasters, wells, caravans of carts, gray villages with samovars, peasant women . . .

The enumeration continues, and later in this passage, one of the most beautiful in the book, occur these lines:

184

The strangeness, and lure, and lightness, and wonder in this word: the road! And it is so wonderful, this road itself: a bright day, autumn leaves, the cool air . . . tighter you wrap yourself in your traveling cloak, and pull your cap on your ears, closer and snugger you huddle in the corner. For the last time a shiver runs through your limbs, and then it is replaced by a pleasant warmth.

The poetry of traveling in *Dead Souls* is clearly personal, and the motif of the traveling carriage rushing through space – and of space rushing by, with objects and people see in a succession of quick glimpses – first appears in the sketches of "Petersburg Notes".

The "Notes" also speak of Moscow, however, does not appear in his fiction; a description of a market in Moscow, in one of the drafts of *Dead Souls,* was deleted in the final version.

Chapter XIV

DEAD SOULS AND OVERCOAT

(THE AUTHOR AND HIS WORK)

Gogol was twenty-seven when he left Russia. By that time he had published *Evenings on a Farm near Dikanka, Arabesques,* and *Mirgorod;* his *Inspector-General* had been produced in Petersburg and in Moscow; he had written *The Marriage* (which he later revises); he had began and abandoned another comedy, *Vladimir of the Third Class,* and an historical drama, *Alfred;* he had written "The Nose" and "The Carriage"; he had published a number of essays and critical articles. And he had begun *Dead Souls.*

This was an impressive accomplishment. The only works of fiction conceived in later years were the unfinished novel *Rome* and one of his greatest achievevents, "The Overcoat." The years abroad were devoted to *Dead Souls* — it took Gogol six years to complete the first volume — to rewriting and revising some of his earlier works (especially *Taras Bulba* and "The Portrait"), to supplying others with glosses and epilogues which purported to reveal their concealed significance, and to writing various didactic and moralistic works.

The main genres of Gogol's work are represented, in a rudimentary form, in the very earliest phase of his creative development: Ukrainian demonology by "The Eve of St. John the Baptist" (1829); historical romance based on Cossack epic, by the earlier fragments of *The Hetman* (1830); humorous realism, by "The Tutor" (1830); and the fragments sketched in 1831 reflect Petersburg imagery. His later development suggests a biological process: a growth out of an embryo, or the evolvment of more complex and higer forms from lower ones. This embryo, or these rudimentary forms, containing all the potentialities of the future development.

During his Petersburg years, Gogol wrote about the Ukraine of the Cossacks, about the Ukraine of the time of his parents and grandparents, and about Petersburg. Only one of his stories, "The Carriage," and *The Inspector* dealt with provincial Russia. But provincial Russia was to be the scene of his major work, *Dead Souls*, of wich he carried with him the first two or three chapters when he left Russia for the second time. In *Dead Souls*, he wrote to Pushkin in October 1835, that he wanted to "show the whole of Russia, be it only from one side." A year later, in a letter to Zhukovski from Paris, he repeated: "The whole of Russia will appear in it!" Gogol had a very limited knowledge of Russia, yet at the very time when he undertook to portray " the whole of Russia," he chose to withdraw to a great distance from a "model" in his memory which he had scarcely studied.

Shortly before leaving Russia in a letter to Pogodin, Gogol stated the view that: "A contemporary writer, a comical writer, a writer of manners has to be far away from his native land." The reason for this, as the context of the letter indicates, was the hostility of his compatriots, of which he complained so bitterly. Some ten years later, in his *Confession* (1847) which was intended to justify, among other things, his expatriation, Gogol repeated this idea in a slihgtly modified form, and added other considerations which have a direct bearing on the problem of his creative method:

Nearly all writers who are not deprived of creativeness have the ability which I shall call imagination – the ability to evoke absent objects vividly, as if they were before our eyes. This ability is active in us only when we withdraw from the objects we depict. This is why poets chose, for the most part, epochs removed from us, and immersed themselves in the past. The past, detaching us from everything that surrounds us, puts the soul in that quiet, serene mood which is essential for creative work. I was never attracted by the past. My object was always the contemporary world and life in its present form. This was perhaps because I was always inclined to the substantial and to tangible usefulness. The further I advanced, the stronger became my desire to be a contemporary writer. But I saw at the same time that in depicting the contemporary world, one cannot maintain that elevated and serene mood which is essential for the creaation of a vast and harmonious work. The present is too much alive, too stirring, too provoking; the author's pen insensibly and unnoticeably slips into satire. In addition, when you are among the others and act more or less together with them, you see only those people who are close to you: you do not see the whole crowd, the mass, you cannot look over the whole. I began to think about how I could get out of the ranks among the others and find a place whence I could view the whole mass, and not only those standing beside me — how, by withdrawing from the present, I could, as it were, turn it for myself into the past.

This was to explain his expatriation: he needed peace and serenity. This artistic method, on the other hand, was one of recreation of the absent, and finally, by withdrawing from the agitation of the contemporary world, he made it static; he made it into a memory — and thus was able to reinterpret and to recreate this frozen reality in his art.

Even if much in this statement is rationalization and self justification, it certainly does express an essential feature of Cogol's personality: his tendency to view the work as static and, if possible, to reduce it to stagnation. His social and political philosophy was a philosophy of immobility; his refuge was Rome with its timelessness and immobility, and he "immobilized" contemporary Russia by withdrawing from it. He was a solipsist not rationally, but emotionally: nothing existed but his own self. The outside world and the others were denied the right to exist, to move; he had to be alone in a motionless world, in his own museum of wax figures, in which he finally perished.

Gogol shut off the source of living experience when he left Russia in June 1836, at the age of twenty-seven, to recreate an image of Russia from the material of his reminiscences. He did not need extensive experience to recreate the world of *Dead Souls:* his scant knowledge of provincial Russia proved sufficient. Later he attempted to renew his contact with reality, to broaden his experience, to become "a contemporary writer." The second volume of *Dead Souls* was to be a contemporary novel (which the first volume, quite obviously, was not).

Gogol's dilemma at this point became insoluble: on the one hand he strove to regain contact with social reality and to observe and depict social change; but on the other hand he clung to his withdrawal and disengagement. He sought a solution by demanding from his compatriots that they supply him with information and experience. Numerous requests were sent to his friends in Russia. Then — this was one of the grotesque interludes in Gogol's tragedy — in the Preface to the second edition of *Dead Souls* (1846), he made a public appeal: all his readers were invited to assist him in his effort by sharing with him their personal experiences, their observations, their knowledge of life in all its aspects, and even to communicate to him any ideas they might have on the further development of the plot of *Dead Souls* and on the destinies of the characters. Those who would respond to this appeal were instructed to put their messages in a double envelope, the exterior envelope

188

being addressrd either to the Rector of the University of St. Petersburg, P. A. Pletnyov, or to S. P. Shevyryov, professor of the Moscow University. The novel was growing into a project with a nation-wide participation.

A few examples of the methods of characterization in *Dead Souls* may reveal some of the aspects of the relation between Gogol's art and his experience.

One useful example is a character which appears in several of Gogol's works: the elderly landed proprietress, the busy housewife, a matriarch ruling over a household engaged in preparing an abundance of food. The male, if he is not altogether absent, plays a purely passive role in this beehive. This generic character is obviously based on observations made in Vasilyevka and its environs; whether the prototype was Gogol's mother, his grandmother, an aunt or a neighbor, is, of course, completely irrelevant.

The character first appears in "The Tutor," a fragment written not later than 1830; the "tutor" is in the employ of an elderly widow who leads a very busy life:

> The whole day, from five in the morning until six in the evening, that is until it was time to retire, was one uninterrupted chain of activities. Before seven o'clock in the morning, she would have inspected all the domestic establishments, from the kitchen to the cellars and the store-room, would have found the time to scold the bailiff, and give feed to the chickens and the home-bred geese of which she was particularly fond. Before dinner, which was never served later than noon, she would turn into the bakery and would even herself bake some loaves or some rolls of a special kind, made with honey and eggs, the mere odor of which produced an inexpressible emotion in the pedagogue who was impassionately concerned with whatever provides sustenance for the spiritual and for the bodily nature of man. And is there not enough to keep a mistress busy between dinner time and evening, what with wool dyeing, and measuring homespun, and cucumber salting, and making preserves, and sweetening fruit brandies? How many skills, secrets and domestic recipes were put into operation during those hours!

In "Ivan Fyodorovich Shponka and His Auntie" (one of the *Evenings* stories), the auntie, a burly spinster in her fiftees, is a matriaarch endowed with extraordinary virility, a feature which her nephew lacks completely. Her benevolent tyranny creates the basic situation in the story. But with all her masculinity, ainte Vasilisa is a housewife performing with great energy her feminine functions: she prepares great amounts of food, preserves, homespun, etc.

The next incarnation of the prototype is Pulkheriya Ivanovna in "Old-Time Squires" (*Mirgorod*). Once more, the generic type is endowed with individual characteristics required by the situation. The story is an idyll. and its protagonists an old, childless couple. Their lives, warmed with love and mutual devotion, are centered around cooking and eating: complecated age-old recipes, culinary refinements, fruit-brandies, and brandies infused with medicinal herbs are a cultural heritage, and the sumbolic language expressing their emotions. Kind old Pulkheriya has none of the masculinity of auntie Vasilisa; she alone, nevertheless, has control over the household and the entire property:

Afanasi Ivanovich concerned himself very little with the manegement of the estate, even if sometimes he went out to the mowers and the reapers and looked at their work rather intently; all the burden of government rested upon Pulkheriya Ivanovna.

One may note the following descriptive details among those not dealing with culinary interests:

The walls in the rooms were adorned with several pictures, large ones and small ones, in antiqeated, narrow frames . . . There were two large size portraits in oil. One represented some archbishop, the other one, Peter III. Out of a narrow frame peered a flyspecked Duchesse de La Valliere.

Most remarkable in the house were the singing doors. As soon as morning came, the chanting of the doors resounded throughout the house. I couldn't say for what reason they sang . . . but the remarkable thing is that each door had its own particular voice; the door leading to the bedroom sang in the thinnest of trebles; the door that led to the dining room wheezed in a basso; but the one that was on the porch emitted some kind of a strangely jarring, and at the same time moaning sound, so that listening to it carefully, one could hear quite distinctly: Heavens, I'm freezing!

[When the old squire's antiquated droshki set into motion] . . . the air quivered with strange sounds, such that one heard at one and the same time a flute, and a tambourine, and a drum; every nail or iron cramp produced such a jingle that one could hear all the way to the windmills that the lady was driving out.

The last representative of the generic type is the widowed landed proprietress Korobochka in *Dead Souls,* the most complete but also the least individualized in the series of housewives. Many of the motifs and descriptive details of the chapter dealing with Korobochka can be traced to "Old-Time Squires." Thus, the portraits of the archbeshop and of Peter III (and also the "rug before the divan with birds resembling flowers, and flowers resembling birds" and "between the windows, antiquated little mirrors in dark frames fashioned like curled up leaves." In Old-Time Squires": ". . . a mirror in a narrow gilded frame carved with leaves . . ." And further:

> Glancing around the room, he now noticed that there were not only birds on the pictures: among them hung a portrait of Kutuzov done in oils and one of an old man with red cuffs on his uniform coat, of the kind worn in the days of Emperor Paul.

More important than the simple repetitions or similarities, which are numerous, is the new treatment of the motifs previously used. The "singing doors" or the "jingling drozhki" motif appears in two variants in Chapter III of *Dead Souls:*

> The hostess's words were interrupted by a strange hissing, and for a moment the visitor took fright; the noise was such as if the room were full of snakes; but glancing upward he was reassured, for he realized that the wall clock had taken the fancy to strike the hour. After the hissing, immediately came a wheezing, and at long last, straining with all its might, it struck two, with a noise such as if someone were hammering cracked earthenware with a stick, whereupon the pendulum tranquilly went on clicking right and left.

In the description of the "singing doors" ("Old-Time Squires"), animism is suggested (the "treble," the "basso," the jarring and moaning voice); in *Dead Souls* the motif of sounds or noises suggesting the beings that produce them is developed with great elaboration, becoming an extended animistic metaphor:

> In the meantime, the dogs carried on in every voice imaginable: one of them, thrusting his head up, drawled out his tune with such application as if he were getting God knows what salary for it; another one banged away in a hurry, like a sexton; in their midst an indefatigable treble, probably belonging to a

191

young puppy, jingled like a mail coach bell. And all of this was topped by a bass, perhaps of one in advanced age, or simply endowed with a mighty dog's nature, for he rumbled like a basso in a choir when the performance is at its height, the tenors rise on tip-toe, eager to bring out a high note, and all and sundry stretch upward, throwing their heads back, while he alone, thrusting his unshaven chin into his cravat, squatting and sinking almost to the ground, from where he lets out his note which makes the windowpanes chake and jingle.

The "singing doors" in the "Old-Time Squires" are primitive compared to this canine choir; the complexity of the description is extraordinary: the auditory impression (the dogs are not seen, but "guessed") leads to the first visual images (accompanied by similes: sexton, mail coach bell), then the bass as transition to the animistic metaphor applied to the whole "choir," to a picture reminiscent of the manner of a Cruikshank, or a Daumier, or of Agin, the very talented illustrator of *Dead Souls* whose work Gogol chose to ignore.

During his visit to Korobochka, Chichikov is offered abundant food. But instead of the infinite details and nomenclatures of "Old-Time Squires," the descriptions of food in the Korobochka chapter are based on selection: Chichikov is offered a great variety of pastries, pancakes, and pies with various fillings. This collection of soft and plump eatables is supplemented by the description of a monumental feather bed into which Chichikov sinks, causing clouds of feathers to fly over the room.

The jingling drozhki of the scene of Korobochka's driving into the town:

. . . through the remote streets and by-lanes of the town jingled along a most bizarre vehicle which would make anyone wonder as to the name it could be given. It resembled neither a tarantass, nor a calash nor yet a shay, but rather it looked like a round-cheeked, bulging watermelon set upon wheels. The cheeks of this watermelon, that is to say, the doors, which bore traces of yellow paint, did not shut properly by reason of the sad condition of the handles and catches, and were fixed, as well as they could be, with some rope. The watermelon was filled with chintz cushions shaped like pouches, or bolsters, or cimply cushions, and was stuffed with bags containing loaves of bread, scones, cakes and dumplings made from steamed dough. A chicken pie and a giblet pie were even sticking out of it . . . The noise and screech from the iron clamps and the rusty bolts aroused, at the other end of the town, a sentry in his box who picked up his halberd and, though only half awake, shouted at the top of his voice: "Who goes there?" . . .

The jingling traveling contraption of the "Old-Time Squires" is combined here with the Korobochka leitmotif of rotundity; it is a watermelon packed full of plump and soft objects, the pies and pillows mentioned in an earlier chapter.

Thus, in the characterization of Korobochka, Gogol uses old motif and factual data, probably for the most part of Ukrainian provenance. There is, in the portrayal of Korobochka, practically no Great-Russian *couleur locale* and it is obvious that the imagery in the chapter is not based on direct observation: this imagery is composed, it is made of elements selected for their symbolic expressiveness and arranged in complex patterns of a highly metaphoric style.

The comparison between similar motifs appearing in "Old-Time Squires" and in *Dead Souls* shows that Gogol moved from a more objective method; descriptive details are hyperbolized, similes merely suggested in the story become extended metaphors in the multi-plane structure of *Dead Souls,* selected symbols forming leitmotifs more and more take the place of objective description.

The resulting impression is not one of real experience; despite all the concreteness and tangibility of the details and the triviality of the subject matter, there is a dreamlike quality in the scene because it is told in a language of symbols: the pillows and pies in Korobochka's carriage are not things, but "shows of things": in the real world round and soft things do not assemble to characterize their owner, they have to be selected, or recreated, or invented. Writing *Dead Souls* in Vevey, in Paris, or in Rome, Gogol "evoked absent objects"; "present objects," with their density and their own dimensions, would have been a less suitable material for Gogol; he had to be free from the "immediate."

A brief analysis of another characterization may be added, that of Manilov. Manilov is the personification of vacuity; he is completely deprived of will power or of any personal opinion, agreeing with anyone and with anything; he is given to daydreaming; he is a cloyingly sweet husband and host; his speech abounds in old-fashioned sentimental clichés which dessolve in a haze of unfinished sentences and incomplete thoughts. The first impression he produces is that of a nice and kind person; then one feels indifference and finally deadly boredom; he is one of those people who are known as "neither one thing or another."

The following landscape is introduced when Chichikov approaches Manilov's estate:

In the distance a pine forest loomed dark, in some kind of a dull bluish hue. Even the weather had made itself altogether fitting: the day was not exactly clear, nor was it gloomy, but it was of a kind of a light-gray color . . .

After a copious luncheon, Chichikov is led into the host's "study":

"Delightful little place," said Chichikov casting his glance over it. The room actually did not want for pleasantness: the walls were painted a kind of a light-bluish color, rather on the grayish side . . .

During the long conversation with Chichikov, Manilov continually smokes his long-stemmed choubouk. Smoking is discussed at length before Chichkov turns to business matters, and the motif of smoking accompanies the conversation. In embarrassment Manilov drops his pipe, then picks it up but

Try as he may to reach a solution and decide what to do, all Manilov could think of was to let out of his mouth, in a very thin stream, the smoke that remained there.

And at another point:

Manilov was altogether at a loss. He felt that he had to do something, to put a question, but what question — the devil if he knew. He wound up at long last by letting out some smoke once more, but through his nostrlls.

Further, in his effort to grasp the situation,

Manilov instead of replying, started to suck at his choubouk so violently that finally it began to wheeze like a bassoon. It seemed as if he were trying to draw from it an opinion concerning the very extraordinary circumstance; but the choubouk wheezed, and that was all.

Thus bluish-gray and tobacco smoke (which is bluish-gray) are leitmotifs in the characterization of Manilov. The chapter ends in a gigantic puff of tobacco smoke: Manilov's fantasy about some kind of a glorious existence he will lead with his friend Chichikov, the fantasy itself dissolving at the end, like a puff of smoke, in utter vacuity.

Manilov is "composed" and symbolically characterized. His style

194

(the sentimental clichés) and the "Temple of Solitary Meditation" in the garden ("with a flat green cupola and light blue columns") is a reminiscence of Vasili Afanasyevich, of the landscape painted by Gogol in Nezhin, and generally of the Karamzinian affectations of Gogol's young years.

At one point, wishing to express the immense joy coused by Chichikov's visit, Manilov speaks of a "day in May, a jubilee of the heart..." –

> Chichikov, hearing that matters had actually now reached the jubilee of the heart, began to feel somewhat embarrassed, and replied with modesty that he could claim neither renown, nor even a distinguished rank.

The "heart" is very frequent in Gogol's letters of the Nezhin days: one may recall his letter to his mother, of June 1825, offering her a present which, he felt certain, she will prefer to any other one – the present of his heart all aflame with the most tender love for her.

In the characterization of Sobakevich, Gogol reveals his device:

> Chichikov glanced around the room once more, and everything in it without exception – everything was solid, clumsy in the extreme, and bore a kind of strange resemblance to the landlord himself.

The device is somewhat vulgarized here. In most instances Gogol did no use direct resemblance, but very subtle associative relations between characters and objects.

A curious detail in the description of Sobakevich's house are the portraits in the drawing room – this time of "Greek generals," the heroes of the war of independence: Mavrocordato, Colocotronis, Mioulis, Kanaris. The war aroused great interest in Russia in the 1820's, but for Gogol it was a personal, not only an historical reminiscence.

One of the "Greek generals" is mentioned in *Hans Kuchelgarten;* he is referred to in the course of a conversation about current events: ". . . about the Greeks and the Turks, about Missolonghi, and the war, and the glorious leader Colocotronis . . . *Hans Kuchelgarten* leads to Nezhin; in Nezhin there was an important Greek colony which was in contact, through Odessa, with the Greek insurgents. Among Gogol's classmates were several young Greek refugees; one of them, Constantine Bazili, was a close friend of his. In March 1827, in one of his letters to Vysotski, Gogol gave a detailed humorous account of political agitation in the Greek colony. There can be no doubt that the names of the Greek leaders were familiar to Gogol in his Nezhin years, and it is very likly that he sow their portraits.

Artistically the use of the name Colocotronis in *Hans Kuchelgarten* is uninteresting and ineffective; and it is "realistic" in the sense that this name was likely to be mentioned in the 1820's in a discussion of political news. The presence of the gallery of portraits in Sobakevich's house, on the contrary, produces an artistic effect: its aesthetic justification is precisely in its incongruity. This, consequently, is another "composed" image — made of "absent objects," of old memories which Gogol "evoked" to give life to a picture of his invention.

In the middle forties Gogol began to compile a textbook of literature. He did not complete this project, but in the notes which he left are several definitions of literary genres, among them the following definition of what he called "The Minor Genres of the Epic":

In the new ages originated a genre of narrative composition occupying, as it were, an intermediate place between the novel and the epic, the hero of which is a person although private and unimportant, but in many ways significant for the observer of the human soul. The author conducts his life through a chain of adventures and transformations with the purpose of presenting at the same time a living and accurate picture of all the significant features and manners of the period chosen, that earthly, almost statically seized picture of the faults, abuses and vices and of everything capable of attracting the glance of an observant contemporary who seeks a lesson for the present in the past, in bygone times. Such works appeared from time to time with many nations. Many of them, although written in prose, may nevertheless be counted among poetical creations. They do not have universality, but they may and do have a full epic scope, wich is manifest in particular episodes . . . Thus Ariosto depicted an almost fantastic passion for adventure and for the marvelous . . . and Cervantes derided the passion for adventures . . . which survived in certain people . . . It [their central idea] was ever present in their minds and therefore acquired a well-considered, strict significance . . . conferring on their works the character of minor epics despite the facetious tone, the levity, and even the fact that one of them is written in prose.

It is not difficult to recognize in this definition Gogol's own *Dead Souls*,which, without mentioning it, he places beside *Orlando Furioso* and *Don Quixote*. The implicit comparison with *Don Quixote* is repeated in *The Confession* in which Pushkin is made to speak of Cervantes in connection with Gogol:

> He had long been urging me to undertake a work of large proportions, and at last, when I once read to him a little description of a little scene, which impressed him, however, more than anything I had read to him previously, he said to me:"How is it that with this ability to guess a man, and with a few strokes, suddenly to make him stand out as if he were alive, how can you, with this ability, not undertake a large work? This is simply a disgrace!" And after this he began to represent to me my feeble constitution, my ailments which might early put an end to my life; he quoted the example of Cervantes who, although he had written several remarkable and very good stories, but who would never have occupied the place he now holds among writers, had he not undertaken his *Don Quixote,* and as a conclusion of all this he gave me his own plot out of which he wanted to make something like a poem himself, and which, in his words, he would not have given to anyone else. This was the plot of *Dead Souls.*

Pushkin, consequently, if one is to believe this not very convincing account, designated Gogol as the Russian Cervantes, and even supplied him with the plot of the Russian *Don Quixote.* If the comparison is to be made at all,it may be observed that Gogol's hero resembles Sancho Panza rather than Don Quixote; but it is the author-image in *Dead Souls* which, perhaps,could be regarded as the counterpart of the hero of Cervantes.

Dead Souls was obviously one of the "minor epics" for Gogol; in his textbook he also supplied a definition of the epic (without qualifications) — according to him the greatest, the most complete and the most universal of all narrative and dramatic genres. But, he adds, after the *Iliad* and the *Odyssey,* the universality and the scope of the true epic have scarcely ever been attained. These remarks seem to reflect Gogol's reaction to the polemics between Konstantin Aksakov and Belinski apropos of Aksakov's statement, vigorously attacked by Belinski, that Gogol re-created the epic genre which had been dead since the days of Homer. With his own peculiar brand of modesty, Gogol seems to reply to his immoderately enthusiastic admirer, Konstantine Aksakov, that he is not another Homer and that there can be no other Homer. His work belongs to a new genre which originated in the new age, a genre intermediate between the Homeric epic and the novel, to which *Orlando Furioso* and *Don Quixote* also belong. The "minor epic," a genre intermediate between the Homeric epic and the novel, is moreover superior to the novel, which "cannot be a high poetical creation. A novel is not an epic. Like the drama it is a work all too conventional." The novel, Gogol pointed out, needs a tightly knit plot and a denouement; it is a whole, built around the fate of the hero; "the novel does not take life in its entirety, but only a remarkable occurence from life. . . ."

And finally, Gogol insist in his definition of the "minor epic" that it is a poetic genre "despite the facetious tone, the levity, and even the fact that one of them [the minor epics] is written in prose." "One of them" is *Don Quixote;* another one is obviously *Dead Souls,* also written in prose, but subtitled by its author "a poem."

This subtitle is justified not because of its "idea" of "significance" (which, according to Gogol, make the minor epic a poetic work), but because it is lyric as much as it is narrative or epic; it is lyric in the precise sense of Gogol's definition of lyric poetry, given in his unfinished textbook:

> Lyric poetry is the portrait, the reflection, the mirror of the highest movement of the poet's own soul, his most essential notations, the biography of his ecstasies. In its highest as in its lowest forms, it is but an account of the emotions of the poet himself.

There is much in *Dead Souls* which is directly, overtly, "an account of the emotions of the poet himself," but not all the personal appearances of the author in *Dead Souls* are purely lyrical; these perconal appearances, or digressions, are functionally different, and there is not one, but several, author-images in *Dead Souls.*

The author-image appeared more than once in Gogol's earlier work, before it was developed in the very complex structure of *Dead Souls.* One may distinguish several variants of the author-image in Gogol's work. In the earlier Ukrainian stories (collected in the *Evenings on a Farmstead near Dikanka*), individualized, fictionalized narrators are introduced — actually fictional characters whose role in a story is to tell it. The narrative itself is stylized (not always consistently, however) in order to support the characterization of the fictious narrator, completely dissociated from the real author.

In "Old-Time Squires" (*Mirgorod*) the narrator is also present —

198

the story is told in the first person — but he is not directly characterized. The style is literary, it does not imitate oral narration by a local character (the *skaz* manner, to use the Russian term, is here abandoned). The story, however, is presented as a real occurrence, a reminiscence of the author who introduces himself as a pseudo-witness of the events described. Furthermore, if not characterized "from the outside," the narrator is not impersonal; he suggests a "sentimental traveler," and certain Karamzinian features are obvious in the style of the narration. The opening paragraphs state the narrator's attitude toward the world of the old-time squires from which he diissociates himself. The following passage from the beginning of the story (partly quoted earlier) is significant:

> I like to descend sometimes for a moment into the sphere of this life so completely withdrawn where no desire extends beyond the paling around the small yard, beyond the fence of a garden full of apples and prunes; beyond the surrounding village huts standing atilt in the shade of willows, elders and pear trees. The life of their modest owners is quiet, so quiet that for a moment one is conquered by the illusion that passions, desires and those disturbing creations of the evil spirit which agitate the world, do not exist at all, and you merely saw them in a bright, glittering dream.

And further:

> Their faces sometimes appear before me even now, in the noise of the crowd, amidst fashionable tail-coats, and then something like a drowsiness overcomes me, and it seems to me that once again I see the past. Their faces express so much kindness, such hospitality and candor, that you cannot help renounce, be it only for a short while, all your bold dreams, and imperceptibly with all your feelings you join them in their lowly bucolic life.

This lyrical digression (or "lyrical introduction") expresses the narrator's emotions connected with the story he tells. They are perceived as supporting the fictional structure and as part of it. It may be remarked, however, that the passage also has a real autobiographical significance as a reflection of Gogol's attitude towards the vanished idyll of Ukrainian country life.

In the "Quarrel" the author-image appears in a short epilogue added to the story: it is not associated with the narrative process. The narrator is not individualized, but of some of the earlier stories of the *Evenings*. The "first person" is used only in the epilogue which begins as follows:

199

Some five years back I drove through the town of Mirgorod. It was a bad time for traveling. Autumn was there with its depressingly damp weather, its mud and its mist . . . I used to be much influenced by the weather in those days: I would be gloomy when it was gloomy. But despite this, as I approached Mirgorod, I felt that my heart began to beat stronger. My God, how many memories! . . .

After a meeting with the two protagonists, the author continues his journey:

The rain poured in torrents onto the Jew who sat on the box covered with a bast mat. I felt the dampness penetrate me to the marrow. The sad looking barrier with a sentry box, in which a veteran was repairing his gray coverings, swept slowly by. Then once more the same fields, green in some places, dug up and black in others, wet jackdaws and crows, monotonous rain, the sky hopelessly shedding its tears. – It's dull in this world of ours, gentlemen!

The author-image, independent from the narration, is first introduced in the lyrical digression of the finale: the author's emotions change the key of the story and thus the "disengagement" is realized: the characters and the situations of the story are removed, they dissolve as the author moves away from the world of the story which is not his creation.

It may be noted that both in "Old-Time Squires" and in the "Quarrel" the author-image with which the lyrical passages are associated is the image of a traveler who visits the scene, but who belongs to a different world, far distant from the world of his characters, essentially static, from which he is free to withdrow.

In *Dead Souls* the author-image and the lyrical motifs are developed with great force and combine with the narration in a pattern which may be approximately described as a rogue novel which is at the same time a sentimental journey. The traveler is Chichikov, but the Poet accompanies him, and during the travels the poetic author-image often takes the place of the hero: the road and swift motion are that special milieu in which this image manifests itself most often. During the stops, the scenes in the static world, the author usually conceals himself and becomes the anonymous narrator.

One may distinguish three main types of the author's interventions in the generally impersonal narration.

200

To the first type belong remarks addressed to the reader, introductory, explanatory, etc., which have to do with, and comment on, the narrative process, e. g.:

But the reader will learn all this gradually in due time if he will only have the patience to read the account presented to him, a very long one, and which later on will unfold . . .

or:

It would do no harm if the reader were introduced to these domestics of our hero. Although naturally, they are not very prominent characters, but are what is known as second or even third-rate; although the movement and the springs of the poem rest upon others, and they may, perhaps, touch them or catch them only here or there — but the author has an especial liking for being circumstantial in all matters, and in this respect, despite the fact that he is Russian, he wishes to be as thorough as a German. This, however, will not take up much time or space, because there is but little to be added . . .

Or, when Chichikov dozes off in his carriage:

The author must confess that he is actually quite happy about this as the circumstance is an opportunity for him to say something about his hero; for hitherto, as the reader has seen, he has constantly been distracted . . .

These comments on the narrative process, for the most part humorous, were not only often used, but often parodied (as they are by Gogol) in eighteenth-century prose (of Sterne or Fielding); they slow down the action and maintain the suspense, suggesting at the same time that the author and the reader are playing a game which amuses them both.

A different type of the author's interventions are the moralistic remarks or discourses on some topic connected with the story. These digressions usually assume a pseudo-serious tone and present some general verities and considerations on the mores of contemporary society, on Russian national traits, etc. An example may be found in the following passage:

It must be said that if we have not yet caught up with foreigners in a thing or two in Russia, we are far ahead of them in the art of dealing with different people. There is no counting all the shades and refinements in our manners. A

201

Frenchman or a German could never in his liftime grasp and understand all the peculiarities and distinctions; he will use nearly the same voice and language addressing a millionaire and the owner of a wretched little tobacco–shop, although, naturally he will duly humble himself before the former. But with us it is different; we have people so judicious that they will speak in a way quite different to a squire who owns two hundred souls than the way they will use with one who owns three hundred, and with the owner of three hundred they will not speak at all as they would with the owner of five hundred . . .

The third type, finally, is the lyrical digression proper, a poetic expression of emotions which are not attributed, or attributable to, any one of the characters; such are the long rhytmic, song–like passages in the last chapter devoted to traveling; the traveler is Chichikov, the emotions and their expression, however, are dissociated from him, they are freed from the "character" and are generalized in poetry which stems directly from the author.

These main types of comment in the first person or of the author's interventions as moralist or as lyricist occur in *Dead Souls* in the more or less traditional forms, but in some instances, they are unusually broad in scope, and the author–image appearing in these passages becomes more and more personal. The traditional comments on the progress of the story (the author speaking in his special capacity of the author of the narration in progress) grow into long discourses on the choice of the hero, on the author and his audience, or on the future developments of the work. As distinct from this image of the "Author of *Dead Souls*," there appears a more intimate image of the author as a human being – and a lyric poet – not directly connected with the story, speaking in his own name about himself and his emotions.

The most complete purely lyrical digression is the long passage introducing Chapter VI on the poet's bygone youth; as in the epilogue of the "Quarrel." The "author–image" in this passage is detached from the narration, the "author," or the "poet" is not technically the narrator. In this passage, he steps down from his commanding position, he forgets his duties of narrator and abandons himself to reminiscence and introspection.

The next, seventh, chapter is introduced by the very long digression in which a parallel is traced between the universally worshipped and adulated writer who chooses the "exeptional," the heroic for his subject matter, and the writer who depicts the drab triviality of everyday life: he is mocked insulted by his contemporaries; he is a homeless wanderer treading lonely path. This is no longer the Poet abandoning himself to the melancholy of reminiscence or to an elated feeling of nature. The monologue introduces a different author-image: the concrete image, and the personal tragedy, of the author of *Dead Souls,* the artist whom his contemporaries persecute and insult because they are insulted by his art, an art they are unable to understand. This is once more Gogol facing the "shouting mob," threatened by a revolt of his wax-figures – the "existers."

The ego motifs and the ego ideals invaded more and more *Dead Souls,* as the work advanced, and finally, overflowing it during the struggle with the second volume, produced the didactic *Correspondence* and ratiocinating *Confession.*

Inspector – the first "contemporary" work, followed by the first revolt of the "existers," a revolt more imaginary than real, was a play – and on the stage there is no room for the author; but Gogol added to his comedy a dramatized epilogue, "Leaving the Theter." The stage in this epilogue represented the lobby of the theater after a performance of *Inspector,* and in this lobby the author appeared in the midst of the spectators, listening to their comments. But the part of the author mingling with the crowd would, naturally, be played by an actor.

In *Dead Souls,* the intrusion of the author's ego and of his personal tragedy make for the artistic greatness of the work.

Gogol writes in his *Confession:*

> I had begun to write without determining for myself a detailed plan, without deciding just what the hero himself lead me to varied persons and characters; that the desire to laugh which arose in me would generate of itself a multitude of funny situations which I intended to mingle with others that would be touching.

One may find some corroboration of this in his letter to Zhukovski, from Paris, November 12, 1836, with an account of the months he spent on Lake Geneva:

> A beautiful fall finally set in Vevey, it was almost like summer. Now it was warm in my room, and I took up *Dead Souls,* which I had begun in Petersburg. I reworked all I had done and gave more consideration to the whole plan, and now I am advancing it calmly, like a chronicle.

Gogol "gave more consideration" to the plan at this stage, but it seems certain that no definite solution of the problem was found. And further in the same letter, Gogol wrote: "Another Leviathan is being conceived . . . but now I am entirely plunged in *Dead Souls.*" The "Leviathan" was perhaps at that time independent from *Dead Souls,* but later on it was to become the grandiose project of its sequence. It is important, in any case, that even during the writing of the first volume, there loomed in Gogol's mind another project, a "super-*Dead Souls,*" and this great work, placed as an ideal reality above the one produced, is reflected and announced in the text of the Chichikov story.

In his *Confession,* Gogol continues the account of this work on *Dead Souls,* "begun without a plan," as follows:

> But at every step I was stopped by the questions: what for? what is the purpose of this? what is this or that character to express? what is this or that scene to signify? . . . I saw clearly that I could no longer write without a perfectly clear and definite plan, that it is ncccesary that one explane well to oncself the purpose of one's work, its substantial usefulness and urgent need, so that, following this, the author may himself flare up with a true and powerful love for his labor.

Whether Gogol's problem was actually one of "purpose" or of "usefulness," it is true that at first he simply abandoned himself to his narration which developed instinctively, spontaneously, and impersonally, and that later the author became more and more conscious of himself with regard to his story — and his preoccupations with the significance of his work for himsilf and for others materialized in the intrusions of the author-image. The various "digressions" develop in the latter half of the first volume, the narrator performing a function and becoming more and more a real person with his own drama.

The greatness of Gogol's masterpiece is perhaps precisely in its lack of a plan: it is not "finished," it is not a closed composition, The principle of the art of the novel is expansion, as E. M. Forster puts it, not completion:

> Not rounding off but opening out. When the symphony is over, we feel that the notes and atunes composing it have been liberated, they have found their individual freedom in the rhythm of the whole.

Dead Souls "opens out" onto the tremendously expanded author-image, liberating the "tunes" — the characters and the situations; they had been given freedom in the concluding pages of the first volume, and could not be harnessed once more to continue the performance in more chapters or volumes.

Chapter XV

O, DO NOT DEPART FROM ME, MY GENIUS!

From his early days, Gogol had the feeling that he was chosen for an exceptional destiny, and he was called to perform a great mission of universal significance. He variously associated this duty or this urge to perform a great task with the image of a superior being symbolizing both the will that commanded him to perform his task and the source of the power he needed to fulfill it.

The consciousness of the superior being within him – of his super-ego – is expressed in a striking form in the letter to his mother, already quoted, written on March 24, 1827. The approach of spring recalled various memories to his mind, among others that of the pleasure of gardening in Vasilyevka (and this was the first recollection of the letters of his father since his death two years earlier):

It [gardening] was the favorite exercise of dear father, my friend, benefactor, solacer . . . I do not know what name to give to this heavenly angel, this pure, exalted creature who inspires me on my arduous path, vivifying me, bestowing upon me the gift of self-cognizance, and who often, during moments of grief, enters me like a heavenly flame, illuminating the clouds of my meditations. At such moments it is sweet for me to be with him, I peer into him, that is into myself, as into the heart of a friend. I test my strength for undertaking a task important and noble – for the good of the country, for the happiness of citizens, for the benefit of fellow men, and until now hesitant and diffident (and for good reason), I flare up in a flame of proud self-consciousness, and it is as if my soul saw this unearthly angel, giving me an implacable guidance to everything in my avid quest . . .

The "avid quest" is given a definite object here; the exalted lines are followed by the somewhat anticlimactic words: "In a year I will enter government service." But the goal could vary, and what is of greater importance is the idealized and completely unreal image of the dead father – the "unearthly angel" who lives with him in a

mystic communion: ". . . he enters me like a heavenly flame . . ."
". . . I peer into him, that is into myself . . ." This mysterious being provides both strength and "implacable guidance" — which suggests not only assistance, but also compulsion.

This letter maybe contrasted with the text written by Gogol some seven years later, his prayer or incantation addressed to the coming year 1834:

> Great, solemn moment. God, how the waves of diverse feelings are merged and crowded around it! . . . No, this is not a dream. It is the fatal, the inescapable boundary between reminiscence and hope . . . Reminiscence is no more, it is flying by, it is overpowered by hope. At my feet is the tumult of my past; above me, through a mist, the future shines undecipherably. I pray thee, life of my soul, my guardian Angel, my Genius! O, do not conceal thyself from me! Wake over me at this moment, and do not depart from me this year which nears so luringly. What wilt thou be, my future? Brilliant, broad, seething for me with great deeds, or . . . O, be brilliant, be industrious, devoted to labor and to peace! But why dost thou rise so mysteriously before me, year 1834? Thou too — be my angel. If indolence and apathy dared approach me, were it only for a short while, oh, then awaken me! Do not let them overpower me! May thy eloquent numbers stand before me like a never silent time-piece, like conscience, so that each of thy figures strike my ear stronger than the tocsin! Thay like a galvanic rod it produce a convulsive shock in my whole being. . . . . .I do not know what name to give thee, my Genius! Thou who, ever since I was in my cradle, hast been flying past, thy songs of harmony reaching my ears, who hast engendered in me thoughts so marvelous, and hitherto unexplained, and nurtured in me limitless and rapturous dreams! O, glance at me! Fair one, cast down upon me thy divine glance. I am on my knees. I am at thy feet! O, do not part from me! Live on this earth with me be it but for two hours every day, like my fair brother! I shall fulfill . . . O, bestow upon me thy kiss and thy blessing.

The Being within, which gives him guidance and inspiration, is no longer Father: it is now an anonymous spirit, or his personal Genius. The prayer is the prayer of a poet for inspiration, but in Gogol's subjective symbolism, "Genius" acquires a concrete significance, a mystical reality. Serving mankind, in the government or otherwise, is not mentioned in the prayer; the ideal of government service did not survive the first contact with reality, and the task of serving mankind through moral and religious edification was to be undertaken later. For the time being the poet abandoned himself to his creative genius.

The themes of predestination and of great achievement often reappear in later years; when Gogol left Russia after the crisis of the *Inspector,* he wrote to Zhukovski from Hamburg, which he reached in June 1836:

How should I not be grateful to Him who sent me to this earth! Such lofty, such solemn sensations, imperceptible, invisible to the world, fill my life! I swear, I will do something that an ordinary man would not do. I sense a leonine strength in my soul! . . . O how much inscrutably marvelous meaning there was in all the happenings and circumstances of my life. How salutary for me were all the misfortunes and vexations . . . I can say that I never sacrificed my talent to the world. No distraction, no passion were able to take possession of my soul were it only for a single minute, nor to turn me away from my duty. There is no life for me outside of my life, and my present removal from the fatherland − it was ordained from above, by the same Providence that sends everything to educate me.

The great "duty," the great task he is required to perform will be identified for many years to come with *Dead Souls,* the first chapters of which he carried with him when he left Russia.

In November 1836, in another letter to Zhukovski, Gogol reported on the progress of *Dead Souls* and on the inception of "another Leviathan:"

A sacred tremor shakes me in advance when I think of it; can I hear anything of it yet? I shall live divine moments . . . but . . . for the present I am all plunged into *Dead Souls.* Colossally great is my creation, and its end is remote. They will yet rise against me − more classes and many different gentlemen; but what is to be done! It is my destiny to wage war with my compatriots. Patience! Someone invisible writes before me with a powerful wand. I know that after me my name will be luckier than myself, and the descendants of the very same compatriots, perhaps with tears moistening their eyes, will address words of reconciliation to my shadow.

Once more: the "shouting mob" and the appreciative posterity of Hans Küchelgarten, and the mysterious power ("someone invisible") whose dictates he follows. During the following years the sequel to

Dead Souls, the volumes to come, were called "something colossal," his labor "important and great," and what was known of his work (i.e. the first volume) – merely a "vestibule of the palace which is being built within me." The subject of *Dead Souls* is "for the time being a secret which suddenly, to the amazement of everyone (for not one single reader has guessed it), will be disclosed in the subsequent volumes . . ."

The theme of being chosen and committed to deliver a prophetic message to mankind sounds with great force in the very text of the first volume of *Dead Souls*:

And for a long time to come I have been preordained by a prodigious power to march hand in hand with my strange heroes, to keep my gaze on the whole of the gigantically streaming life, to gaze at it through a laughter perceptible to the world, and through tears invisible to it and ignored! And far distant is yet that time when in another surge the awesome storm of inspiration will rise from a head enveloped in sacred horror and radiance, and when trembling and abashed they will harken to other words coming to them like a majestic thunder.

What actually came instead of the thundering prophecy was the somewhat dampened explosion of the *Correspondence* (and more visits of more landowners in the surviving chapters of the second volume of *Dead Souls*). But again: he is "preordained by a prodigious power . . ."

In connection with the work on *Dead Souls*, the mysterious force within him (Father, personal Genius, Divine Providence) became associated with Pushkin, who died some six months after Gogol left Russia. When the news of Pushkin's death reached him in Rome, Gogol wrote to Pletnyov, on March 16, 1837:

All the delight of my life, all the superior delight, has disappeared with him. Never did I undertake anything without his advice. Not a line was written without my imagining him before me. What he would say, what he would remark, what would receive his indestructible and eternal approval – that is what preoccupied me and stimulated my powers. A secret tremor of a joy inaccessible on this earth would seize my soul . . . God! this present labor of mine, inspired by him, his creation . . . I am without strength to continue it. Several times I grasped my pen – and the pen fell from my hand. My anguish is inexpressible.

And two weeks later, in almost identical terms, to Pogodin:

You grieve as a Russian, as a writer, but I, . . . I am unable to express one-hundredth fraction of my grief. My life, my superior delight have died with him. The luminous moments of my life were the moments when I created. When I created I saw before me only Pushkin. It meant nothing to me — all the gossip, I spat at the contemptible mob known as the public; only his eternal and infallible words were dear to me. Nothing did I undertake, nothing did I write without his advice. Anything I have that is good, I owe it to him. And my present labor is his creation. He bound me by an oath to write, and not a line of it was written without his appearing before my eyes. I lured myself with the thoughts of how he would be pleased, I guessed what he would like, and that was my first and my highest reward. Now I do not have this reward to look forward to. What is my labor? What is my life now?

It was ten years after Pushkin's death that Gogol told in his *Confession* the story of the plots of the *Inspector* and of *Dead Souls* which Pushkin had "given" him. But regardless of what Pushkin actually contributed in supplying plots or advice, in the two letters written at the time of Pushkin's death, Gogol obviously spoke of a subjective experience: his words about Pushkin's inspiring "presence" were not meant to be taken literally. Pushkin's image, however, following the now familiar pattern, becomes the source of Gogol's creative power, and at the same time the compulsive force which urges him to carry on his labor. The great poet had made him promise under oath to fulfill his great task.

The idea of carrying out Pushkin's will and of bringing to completion what Pushkin had conceived and had transmitted to him (in other terms, of being Pushkin's heir, or, by an obvious association, his son), this idea will be taken up again and again in later years, sometimes in connection with appeals for financial help; thus, in a letter from Rome, dated April 6, 1837, and addressed to Zhukovski

I must continue the vast labor I began, which Pushkin made me promise him to write, the ideas of which are his creation and which, from that time, has become a sacred inheritance for me.

This is followed by a request that Zhukovski intercede on his behalf before the Emperor and solicit a pension or some other form of financial support for him.

The difficulty of performing the great task imposed upon him was increasingly felt by Gogol as an impediment caused by physical symptoms, for the most part connected with the digestive system. His letters are filled with complaints about his health, and in one instance at least an implicit connection is made between his condition and Pushkin's death (it may be noteworthy to recall that Gogol was twenty-eight when he wrote the lines quoted below):

> I fear hypochondria, it follows me at my heels. Pushkin's death seems to have removed from everything I glance at half of what could give me pleasure. My stomach is vile to an impossible degree and decidedly refuses to digest, although I now eat very moderately. My hemorrhoidal constipations have returned after I left Rome, and would you believe it, if I do not go to the privy I feel throughout the day as if some kind of a hood had been forced upon my brain which prevents me from thinking and beclouds my thoughts.

There is nothing cynical in the implicit association: Gogol was tormented by the demands of his super-ego and suffered from a feeling of impotence to perform his great task, his sacred duty. In his subjective symbolism the periods of depression were the periods when he was abandoned by the diversely identified Supreme Being (one will recall in his New Year's Eve prayer the supplication to his Genius not to depart from him); but while abandoned, he was not released from the duty imposed upon him, he was left to struggle alone. Pushkin's death was evidently interpreted as such an abandonment. He stressed in his letters that, without Puskin's mystic presence, he was no longer able to pursue his labor. The feeling — and the dread — of being powerless is connected on one level with Pushkin's death and on another, more primitive level, it takes the aspect of physical symptoms which obscured his mind and interfered with his creative work. Gogol's life became a nightmare.

Gogol writes in his *Confession* that in his young years his "laughter" (or his humor) was light-hearted and thoughtless, but that Pushkin made him "take a serious look at matters," and that after accepting the gift of the two plots, he began to consider seriously the problem of the purpose of his art, to arrive finally at the conclusion that he was wasting his talent, and that his laughter must be aimed at that which deserves to be exposed to universal ridicule.

This, it must be said, is the least convincing part of Gogol's story of his relationship with Pushkin; Pushkin would have been the last man to suggest to Gogol that he "look at matters seriously," or that he "laugh with a purpose," for nothing was more alien to Pushkin than the view that art must have a purpose.

On the other hand, everything seems to indicate that Pushkin saw in Gogol a comic writer *par excellence*. Thus, in his diary, under December 3, 1833, Pushkin noted: "Yesterday Gogol read to me his tale about how Ivan Ivanovich quarreled with Ivan Timofeyevich [i.e. Nikiforovich] — very original and very funny." When the second edition of the *Evenings* appeared, Pushkin wrote in his *Sovremennik*: "How astonished we were by a Russian book which made us laugh — we who had not laughed since the days of Fonvizin!" In this very short article he also mentioned *Arabesques*, calling Gogol's "Nevski Prospect" "the most complete of his works," and concluded:

> Following them appeared *Mirgorod* where we all avidly read "The Old-Time Squires," this humorous and touching idyll which made us laugh through tears of melancholy and tender emotion, and *Taras Bulba*, the beginning of which is worthy of Walter Scott. Mr. Gogol continues to make progress. It is our wish and our hope that we shall have frequent occasions to speak of him in our journal.

The following footnote accompanied the article: "In a few days his comedy, the *Inspector*, will be performed in the theater here."

Pushkin's innocent and obvious remark on "Old-Time Squires" — a humorous story with a sad ending — was repeated by Gogol himself in *Dead Souls* and became the favorite cliché of "laughter through tears;" it was stretched to mean that under the surface of a humorist, Gogol wept in secret over the miseries and injustices which plague humanity. This was hardly what Pushkin meant (even if he knew that Gogol was "a great melancholiac"); and if Gogol, the unhappy humorist, shed tears in secret, it was not over the sufferings and miseries of mankind.

One may add one more of Pushkin's appraisals of Gogol, a short note introducing "The Nose" in *Sovremennik*:

> N.V. Gogol refused for a long time to publish this joke; but we found in it so much that is unexpected, fantastic, gay and original, that we persuaded him to allow us to share with the public the pleasure we were given by his manuscript.

Very significant psychologically is Gogol's letter to Pushkin announcing that he had begun *Dead Souls*: it seemed to him, he wrote, that his novel "would be very funny." Gogol was unusually sensitive to his friends' attitudes toward himself, and his letters reflect in a striking manner his "adjustments" to his various correspondents: one may recall the pathos and lyricism of the references to *Dead Souls* in his letters to Zhukovski. In announcing his novel to Pushkin as "funny," he was attuning his letter to Pushkin's view of himself.

Gogol wrote in *Correspondence* that in his true essence he was understood by Pushkin alone. But a different opinion was expressed by Aksakov:

> Zhukovski did not completely appreciate Gogol's talent. Nor did even Pushkin, I suspect, especially because Pushkin died having read only the sketches of the first chapters of *Dead Souls*. They both admired Gogol's art of seizing imperceptible traits and giving them life and relief, they admired his humor, his drollery — but that was all. As for serious significance, it seems to me that they did not recognize any in him.

Pushkin's attitude toward Gogol was very friendly, and there is no doubt that he saw in him an exceptionally gifted, promising young author, but he obviously could not, and did not, give him that recognition to which Gogol aspired. Gogol's statements about Pushkin, after the poet's death, were, in part at least, a wish fulfillment. Gogol had deified Pushkin in his very early days; he wrote his ecstatic essay on *Boris Godunov* before he met Pushkin; but it was during the years that followed Pushkin's death, in retrospect, that Gogol imagined this intimate communion, almost a merging of the two personalities.

Gogol's identifying himself with Pushkin reveals its full significance in the light of the passage in *Dead Souls* about the romantic or heroic writer and the poet of triviality, that is himself. He insists with great pathos that the writer who deals with every life may be a great poet even if his subject matter is trivial of vulgar. No better support could be given to this idea than the support of Pushkin's authority: *Dead Souls* ("a poem") materialized through Gogol, but it was conceived and mystically directed by Pushkin, the greatest of all Russian poets.

Being merely a comic writer was not acceptable to Gogol. He did not want to be an entertainer like his father Vasili Afanasyevich, even if he was to entertain the whole of Russia, and not only Dmitri Prokofyevich Troshchinski and his entourage in Kibintsy. Gogol wanted to be Troshchinski himself. Gogol wrote in his *Confession* that the author must make clear to himself the purpose of his work and its usefulness, so that he may "flare up with a true and powerful love for his labor . . ." and, he added:

. . . in a word [it is necessary] that the author realize and convince himself that in working on his creation he fulfills that duty for which he has been called to this earth, for which he has been given ability and power, and that in fulfilling it he serves at the same time his country as if he were actually employed in government service.

Gogol's *Confession* joins at this point, after twenty years, the letters of the Nezhin period: the writer discovered that being a writer could be an equivalent of serving humanity in a government position, or, which is very nearly the same, of ruling humanity from a position in the government. Different ego-ideals could be combined and reconciled: one could be Troshchinski and Pushkin at one and the same time. His *Inspector*, he wrote, perhaps with some amount of exaggeration, "produced a tremendous effect." He had dealt a powerful blow to abuse, corruption and injustice, and he had accomplished this without taking service in the Department of Justice as he had decided to do in his young days, under the double influence of Minister Troshchinski and of Professor Belousov. But an author could rise to an even higher position, dominating the rest of humanity (the "existers" or the "mob"); and he could exert his power from afar, from above – seeing everything, giving advice and castigating evil, yet himself unseen and invulnerable.

Chapter XVI

THE TOWERS. UNREALIZABLE DESIRES.

USEFUL FRIENDS.

An image appears in Gogol's writings with an insistence which suggests a symbolic projection of the subconcious: the image of a tower of extraordinary height. An early example may be found in his essay "On the Architecture of Our Time" (1832 or 1833) in which he recommends the building of very high towers, especially in capital cities:

> Gigantic, colossal towers are essential in a city, regardless even of the important destination they have for Christian churches. Besides adding to the appearance and being an adornment, they are needed in order to confer to the city a sharp distinctive mark, which serves as a lighthouse, showing the way to everyone, preventing one from losing direction. The need for them is even greater in the capitals for the observation of the environs. We ordinarily limit ourselves to a height enabling to survey only the city itself, whereas for a capital it is necessary to see at least as far as 150 versts [approximately 100 miles], and for this, with perhaps only one or two stories added — everything would be changed. The scope of the horizon is augmented, as you rise, in an extraordinary proportion. The capital gains a substantial advantage by surveying the provices and foreseeing everything in advance.

There is a distinct schizoid flavor in this fantasy, which is only accentuated by the "practical" considerations added in support of aesthetics: the poet/architect was also concerned with the government keeping an eye on the country (which Nicholas I government did quite effectively). It is remarkable that Gogol ridiculed the idea of a super watchtower in Manilov's reverie in *Dead Souls*, which follows Chichikov's departure:

> For a long while Manilov stood on the porch, his eyes following the receding carriage, and even when it had passed out of sight completely, he was still standing there, smoking his pipe. At length he went inside, sat down on a chair and abandoned some slight gratification to his friend. Then his

thoughts passed on imperceptibly to other subjects and finally strayed only God knows whither. He was thinking of a life of friendship, of how sweet it would be to live with one's friend on the bank of some river; then, across this river, a bridge began to be built, then a colossal house with a belvedere so high up that one could even see Moscow from its top, and drink tea there in the evening, discoursing about some pleasant subjects; then, together with Chichikov, they drove in fine carriages to some reception where they enchanted everyone by the agreeableness of their manners. And, so it appeared, the Emperor, upon learning of this friendship they entertained, made them both generals, and what came after that, God alone knows, he could find no way to figure it out himself.

Still another "tower-image" occurs in "Leaving the Theater;" the "author of the play" overhears the following remarks exchanged by the spectators crowding toward the exit:

> *The first*: You know what they say — that a similar incident happened to the author himself, in some small town; he was jailed there — for debts.
> *A gentleman from another group* (breaking into the conversation): No, it wasn't in jail, it was on a tower. Those who were driving by saw it. They say it was most unusual. Imagine: the poet on an extraordinarily high tower, mountains all around — a perfectly delightful situation — and he was reading his verses from there. Wouldn't you say this discloses some kind of a peculiar trait of the author?
> *A positively disposed gentleman*: The author must be an intelligent man.
> *A negatively disposed gentleman*: Intelligent? Not at all. What I know is that he held a position, and they all but kicked him out — couldn't write an application.

Once more, the schizoid fantasy is ridiculed and attributed to others; in this caricature, however, he himself, "the author of the comedy," is placed on the high tower. And in his *Confession,* Gogol was to write that the main reason for his leaving Russia was that he needed to place himself in a position whence he could overlook "the whole," "the mass." The tower offers an advantageous position not only for the epic poet, but also for the statesman (especially if it is erected in the capital), for he can view the provinces from this elevated point, and thus even foresee the future. But the epic poet actually is also a statesman. In an ideal sense, he sees far from his tower, and he does not merely recite verses, as the stupid "existers" believe, he also gives guidance to his country.

These symbols could be derided as false and ridiculous rumors about the author being in jail or on top of a tower. It was his own fantasy, however, that Gogol ridiculed, and his tower was also his jail. He was, in his seclusion, his own prisoner. He would admit no one to his prison, or to his tower. Manilov also dreamed of the belvedere high enough to see Moscow, but he wanted to share this elevated position with his bosom friend Chichikov; he was a fool, among other things, because he believed in friendship. Gogol did not, in his later years. In a letter to Alexandra Smirnova, written in December 1844, Gogol gave a detailed analysis of his relations with his literary friends in Russia, some of whom had cared for him and served his interests for years with devotion and effacement. This little treatise on human relations, a remarkable piece of saintly cynicism, reads partly as follows:

> Knowing how to evaluate them, I knew how to obtain some advantage from each of them, and as for a later time, for the time when I would gain more wisdom and would be able to instruct them in something they lacked . . . To none of them did I confide my intentions, or my plans regarding either myself or all that concerned my personal destiny, considering this unnecessary for many reasons: first . . .; second . . . because even then I was able to feel in what way a man may be useful to me, and consequently, just what it was proper to tell him and not to tell him. And finally, third, even then I felt that we must love all men, more or less, according to their merits, but that as our true and closest friend, to whom we could confide everything, up to the least movement of our heart, we must choose none but God alone.

Three years later he wrote to Aksakov:

> I loved you much less than you loved me. I was always capable, or so it seems to me, of loving all people in general, because I was unable to feel hate toward anyone; but to love someone especially, in particular, I only could out of interest. If someone afforded me some substantial benefit and through him my knowledge expanded in some way, then I loved this man, be it even that he was less worthy of love than another one, even if he loved me less. What is there to be done? You see what kind of a creature man is: it is his own interest that counts most for him. Who knows? Perhaps I would have loved you much more if you had done something for my mind, say, by writing notes about your life which would remind me what

kind of people I should be careful not to omit in my creation. But you never did anything of this kind for me.

Having suppressed (or sublimated) all his needs or desires, Gogol insisted on being given, on being fed, this mental substance which, he felt, he was beginning to lack, and he was capable of "loving" (it is difficult to say what the word meant for him in this context) only those who provided him with this nourishment. The letter to Aksakov actually goes beyond Gogol's frequent requests for documentation or "statistics" (a word often used in his letters of the later years): Aksakov was to write his memoirs and deliver them to Gogol. He was, in other terms, to give over to Gogol his own life, his substance, which Gogol might use as material for his work, as nourishment; then he would have loved Aksakov. The same kind of resentment that he felt against this man of endless kindness and patience is also expressed in the *Confession* , this time directed against his readers and against society in general for not responding to the appeal he published in the Preface to the second edition of *Dead Souls*. The response was silence or mockery. Many were those who completely failed to understand his position; they

> . . . expressed their amazement over the fact that while I am so eager to have information about Russia, at the same time I stay away from Russia; but they did not consider that, aside from my failing health which requires a warm climate, I needed this removal from Russia in order that in my thoughts I may be more vividly in Russia.

To grasp this was actually rather difficult for the majority of Gogol's countrymen. Apparently the visibility from his tower was insufficient: he could see "the whole," but the details of the lives of the tiny creatures below escaped his observation. And Gogol's art could not live on "the whole." The only solution was to descend from the tower. But the tower was also a shelter: the poet and the prophet dominating humanity and demanding a tribute in the form of ideas and experience from humanity was also a hopelessly lonely and feeble human being hiding in his hole. Suffering in his body and in his soul, unable to fulfill the demands he made upon himself or to free himself from these demands, unable to love or to be loved, fearing death and finally abandoning himself to death as his only escape.

Withdrawing from the world and rising above it, Gogol strove for complete freedom from all desires, for the freedom of asceticism. When he was eighteen, he once wrote to his mother:

Man is strange with regard to his inner desires. He sights something in the distance, and the yearning for it will not abandon him for a single moment. It will trouble his peace and compel him to exert all his powers for the attainment of this essential. So it is with me at times: something, seemingly a trifle, but which is precious, be it only for me alone, will torment me with pining for it and with chagrin at my inability to possess it.

Later the theme of desire and frustration was to become one of Gogol's favorite themes. In one of his notebooks he jotted down (probably in 1832) under the heading "Comedy – general material:"

. . . already he wants to attain, to seize with his hand, when suddenly – an interference, and the withdrawal of the desired object to an enormous distance.

Poprishchin, in "The Madman's Diary," echoes him more or less:

You find your sorry riches for yourself, you think you are going to reach them with your hand – and they are snatched from you by a Kammer-Junker or a general.

Chichikov's dominating feature is his acquisitiveness. He yearns for wealth (and for respectability when he will be able to afford it). But he also has an almost libidinous craving for things that provide physical comfort and pleasure: perfumed soap, eau de cologne with which he sponges his plump body, shirts of fine linen, a frock-coat for which he chooses the finest cloth of the most fashionable color, known as "Navarino smoke with a glow," and which he lacerates in his despair when he is put in jail. Poprishchin, discovering that he is King Ferdinand VIII of Spain, cuts his uniform coat to pieces in the belief that he is tailoring a royal mantle for himself; and poor Akaki Akakiyevich is robbed of his new overcoat, his precious possession, the "poor man's treasure."

The motif of craving for wealth and possession and of frustration stems from different sources; it appears in different variants and with different significance. One of these sources is folklore with its stories about the search for hidden treasures and the belief in the diabolical nature of the hidden gold. Another factor may have been the destructive intrusion of capitalist economic relations (of money, or of "gold") in the patriarchal economy of the Ukraine.

And finally, the stories of Akaki Akakiyevich ("The Overcoat"), of Poprishchin ("The Madman's Diary"), of Khlestakov (*Inspector*), of Chichikov (*Dead Souls*). These are stories about men who were at the bottom of the formidable social and bureaucratic pyramid of imperial Russia and who aspired to gain more power, or more money, or more dignity — through embezzlement, like Chichikov; by purchasing a new garment, like Akaki; by pouring forth his fantasies of grandeur before a credulous audience, like Khlestakov; or finally, like Poprishchin, by ascending to the Spanish throne in his insane imagination.

But not only those who are humiliated are tormented by desires. In the unfinished *Vladimir of the Third Class* a bureaucrat occupying an important position is driven to insanity by his craving for a decoration. Desires for earthly possessions or honors are always destructive; they can never be satisfied, and the only salvation is in freeing oneself from all desires and ambitions.

For Gogol, love is the most dangerous and the most destructive of all desires. But he does not always treat amorous desire (or frustration) as something differing its very essence from desires for the possession of material objects. In the case of Akaki, the lonely and miserable office clerk, his dream of the new overcoat which he will soon possess (the expectation, it must be emphasized, not the actual possession) is compared with marriage; from the moment he had taken the momentous decision to order the garment

> . . . his very existence somehow became fuller, as though he got married, as though some other person was present at his side, as though he was no longer alone, but some pleasant helpmate had consented to tread the path of life together with him — and this mate was none other than the selfsame overcoat with its thick cotton-wool padding and its lining that would last a lifetime.

Chichikov, on the other hand, a middle-aged bachelor, like Akaki, is a jovial, wonderfully groomed and sociable bachelor who has very little interest in the pleasures of love; his pasion is acquisitiveness. We are told, apropos of his meeting the very pretty young daughter of the Governor:

> One cannot say with certainty whether the feeling of love had really awakened in our hero. It is even doubtful whether gentlemen of his sort — that is to say those who are not exactly stout, but who couldn't be called thin either — are capable of love. But for all that, there was here something peculiar,

something of such a nature that he was unable to account for it himself . . .

The notion that men who are neither stout nor yet lean do not fall in love is quite obviously absurd. It is a typically Gogolian piece of aphoristic nonsense. But it is also more than that: Chichikov is consistently described as having no extreme, or even very definite characteristics: his introductory description (or rather pseudo-description) follows the "neither–nor" formula which is repeated in the pasage quoted above with the addition that such a "neither–nor," or neuter, man is very unlikely to fall in love. Chichikov's "neutrality" is described as a perfect balance. He is at peace with himself and thoroughly pleased with his physical self, deriving great enjoyment from shaving and from dressing, lovingly contemplating (for a full hour on one occasion) his perfectly round and smooth face in the mirror.

Major Kovalyov in "The Nose" is also well pleased with his appearance and loves to inspect his face in the mirror, to discover one morning that it presented "instead of a nose, a perfectly smooth place." Chichikov is not allowed such departures from the plausible. But his perfect smoothnes, wonderful humoral balance and physical contentment are disturbed by the appearance of the young girl. He is dazed and shaken. The competence and the adroitness of this somewhat overweight and overage petit-maître abandon him. He is helpless, and his defeat is immediate: after listening to him a minute or two, the girl yawns. Later fantastic rumors spread: Chichikov is accused of having planned to abduct the Governor's daughter. Gossip makes a hero of a cloak-and-dagger romance out of him, a dangerous and mysterious figure – an enormous shadow of the real Chichikov.

Chapter XVII

LOVE: THE WHITE AND THE TRANSLUCENT

The theme of love occupies a very small place in *Dead Souls*. Yet even in the brief episode of the encounter with the Governor's daughter one finds nearly all the components of Gogol's erotic imagery.

Chichikov sees the girl at a ball:

> It appeared to him, as he later confessed, that the whole ball, with all its hum and noise, was removed somewhere into the distance for a few minutes; the fiddles and the horns were grinding away somewhere in another world, and a mist overcast everything making it look like some canvas hastily primed by a painter. Out of this dim, negligently daubed field emerged, clear and finished, the fine features of the entrancing blende: her ovally rounded face, her waist – thin, so thin – such as a girl has during the first months after leaving boarding school; her white, almost plain little dress, lightly and deftly hugging all her youthful and graceful limbs which showed their pure lines. She seemed to resemble some kind of a toy finely carved out of ivory; she alone shone white and emerged translucent and luminous from the blurred and opaque throng.

The feminine image is unreal ("a toy carved out of ivory"), but at the same time it possesses a reality superior to the reality of the world of matter; other human beings belong to this material world which is dimmed and blurred (made unreal) by the luminous and translucent image of the girl.

This luminiscence, this translucence, and especially whiteness, are almost inevitable in Gogol's feminine images. Thus, in the early "May Night" (one of the *Dikanka* stories) this description of dancing fairies (seen in a dream):

> In a silvery mist gleamed maidens, light as shadows, in garments white as a meadow covered with lilies of the valley, . . . they were pale; their bodies seemed to be sculptured out of transparent clouds, they seemed to shine through in the silvery moonlight.

222

In "Viy:"

Out of the reeds emerged a mermaid; he saw the gleam of her
back, and of her leg, bulging and resilient, all made of glitter
and tremor . . . now she turned over on her back — and her
cloud-like breasts, matte like unglazed porcelain, were
translucent in the sun around the border of their white,
resiliently delicate circles. In the water, tiny bubbles covered
them like tiny pearls.

In "The Madman's Diary:"

Holy saints, how she was dressed! The dress on her was as
white as a swan — oh, and so fluffy! And when she glanced —
the sun! By God, it was the sun!

And in another passage:

If I could just peep . . . into her boudoir . . . [and see] her
dress negligently dropped, looking more like the air than like a
dress. If I could peep into the bedroom . . . that is, I guess,
where the marvels are, that is where a paradise must be such as
one won't find even in Heaven. Just to have a look at the little
stool on which she places her little foot, rising from her bed,
and how on this leg a stocking is slipped on, white as snow . . .
oh my ! oh my! but no, but no . . . silence.

In one of the early Petersburg fragments:

But white — nothing can be compared to it. Nothing can be
higher than a woman in white. She is a queen, a vision, she is
like the most harmonious dreams. A woman is aware of this
and therefore there are minutes when she transforms and
becomes white. What sparks run along your veins when in the
dark, because then everything seems to be darkness. All the
sensations are then concentrated on the fragrance emanating
from it and in the rustle, barely audible, yet musical, which it
produces. This is the highest and the most voluptuous of sensual
experiences.

Of sculpture, in his essay, "Sculpture, Painting and Music" (*The
Arabesques*), Gogol writes:

White, milky, its translucent marble exhaling beauty, langor

223

and voluptuousness . . . everything in it is merged in beauty and sensuality . . .

A further step toward symbolically diffuse (non-genital) eroticism of color and form is made in Gogol's essay on architecture:

. . . the pagan, the round, the entrancing, the voluptuous forms of cupolas and columns . . .

And further in the same essay:

And the cupola, the best, the most charming of all creations of taste, voluptuous, airily bulging . . . I love the cupola, that beautiful, huge, lightly bulging cupola . . . Nothing can adorn a mass of buildings as voluptuously and captivatingly as such a cupola . . . Dazzling whiteness communicates an inexpressible charm and fullness to its lightly bulging form — then it rounds in the sky even finer, more luxuriantly, more cloudlike.

A key to the rather obvious symbol of the "white cupola" is the following passage (from a first draft of one of the *Hetman* fragments):

On her breast and her arms quivered a shirt, white as snow, as if nothing but the finest and the purest linen could cover cascade . . . He saw the young bosom raise the cupola-like breasts, breathing voluptuously . . .

A further investigation of this imagery as a possible expression of Gogol's subconscious would be beyond the scope of this study. The passages quoted above do show, however, a constancy in Gogol's imagery, and it is particularly significant that some of the images of the early Ukrainian stories are carried over into *Dead Souls*, so different in its themes and its texture.

The very nature of Gogol's feminine image precludes the possibility of a communion between the two sexes, of happy love. Woman does not belong to the world of matter which is the world of man. Man, however, can be "charmed" (in the literal, or magic sense) by this extra-material femininity, and unless he guards himself from these charms, he is destroyed.

Another characteristic aspect of Gogol's treatment of the love theme appears in *Dead Souls*, if only as an allusion: Chichikov is introduced to the Governor's daughter by her mother, and there is a faint note of invitation or encouragement in her words. The "matchmaker" is part of Gogol's very peculiar erotic pattern. The motif is particularly important in "Shponka," in Viy," in *Marriage*. In "Shponka," husky and virile "auntie" Vasilisa tries to force her nephew to unite in holy matrimony with the daughter of a neighboring squire. The story ends, or rather breaks off, in Shponka's dream in which he sees himself married; in his bedroom he finds endlessly multiplying "wives" (with goose-like faces):

> He ran out into the garden; but it was hot in the garden. He took his hat off, and he saw that there was a wife in his hat too. He thrust his hand into his pocket to get a handkerchief — and in the pocket too there was a wife . . . Then he was jumping on one leg; and auntie, looking at him, was saying with an air of importance: "Yes, you have to jump, because you are a married man at present." He turned towards her — auntie, however, was no longer auntie, but a belfry. And he felt that someone was hauling him up onto the belfry with a rope. "Who is that pulling me?" plaintively said Ivan Fyodorovich. "It's I, your wife, and I'm hauling you up because you are a bell." — "No, I'm not a bell, I'm Ivan Fyodorovich!" he cried. "O yes, you are a bell," said the colonel of the *** infantry regiment, as he passed by.

Meek and helpless Shponka is entirely on the defensive; the initiative is in the hands of the older woman — the matchmaker — and at one point of Shponka's grotesque nightmare, the matchmaker (in the guise of the belfry onto which Shponka is hauled) is substituted for the bride. The situation has a parallel in "Viy," a story of witchcraft and death, widely different from humorous and realistic "Shponka." Khoma, a seminary student, becomes the prey of a hideous witch; he is forced to carry her on his back, and as he gallops along through the air, erotic visions appear to him (see the passage with the mermaid quoted above):

> . . . he galloped full speed. Sweat poured from him. He was gripped by a diabolically sweet feeling, he felt a piercing, a tormenting and dreadful delight . . .

Finally, he frees himself, by reciting prayers; he is now the stronger, and after taking a ride in his turn, he picks up a log and hits the hideous old woman again and again. Under his blows she is transformed into a young beauty who lies moaning before him, her eyes filled with tears. It is at this moment that Khoma flees, leaving the witch to die. The rest of the story tells of the vengeance of the

225

forces of evil: Khoma is destroyed.

The similarity between the erotic fantasies in "Viy" and the grotesque "Shponka" is, in the first place, that the man is dominated by an old woman endowed with great power; and further: "auntie" Vasilisa wants her nephew to marry; Khoma, under the power of the witch, has erotic visions (the mermaid) and experiences, a "piercing" and "tormenting" delight. Thus the older woman supplies the man with a desirable, or at least an acceptable, object; she does not claim the man for herself. The man, however, flees (Shponka in his dream, in which his bride-to-be becomes multiple and "goose-headed"). And finally, the two images, of the old and of the young woman, are confused or identified.

In *The Marriage*, hesitant Podkolyosin is vigorously handled by his friend Kochkaryov and by a professional matchmaker who unite their efforts to induce him to marry a young girl who is willing, but completely passive. Kochkaryov yields after endless vacillations, and even, when according to custom he is made to kiss the bride, he flares up with a sudden enthusiasm and insists that the wedding take place immediately, without losing another minute. But only a few moments later, left alone in the drawing room, he makes an escape through the window — the most obvious thing to do for a Gogolian hero, once coercion has been removed. In one of the scenes of the comedy, it may be added, the gentlemen brought by the matchmaker to view the prospective bride and the enterprising Kochkaryov crowd before the bedroom door; Kochkaryov looks through the keyhole (the young woman is dressing) and reports:

Can't see a thing, gentlemen. Something white, but can't make out what it is — might be a woman or it might be a pillow.

"Nevski Prospect" deserves a special mention in the discussion of the love theme in Gogol. The part of the "matchmaker" in this story is played by the demon of delusion, the demon of the big city, who "sets the street lamps burning for the sole purpose of making everything appear in a false light." The demon is seconded by poor Piskaryov's friend, the jaunty young lieutenant who prompts him to follow the mysterious beauty ("Perugino's Bianca"), actually a vulgar harlot. Then Piskaryov discovers the horrible truth, and he flees the brothel where he had unwittingly followed the young woman. But the shock he experienced does not deliver him from his passion; he seeks an escape in dreams, and in one of his dreams the young woman appears to him (the setting is a brilliant ball in some palatial residence: liveried lackeys, glittering staircase, marble columns, etc.) as the very image of beauty and purity; she dances, then approaches

– an ethereal vision – and takes a seat. Piskaryov admires the glorious whiteness of her hand and murmurs (or thinks): "If only I could touch it – and nothing more! No other desires – they would be an outrage . . ." This time poor Piskaryov's passion is blocked by the excessive purity of the image that he himself had created in his dream. Thus the horror before sordid reality resulted, in Piskaryov's case (and possibly also in Gogol's) in an over-idealization, with equally negative results.

Gogol's (or Piskarov's) aversion for venal love was by no means general among artists, writers and poets of his day. It was certainly not shared by Pushkin or by Lermontov. If the former sang of the brothel in a few gaily lewd verses, the latter produced a long narrative poem. obscene, but powerfully lyrical, in which the hero, Sashka (this is the title of the poem) discovers a young beauty in a brothel, as sordid as Gogol's. The squalor of reality, however, is conquered by passion: Lermontov's hero makes no attempt to escape into a world of dreams. An episode in the poem, written some five years after Gogol's "Nevski Prospect," offers a curious analogy with Piskaryov's dream: Lermontov's harlot askes her lover to take her to the theater, and the young rake promises to do so – he wishes to defy the high society to which he belongs – and sends his valet to buy the best clothes for the girl to wear on this occasion. Gogol's hero in his dream substitutes the ideal and inaccessible being he encounters at the ball for the prostitute. In Lermontov's poem, the prostitute "dreams" of becoming, were it only for one night, a woman of society, and her lover agrees to make this dream a reality.

As a writer of fiction, Gogol was objective enough to recognize that man and woman can meet without the latter necessarily destroying the former unless he makes a safe escape; he could not simply deny the experience of humanity even if it was so unlike his own experience. But he takes a very definite attitude toward "happy love" and matrimony. Some of his early stories in which union in love and happiness are admitted can be disregarded; they are obviously impersonal and repeat motifs borrowed from folklore or from literary sources.

In his more mature works, happy couples are ridiculed for their smugness, their platitudinous sentimentality, for the cheapness of their commonplace happiness. Such are the Manilovs, such is the landowner married to a pretty young woman in "The Carriage," such are the Lenitsyns in the second volume of *Dead Souls* whose innocent babe soils Chichikov's new frock coat. An exception is made for the "Old-Time Squires;" but age has eliminated sex from their lives and their sensuality is focused on food.

There are women in Gogol's works who are neither madonnas nor witches, such as the Burgomaster's wife and daughter in the *Inspector* or the amiable matrons in *Dead Souls*, but they are clearly outside of the world of Gogol's own emotions. The "existers" had their spouses and their sweethearts: the feminine "existers." They were, for Gogol, sexless because they were made of dull, heavy matter, not of the translucent, cloud-like, marble-like substance of his own diffuse eroticism.

It is generally admitted that Gogol had no sex life, or possibly that he had a sexual experience in his early days which he did not seek to repeat. In his letters one finds the story of his consuming passion for a mysterious angel-like creature which he "confessed" to his mother to explain his sudden departure for Lubeck in 1829, and, in a letter to Danilevski (March 1832), something about a "norther queen of his southern heart." But later, when his friend wrote to him about one of his many amorous adventures, Gogol replied as follows:

I well understand the state of your soul, although myself, the fates be thanked, I have not experienced it. I say "be thanked" because this flame would have reduced me to cinders instantaneously. I would be unable to find delight for myself in the past, and would endeavor to change it into the present, and would be the victim of this effort and that is why I have, to my salvation, a strong will-power which twice has prevented me from glancing into the precipice. You are lucky, your lot is to partake of the greatest blessing in the world — of love.

This is a sad confession, and its embarrassed verbiage adds its melancholy. The first lines of the passage — about being reduced to cinders — have often been quoted. Merezhkovski used them to suggest that

. . . the force which kept him away from women was not a lack, but on the contrary, some peculiar orgiastic excess of sensuality.

This is a questionable view, to say the least (very convincing objections to Merezhkovski's theory have been made by Gerhard Gesemann). Complete renunciation of sex life resulting from excessive sensuality would be something very peculiar indeed. Actually what Gogol says when he speaks of "flame" and of "cinders" is that he fears sex, and he certainly did.

He did not lack sensuality, but he was incapable of what the Freudians call object-cathexis. His sensuality remained diffuse —

228

objectless. A remarkable example of his diffuse eroticism is a fragment he wrote, probably in 1839; it reads as follows:

Exalted, celestially booming, marvelous night! Do you love me? Do you gaze, as you used to, at your loved one, whom years and losses have not changed, do you shine and gleam into his eyes, and kiss him on his lips and his brow? And you, moonlight, do you laugh as before, as you used to ? O, God, God, God! Are those the same sounds scudding and trembling in you? I swear — those sounds I heard, I heard them alone, I was then in front of a window: on my breast the shirt torn open, and my breast and my neck exposed to the refreshing night wind. O, so divine, so wonderful and rejuvenating, languorous, exhaling caress and fragrance — O, paradise and heaven — wind of the night, breathing a joyful chill — furtively it would embrace me and seize me in its embrace, then flee, then once more would return to embrace me, while the black, gloomy masses of the forest, bending, looked on from afar, and solemnly unperturbed was the air. And suddenly the nightingale . . . O heavens! Now everything is ablaze! What a flare! Ho, how it thunders! . . . And the moon, the moon! . . . Give me back, O give me back, restore to me my youth, and young strength of my powers, myself, myself with all my freshness, the one that I was! O, but irretrievable everything is in this world!

Chapter XVIII

THERE IS NO LIFE FOR ME OUTSIDE OF MY LIFE

In 1839, a strange episode occurred in Gogol's life. That year the heir to the Russian throne, the future Emperor Alexander II, was traveling in Europe accompanied by his tutor, the poet Zhukovski, and, among other memebers of his suite, the young Count Joseph Wielhorski, the son of a very cultured family of Russianized Polish aristocracy. Young Wielhorski fell ill with consumption during the journey and had to be left in Rome where he died a few weeks later. Gogol, who knew the Wielhorskis through Zhukovski, stayed with the youth and cared for him during these last weekd of his life. He conceived an exalted passion for the dying young man which he endeavored to express in a few pages he wrote, known as "Nights in the Villa." Following is an excerpt from this strange document:

They were sweet and languorous, these sleepless nights. He sat in an armchair, ill. I was with him. Sleep dared not touch my eyes. It could not, so it seemed, but respect in silence those sacred vigils. It was sweet for me to sit beside him, to look at him. The last two nights we had been saying "thou" to each other. How much nearer to me he became after this! He was sitting there ever the same: gentle, quiet, resigned. God! How gladly, how joyfully I would take his illness upon myself! And if my death could restore him to health, with what readiness would I throw myself into it!

I have not gone to see him this night. I decided at last to sleep at home. O! how base, how vile was this night, together with my contemptible sleep! I slept badly although I had spent a whole week without sleep. I was racked by thoughts about him. He appeared to me, imploring and reproaching. I saw him with the eyes of my soul. With haste I went to him next morning, feeling like a criminal. When he saw me he was in his bed. He smiled his usual smile of an angel. He extended his hand and pressed mine lovingly. "Traitor!" – he said to me – "you betrayed me." "My angel!" said I, "forgive me. I suffered with your suffering. I was tormented this night. My repose was not

230

peaceful: forgive me!" Gentle one! He pressed my hand! How completely I was then rewarded for the torment inflicted upon me by the night I spent so stupidly! – "My head is heavy," he said. I began to fan him with a branch of laurel. "Oh, it is so refreshing, so nice!" he said. His words were then . . . O, what they were! What would I not have given then, what worldly blessings, those despicable, those vile, those base blessings . . . no! they are not worthy to be spoken of! You into whose hands these lines will fall – if, perchance, they do fall into someone's hands – these feeble, discordant lines, this pale expression of my feelings – you will understand me. Or else you will not chance upon them. You will understand . . .

It would be a mistake to interpret Gogol's feeling toward the youth as homosexual; rather, it would seem, it was another manifestation of his diffuse, sexless libido, which for a short while found a human being which the approach of death had purified and made "translucent" and which did not present the terrible threat of femininity. But the memory of the dead youth soon vanished. Once more Gogol was alone.

Years later, in 1846, he wrote another prayer; he once said in a letter that he could confide in none but God, his only true friend; now he prayed for the strength to love God:

Send me, O Lord, Thy blessings for this coming year! Turn it into fruit and into labor fecund and beneficial, to serving Thee, to the salvation of souls. Be merciful and release my hands and my reason, sending unto it Thy supreme radiance and the prophetic discernment of Thy great wonders. May the Holy Ghost descend upon me and move my lips and sanctify all in me, reducing to cinders and destroying my wickedness, and my filth, and my infamy, and turn me into a temple holy and pure, worthy, O Lord, of being Thy abode. O Lord, do not part from me! O Lord! Remember Thy love of old. Lord, give me Thy blessing and the power to love Thee, to sing and to praise Thee, and to bring all to praise Thy Holy Name.

Gogol wrote to Sergei Aksakov in May 1844:

Of myself I will say that my nature is not all mystical. Misunderstandings arose because I fancied too early to speak of things which were all too clear for myself but which I did not have the power to express with my stupid and obscure words . . . But internally I never varied in my main attitudes. From the age of twelve, perhaps, I have been following the same

231

path as at the present time, without ever swaying or vacillating in my essential opinions . . . And now I can say that in my essence I am the same I always was . . .

It is best then not to speak, words are powerless, they sow strife among men and create confusion. That he is not a mystic by nature is also a remarkable statement; he did not think of himself as of a mystic: he tried to clarify for himself the affairs of his soul and to manage them and keep them in good order according to the precepts of his own irrational rationality. His thoughts and his deeds were all recorded in a ledger which he endlessly consulted, revised and adjusted, until his final bankruptcy.

There is a remarkable insistence in Gogol's pointing to his early years, as he does in his letter to Aksakov, as to the time when what he thought essential in his personality and his destiny had taken a definite shape, when he chose the path which he followed without deviating from it throughout his life. This interpretation of his life as a meaningful and consistent whole is not entirely justified: there is in it much ex post facto rationalizing. But it does seem true that his early years were formative in the full sense of the word, and that they left a deep imprint on his personality predetermining in many ways its further development.

The remarks which follow do not purpose to explain Gogol's personality through his biography. The primary causes which shaped his personality cannot be determined, but it does seem that in the circumstances of his early life certain patterns were formed which had a powerful influence on him and which he repeated and recreated in his later life. Precisely this may account for his very strong feeling of predestination, of a power which had preordained and guided him.

In his letter to Aksakov Gogol says that he entered upon the path he followed ever since the age of twelve. This was also the age of Tentetnikov when Gogol begins his story in the second volume of *Dead Souls*. Nikosha Gogol was sent to school in Nezhin at the age of twelve, and his repeated references to this age indicate the psychological impact of the event. It may be noted that he never referred to the school in Poltava, nor to his brother Ivan, nor to his death. The death of his brother (and of several other children) seems to be a completely repressed memory, and it is possible that it was behind some of his fears and some of the fantastic imagery of his stories.

In Nezhin, Nikosha found himself separated from the paternal home, left to himself to find an adjustment to a strange environment (his frantic and tearful call for help was not answered). The rest is an obvious and a banal story of a boy with a frail constitution, used to the care and protection of the parental home, having no older brothers, for whom the first contact with a boarding school is a contact with a hostile environment. Nikosha worked out an adjustment, but he did this by his own means, without the help of his parents. Physically he was frail, like his father, and complaints about aches and pains were usual in the family in which domestic medicine was traditionally cultivated. In one of his earliest letters, written in 1820 in Poltava, Nikosha wrote: "Thanks to your parental care, I feel, thanks to God, perfectly well. I continue the decoction you left, dear father, according to your instructions."

His small stature, his frail physique and his concerns about his health, separated him from the crowd of the stronger boys, and this "being different" was stylized as being strange, mysterious, bizarre. He was superior in his artistic abilities, and he could use his talent for mimicry as a weapon against those who were stronger and more aggressive.

As years went by, his studies acquired more significance. The arts were cultivated, and an aestheticism of the sublime variety offered itself as an ideal to young Gogol. Another idealism, a civic idealism, was inspired by Belousov's teaching. Neither ideal, however, could eliminate Nikosha's natural instinct for humorous mimicry, for acute observation, for exerting his power over reality by imitation, mockery and distortion. The education he was receiving, whatever the merits or the shortcomings of the school, separated him from the backward, provincial world of the neighboring landowners, or of the Nezhin citizenry, of the "existers."

The death of his father, when Nikosha reached the age of sixteen, was an event of great importance. His mother pointed out to him that he was eventually to take upon himself the responsibility of the head of the family. But he was not particularly eager to assume this responsibility, which is quite understandable. The place of the head of a family had nevertheless become vacant and it had been offered to him.

On the other hand, it had been decided early that, once his education was completed, he would go to the capital and enter a career in the government, that is, that he would renounce the shelter and the security of the parental home, leaving the rest of the family, the soil and its fruit, and would support himself by his own toil. He was to face his destiny alone, and he was preparing himself for this from his very early years. His was the destiny of an individual who was breaking away from the ancestral tradition, from the soil, from his family, to make his way by his own means in a strange world. His life would not follow a pattern, it would not continue a tradition — it had to be given a significance on its own terms. But the abandoned soil — and the past with which his problematic ancestry was a link — were romanticized and idealized.

His attitude toward his family and toward home was ambivalent. On the one hand, he was abandoning his mother and his small sisters and did not accept the vacant place as head of the family, and this was an unfulfilled obligation. On the other hand, if he had accepted an independent future away from home, and had even formed a brilliant and exalted image of his future, he felt nevertheless that his leaving home was a sacrifice — he was going alone into the unknown world, and the others were staying in the comfort and security of the ancestral home.

The failure to fulfill the duties of head of the family will be compensated by emphasizing his sacrifice, and also by offering his mother guidance and advice on the management of the property, on the education of his sisters and on various other matters, practical as well as spiritual: he was a paterfamilias by correspondence.

When he was taking leave from home he wrote to Kosyarovski on September 8, 1828, that he might be absent in distant lands as long as ten years: ". . . if I make my fortune, if I am in a condition to help my relatives and my sisters, then I will come back; if not — I will suffer need, and whom does need not improve and make rich? . . ."

Gogol made repeated gestures of renouncing his rights to the family property. He began by gestures which were valid only for himself, as symbols of self-sacrifice. He continues to make demands for money (however only until 1831), and even embezzled the 1,450 rubles his mother sent him. But later the symbolic gestures of renunciation and sacrifice were followed by real acts. In 1832, he sent some money home and took two of his sisters to Petersburg, placed them in the Patriotic Institute and arranged for his entire salary to be withheld to pay for their board and tuition, living on the meager income from his books in the meanwhile. In later years, after his emigration, he donated (anonymously) his entire literary income to needy students, himself living on money borrowed from his friends.

In his *Confession* , recalling his early years, Gogol tells of his thoughts about the "sacrifice" he would have to offer, and he associates these thoughts with those of a lone journey to distant lands. These thoughts, he writes, made him feel melancholy; but he felt that "for the sake of serving my fatherland I would have to be educated in some place far distant from it."

This is closely riminiscent of the thoughts expressed in the letter to Kosyarovski – that he would spend years in foreign lands, and return when he would be able to help his family.

The substitution of his country for his family, in the *Confession*, is highly significant. There is a striking parallel between Gogol's attitude toward his family and the attitude he later assumed toward his country. In both situations he feels that he has a duty to perform. In both cases, he assumes from afar, in absentia, the role of guide, of advisor who must be followed and obeyed, who is loving and critical, and endowed with supreme wisdom.

He is the absentee paterfamilias, the absentee landlord, educator, statesman, regulator of all matters public and private; but he is also a homeless wanderer, a lonely sufferer before God, a Hans Küchelgarten, weary of his long journey. There was, however, no Luisa waiting for him, there was no idyllic shelter for the defeated romantic.

The only works of fiction Gogol created in his later years were the unfinished novel *Rome* and one of his most perfect works, the *Overcoat* with its hero, Akaki Akakiyevich.

Gogol, however, still believed that he was chosen to create a "Leviathan" task, a greater task than he had ever performed. This "Leviathan" would be the second volume of *Dead Souls*.

He toiled and toiled on this volume for years, creating more and more landowners, trying to endow them with positive traits. These new positive traits did not blend with Gogolian peculiarities.

Gogol became desperate. He hated these puppets, destroyed them and tried again and again. His genius had definitely abandoned him. He turned to God and religion, and spent hours in prayer. He made a pilgrimage to Jerusalem, suffered from cold and the discomfort of traveling and returned in a much worse state than when he left.

His health was rapidly deteriorating. He was suffering from chronic diarrhea (which had often plagued him during his life) and his mind became confused. He refused food and rejected all help and died in 1852 at the age of 42 after long and tortuous agony.

Even if fictional writing has a very uncertain value as biographical or psychological evidence, it seems interesting to quote the following passage from *Dead Souls* describing this fading of interest in the outside world, this "loss of appetite" for new impressions:

> In former days, long gone by, in the years of my youth, in the years of my childhood that vanished swiftly and irretrievably, it was a joy for me to drive up for the first time to an unfamiliar place, no matter what it was: whether a little

hamlet, or some forlorn little town, a village or some suburb — many a curious thing was discovered by the curious eye of a child. A building, anything, if it only bore one mark of a noticeable peculiarity, anything would arrest my attention and impress me. Whether a stone government structure built in the familiar style, half its windows blind, sticking up lonesomely amid a cluster of one-storied little houses of hewn log, the dwellings of the townsfolk; or the round, regular cupola, covered over with white sheet-iron, high above the new church daubed white as snow; or the market-place, or some dandy from the neighborhood chancing in the town — nothing eluded my fresh, keen observation, and sticking my nose out of my traveling cart, I would stare at some queer frock-coat, of a cut heretofore unseen, and at wooden bins containing nails, or sulphur — a yellow speck in the distance — or raisins, or soap, all of this glimpsed through the door of a grocer's together with jars of stale Moscow-made sweets; and I would also gaze at an infantry officer passing by, drifted here from some provincial center, God only knows which, to suffer from small-town boredom; and at a merchant wearing a short, warm overcoat, who dashed past in a carriage; and my thoughts would fly after them all, following them into their drab existences. An office clerk would pass by, and there I was, ruminating: Where is he going? Is it to a party at some colleague's of his or straight home, the idea being to spend a half hour or so out on the porch, in the dusk, while it is not yet quite dark, and then to sit down to an early supper with his mother, and his wife, and the wife's sister, and the whole family — and what will the talk be about when the wench, a string of beads around her neck, or a lad in a thick jacket, will bring in — once they are through with the soup — a tallow candle in a candlestick, solid and of lasting service. Driving up to a village, the property of some squire, I looked with curiosity at the tall and narrow wooden belfry, or at the wooden church, old, dark and sprawling. From afar, through the foliage, the red roof and the white chimneys of the landlord's house glimpsed at me enticingly, and I waited with impatience for the gardens that masked it to part to either side and to reveal in its entirety an appearance which in those days — alas, how distant! — did not look at all ordinary to me; and from it I tried to guess what the squire might be like himself; is he stout, and does he have sons, or all of a half dozen daughters, with their ringing girlish laughter, their games, and naturally the youngest sister, a beauty; and did they have dark eyes, like September in its last days, and peer into the calendar, and discourse — boring the young folk — about rye

236

and wheat.

Now it is with apathy that I drive up to an unfamiliar village and with apathy do I look at its ordinary appearance; to my gaze, now cold, everything is bleak, I am not amused, and what in bygone years would have brought animation to my face, would have caused laughter and unceasing speeches, now glides past me, and my motionless lips preserve an impassive silence. Oh, my youth! Oh, age of freshness!

Gogol was only thirty-two when he wrote this passage.

NAME INDEX

Raphael, 95
Redkin, Peter, 87
Romodanovski, Grigori, 41
Rossini, Gioacchino, 92
Rousseau, Jean-Jacques, 103
Rozanov, V. V., 13, 14
Ryleyev, K. F., 103

Saint John the Baptist, 31
Sabatier de Castres, 88
Samoilovich, Ivan, 43
Schad (philosofer), 102
Schiller, Friedrich von, 89, 124
Scott, Walter, 158, 167, 212
Seldner (teacher), 78, 79
Senkovski, O. I., 180
Sevryugin (teacher), 92
Shakespeare, William, 15, 16, 150
Shapalinski, Casimir, 100, 101, 104, 109
Shchepkin, M. S,. 174, 175, 178, 179
Shenrok (Gogol's biographer), 123
Sheridan, Richard, 92
Shevchenko, T. G., 94
Shevyryov, S. P., 189
Singer (teacher), 89, 101, 103, 104, 106
Sismondi, Jan Charles, 167
Skalon, Sofya, 68
Smirnova-Rossette, Alexandra, 161
Sobieski, Jan, 41, 43, 45, 53
Somov, Orest, 143, 144
Sophocles, 91, 124
Sotski, Andrei, 43
Southey, Robert, 29
Sreznevski, Izmail, 172
Sterne, Lorence, 201
Stilman, Leon, 58
Svinyin, Pavel, 31, 180

Tarnovski (Gogol's schoolmate), 106
Thierry, Augustin, 171
Thoyras, Rapin, 171, 172
Tieck, Ludwig, 124

Titian, 16
Tovstogub, A. I., 51
Trokhimovski (doctor), 24
Troshchinskaya, Anne, 60, 64
Troshchinskaya, Nadezhda, 65
Troshchinski, A. A., 67, 68, 70-72
Troshchinski, D. P., 11, 25, 60, 63-72, 75, 77, 117-119, 136, 141, 213, 214
Tryssylo, T. F., 37

Uhland (German poet), 29
Uvarov, S. S., 161-163

Veltman, Alexander, 180
Vengerov, S. A., 12
Volynski, Pavel, 103
Voss, J. H., 125
Vyazemski, 181
Vysotski (Gogol's friend), 92, 100, 117, 119, 120, 122, 132, 138, 196

Weber, Carl Marta von, 92
Winckelman, Johann, 124
Wieland, Christoph Martin, 89
Wielhorski, Joseph, 230

Yakovlevich, Jan see Jan Gogol
Yanov, G. (Gogol's pseud.), 55
Yanovski, A. D., 44, 45, 47, 51-55, 57-59, 77
Yanovski, D. I., 51-53, 57
Yanovski, Kirill, 54
Yanovski, Merkuri, 54
Yasnovski (school principal), 104, 109, 111
Yevstafi, 43

Zagoskin, M. N., 91
Zeuxis, 124
Zhukovski, V. A., 29, 58, 88, 89, 93, 94, 144, 159, 160, 187, 203, 208, 210, 213, 230
Zyablova (actress), 93